The Blue Marauders

The Blue Marauders

Ted MacVeagh

STONE POND PRESS

YA Ted
MACVEAGH

STONE POND PRESS

PO Box 183, Thetford, VT 05074

Text and Cover Design: Linnea Spelman

First Edition, 2016

For information contact Stone Pond Press or visit
www.stonepondpress.com

Publisher's Cataloging-in-Publication
(Provided by Quality Books, Inc.)

MacVeagh, Ted, author.
    The Blue Marauders / Ted MacVeagh.
    pages cm
    SUMMARY: Nick and Erik, kids from a small town, form
a travel soccer team to compete with the well-organized,
well-financed soccer powers of the Tri-State League.
    Audience: Ages 12-14.
    LCCN 2016900819
    ISBN 978-0-9972236-0-6

    1. Soccer teams--Juvenile fiction. 2. Soccer matches
--Juvenile fiction. 3. Soccer stories. [1. Soccer--
Fiction. 2. Soccer teams--Fiction. 3. Soccer matches--
Fiction. 4. Small cities--Fiction.] I. Title.

PZ7.1.M2485Bl 2016   [Fic]
                          QBI16-900020

For Katy

CHAPTER 1

A Team of One's Own

Nick was pedaling hard. It was more than two miles straight uphill to get from his house by the river to the school. Nick didn't mind the ride; he'd been biking back and forth to school since the beginning of sixth grade. At first his dad had insisted on biking with him to make sure he was safe. On the third day, lagging behind and breathing hard, his dad stopped halfway up and called to his son, "You'll make it okay from here, Nicky. I'm heading back."

Now, during the summer, Nick considered the bike ride part of his baseline workout. On Mondays, Wednesdays, and Fridays, he biked up the hill to meet his soccer friends from school. Anyone who arrived early would run the high school loop before practice. Erik, who lived in a white colonial house on the town green, just a few hundred yards from the school, usually got to the field first, but today Nick wanted to be there before anyone else. He couldn't wait to tell the team his news.

Nick coasted into the elementary school parking lot, hands in the air, and maneuvered through the gate and past the playground. Without braking, he scissored one leg over the frame and leapt off, letting his bike skitter to a stop along the path.

Nick shrugged off his backpack and got out his soccer ball. It was an old leather Mitre with the paint peeling off, but it kept its air and it flew straight. Nick dropped the ball onto his feet and caught it neatly on his toes. He flicked the ball back into the air and did fifteen quick juggles with his right foot before knocking it high on his last juggle and leaping to volley the ball out of the air as far as he could. He caught it full on, and the ball sailed away across the field. It was a good day.

As Nick stood admiring his kick, Erik emerged on the far sideline, from a path that led to the town green. Erik noticed the ball in the middle of the field, and the boys locked eyes briefly. The ball was closer to Erik, but he was carrying a backpack and a ball bag. Suddenly they both started sprinting.

Halfway there, Erik dropped his bags. Nick tried to match the increase in pace, but Erik reached the ball first. With his right leg extended, and Nick bearing down, Erik flicked the ball to the right with the outside of his right foot as his body swerved left to avoid a collision. Nick threw his left leg out lunging for the ball but he was moving too fast to change direction, and it curled outside his left foot as he slid past.

Erik swerved back to his right and controlled the ball. He put his foot on top of it and waited for Nick to turn around.

"Slowing down, Nicky?"

Seen from afar, as they stood grinning at each other, they might have been mistaken for brothers. They were both medium height, with skinny, muscular frames and nut brown hair cut short. But Erik was paler with light green eyes. Nick's eyes were a deep, dark brown. And when they moved, more differences became apparent.

Erik held himself straight and ran with tight hips. There was no wasted energy. Every motion was precise and calculated. Nick was much looser. His arms jangled by his sides while his hips and shoulders undulated to some unheard rhythm. When Nick accelerated, his body flowed so smoothly the speed was hard to notice.

"Yeah, I guess I can't give you more than a ten-yard head start," Nick said.

"Yo, Yo, Yo!"

Nick and Erik turned to see Dylan jump out of his mother's minivan. Dylan was a tall, thin, black kid, with big feet, big hands, and large, intense eyes.

"Hey, Dyl." Nick kicked him the ball. "You won't believe the news."

"What news, buddy?" Dylan said.

"Can't tell you yet. Not until Will's here at least."

Dylan looked at Erik. "What's up?"

"No idea."

Dylan's main sport was baseball. He had a killer fastball and could throw a curve and a knuckler. Thanks to his size and speed, he was also a solid soccer player. He loved sprinting up the wings to terrorize the opposing defense. But his game had limitations. Whenever he trapped or dribbled the ball, it seemed to find some hard, bony part of his body and bounce several yards away.

"C'mon, Nick. What's the word?"

"I'm waiting 'til Will's here. It's good news."

Dylan rolled his eyes. He turned to the goal and toed the ball hard into the middle of the net.

"Not with your toe, Dyl," Erik said.

"That was no toe, Steiner."

Erik looked at Nick and shrugged. Dylan still refused to accept that he ever hit the ball with his toe. The boys formed a triangle and passed the ball back and forth.

A rusty red pick-up pulled into the school driveway, and Will climbed out. Will was short and stocky, with a handsome pink face, an easy smile, and a mop of blond hair that fell over his eyes. Off the field, he was a quiet kid. On the field, he threw himself around with abandon, happily crunching shins, knees, heads or any other body part with his opponents, and naturally he had no fear of an inflated plastic ball. Nick and Erik loved playing with him.

"Hey," said Will.

"Hey, yourself," said Nick.

"So? Will's here. What's the scoop?" Erik said.

The boys moved in closer to Nick.

"My dad signed us up!"

"For what?" asked Dylan.

"For the Tri-State League. As a team! We don't have to join the Thunder and get broken up. We'll have our own team. We'll practice right here in Lancaster. And the cool thing is, that way Will can play too."

Everyone considered the news.

The Thunder was the travel soccer team based in Milford, the commercial center of the region and the home of Hereford College and the Milford Medical Center. Local kids from the Central Valley who wanted to play serious soccer always joined the Thunder, even if it meant driving forty-five minutes to practice. The Thunder had multiple teams at every age level, perfectly groomed fields, and experienced, high-quality coaching. All the Thunder home games were videotaped and posted on their website. They competed for the Tri-State championship every year.

Lancaster had nothing comparable. Like other small towns in the area, Lancaster ran a rec league for kids through sixth grade, but anyone who wanted to play soccer after that was expected to play for the Thunder.

And joining the Thunder wasn't easy. The Thunder started its program for second graders, but didn't allow non-residents to participate until seventh grade. By the time kids from outside Milford got on a team, they could be behind in their skills. Also, the Milford players formed a clique that wasn't always friendly to kids from the surrounding areas.

Nick, Erik and Dylan had tried out for the Thunder in June. Nick and Erik were put on different Under-13 "A" teams. Dylan, much to his annoyance, was put on a "B" team. Will didn't even try out. He would likely have made one of the A teams, but with his dad working and no mom at home, Will had to help look after his sister. There was no way he could spare the time it took to get back and forth to Milford for practice.

"Wow, that's great!" said Dylan. "We'll play in the A league, right?"

"Of course, man," Nick replied.

"Ha! The Thunder claps think they're too good for us. We'll whip 'em!"

Erik was more cautious. "When did your dad set this up?"

"Earlier in the summer, I guess," Nick said. "When we were complaining about being on separate teams."

"Did you know about it?"

"No, he kept it a surprise. Didn't want to get my hopes up in case it didn't work."

"And he figured everything out?"

"Like what?"

"Well, who will coach? Where'll we play? Who's going to be on the team? Can we really compete against the other travel teams?" Erik tried not to look at Dylan, but he was their fourth best player. If the Thunder coaches didn't think Dylan was ready for A league, then Gabe, Leon, and Parker sure weren't.

"We can definitely compete," Nick said, hotly. "As for a coach, can't your dad do it again?"

"Travel soccer is different from rec league. He's not much of a soccer guy."

"That doesn't matter. We can coach ourselves mostly. We've been doing it all summer." Nick turned to Will. "What about you? Can you play if we're in Lancaster?"

"I'll have to check with my dad. He needs me to help out with

Angie." Will's sister, Angie, had been born with spina bifida and a host of related developmental problems. State aid paid for a special school that went right through the summer. But two afternoons a week Angie arrived home before Will's father got off work. "But, sure, if practices are right here in town, I think so. It's great news, Nick."

"Fantastic," Dylan agreed.

Everyone looked at Erik.

"Okay, it's great news. I'm just thinking of the practical problems. I'll ask my dad about coaching. Do you think they'll let us play on the school field?"

"We'll find somewhere," Nick said.

"C'mon," said Dylan, tapping his wrist where a watch might have been. "Let's do the loop. The others'll be here soon."

"Wait," Erik said. "So if we have a travel team, what's our name?"

"We're the Blue Marauders. And we're going to rock the league!" Nick let out a yell and took off at a run.

THE BOYS DISCUSSED the team name during the loop run. Nick's dad had come up with the Blue Marauders, but Nick liked it too. Lancaster's teams always wore blue, and Nick wanted the team to be identified with the town. He also liked the idea of marauding around the state, destroying the other teams.

Erik said the name reminded him of the Scottish warriors who fought the English. "The Picts. They painted themselves blue and were totally bad-ass."

Nick wondered if that was why his dad had chosen the name. Nicky and his dad were McCoys, but Scottish not Irish McCoys, his dad said. The family was Presbyterian and, supposedly, from Aberdeen a long way back. Nick had never seen much evidence of this. The history got murky just a couple of generations back. But his dad persisted in the family lore and kept up with some Scottish traditions, including eating oatmeal for breakfast, hating the British, and pretending to like the bagpipes.

WHEN THE BOYS got back to the soccer field, Abbey was there taking shots on Jamie. Jamie Farrell-Macquarie was the goalie. He had been born in China and was adopted as a baby by a pair of ex-hippies who ran a local organic farm. Jamie was shorter and thinner than most goalies in seventh grade, but he loved the position. Unfortunately, the fact that he was quick and fearless and had a great eye for the ball had not been enough to win him a roster spot as a keeper on the Thunder. At the try-outs he'd gotten lost in a crowd of bigger kids and been put on one of the B teams as a field player. Jamie wasn't sure he wanted to play soccer if he wasn't a goalie.

Abbey knocked a penalty kick past Jamie into the top left corner. Abbey was, most importantly, a girl. She was taller than most of the boys, and she had dirty blond hair that she kept in a ponytail running straight down her back. Whereas the boys all wore baggy shorts that got longer each year, Abbey's shorts seemed to keep getting shorter. She played with the boys last year because all rec soccer in Lancaster was co-ed. They didn't have enough kids to field more than one team.

Abbey was a strong defender with a knack for winning head balls. She also had a great playing relationship with Nick and Erik. When they made a break, her passes over the heads of the defense would hit them in stride. Abbey had tried out for the Thunder girls' team and, to no one's surprise, won a spot on the A team. The head coach had even taken her aside to tell her how much he looked forward to working with her.

"Hey, slackers!" said Dylan. "You missed the run."

"Some people have lives, moron," Abbey retorted.

Dylan knew that Jamie worked at his parent's farm until noon, and Abbey had piano lessons in the morning, but he wasn't put off.

"Nick here has some killer news."

"We're forming a Lancaster team. To compete against the Thunder. Our own team in the Tri-State League." Nick looked apologetically at Abbey. "Sorry, it's the boys' league."

Dylan was impatient. "The Blue Marauders, man. Me, Erik, Nick, Will, Jamie in goal. Then Gabe, Leon and Parker. We just need a couple others and we're ready to rock."

"You'll play, won't you, Jamie?" said Erik. "We're going need you."

Jamie smiled broadly, "Sure. That sounds great."

"It's a shame Abbey can't play," said Nick.

"That'd really crush the opponents," Dylan grinned. "To get beat by a Lancaster girl."

"Abbey's not just a regular girl," said Will.

"Like she'd play with us anyway," said Nick. "The season hasn't even started and I hear she has the girls' MVP trophy all wrapped up. But you'll still cheer for us, won't you Abbey?"

Abbey, who had stood silently during the ribbing with a ball at her feet, suddenly kicked it as hard as she could right at Nick. There was no chance to duck, and Nick took it in the stomach. He bent double, coughing and laughing. The boys around him also broke into laughter.

"I think you just lost a fan, McCoy," Dylan said.

"What the hell, Abbey?" Nick said, red faced but grinning. "None of your shots at Jamie were that hard."

"Or that accurate," said Erik.

GABE AND LEON arrived together. They made a funny pair. Gabe was heavier and more developed than the other kids. He had a pale round face, blue eyes under heavy lids, and the beginnings of sideburns. Leon was small and dark, with jet black hair hanging down around his shoulders. Gabe's family was French Canadian and his father was the local police chief. Leon's parents were from Mexico and worked at the high school. His father taught Spanish and his mother was the school nurse. Gabe was an intimidating defender who played without finesse. He crashed his body into opponents and sent them flying into the dirt. Leon played forward and was a skillful dribbler. Even Erik and Nick had a hard time getting the ball away from him. But the rest of his game was ineffective. His shots and passes were weak. Both Gabe and Leon had tried out for the Thunder and been placed on a B team. Predictably, Gabe had been loudly outraged, Leon quietly accepting.

Gabe strode into center of the circle of boys. "Hey, what did I miss? Are we pounding McCoy?"

"We're starting a team," said Erik. "To play against the Thunder."

"The Blue Marauders," said Dylan. "Are you in?"

"Hell, yeah!" Gabe was still mad at not making an A team.

"What about you, Leon?" Nicky asked.

"Sure. But don't we need more players?" Leon said.

"With Parker we've got eight," said Dylan. "When does the season start?"

"Like a week, right?" Erik replied. "I think my first Thunder game would've been August 29th, the Saturday before school starts."

"That's ten days," Nick said. "We better get to work. Hey, Erik, tomorrow, you and I should call around and see who else we can get."

"All the good players have already joined the Thunder," said Erik.

"Ah, c'mon. There's plenty of people who would love to play for us."

"Let's have try-outs," Gabe suggested. "If you make some posters, my dad can put them up while he's driving around. Maybe some of the kids in the other towns don't want to drive all the way to Milford."

"Cool, try-outs. Like a real team." Will was pleased by the prospect.

"We are a real team," said Nick. "By the end of the season we'll be the realest thing in the league."

"Are we just going to talk or are we going to practice? Let's go already." It was the first thing Abbey had said since finding out about the new team.

AFTER PRACTICE, ERIK walked slowly back to his house, thinking over the Blue Marauders. It was true that he and Nicky had spent the summer complaining about being on different teams, and it was true about the Milford bias of the Thunder. Erik really was excited about starting their own team in Lancaster.

But it was also true that he had been looking forward to playing with the Thunder. The Thunder was well known throughout the state, and Erik was excited about competing on a bigger stage. He wanted to broaden his horizons, meet new people, and have coaches who really understood soccer.

Erik's dad had coached the rec league team, but he didn't know much about soccer. He did his best. He read coaching books and watched videos, but he'd never played. Erik was sure that his own technical and tactical knowledge of the game exceeded that of his dad.

At supper that night, Erik talked to his parents.

"Dad, I don't think I'm going to play for the Thunder. Mr. Mc-Coy entered a Lancaster team into the Tri-State League. We were talking about it at practice. We're calling it the Blue Marauders."

"I think that's wonderful," Erik's mother said. "I wasn't looking forward to getting you to Milford for practice."

"But there are some details that need to be worked out. We need a field and some more players. And we need a coach."

"That's quite a few details," his father said.

"Nick says it'll work out. We can run the drills. We just need an adult to organize things."

"Well, maybe it's for the best. You two have been moping all summer about being on separate teams."

His mother chimed in again. "Does this mean your friend Will can play?"

"Yeah. That's a good thing." Erik paused. "Dad, I promised Nick I'd ask you about coaching."

"Don't sound too enthusiastic."

"Sorry, Dad."

"Don't worry. I just want to make sure you've thought this through."

"Yeah, it's cool. We'll have our own team. It's going to be great."

"But?" his father prompted.

"But what?"

"That's what I'm asking."

"Well, we need a field and some more players."

"And you need a real coach. Which I am not."

"I guess."

"Well, let's say you find a field and some players. And let's say I agree to coach. Under those circumstances, would you rather play for the Marauders or the Thunder?"

Erik hesitated, torn between ambition and friendship, before saying, "The Marauders." Then he added, "I just want to be good. I want the team to be good."

"There are no guarantees in life, Erik. But we can try. How about if I talk to Nick's dad, and see if we can figure out a field. If we get that far, I'll coach until you can find someone with more time and experience."

"Thanks, Dad."

NICK RODE INTO his driveway at a terrific pace and jumped neatly off his bike before it clattered into the shed.

"Don't do that!" Nick's mother emerged from the shed, holding pruning shears. She went to work early on Wednesdays and Fridays so she could be home in the afternoons to take care of Nick's sisters, 6-year-old twins, after day care. Nick's father was responsible for Mondays and Tuesdays. Nick had them on Thursdays.

"Ahh, Mom."

"You'll ruin your bike!"

"It's just an old junker. It'll be fine."

"I'm not buying you a replacement. And where's your helmet?" Nick did not answer. "Okay, that's it. I won't have you bombing down Lancaster Hill without a helmet. No bike for a week!"

Nick was used to this sort of threat. It usually came to nothing. "Mom, is Dad home?"

His mother, having issued her threat, was mollified. "No, he won't be in until after supper. He has a late job in Canterbury." Nick's father worked running heavy equipment for construction companies. He was known as one of the best operators in the region.

Nick ducked into the house before his mother could get back on the subject of the bike. His sisters were playing Candy Land.

"Will you play?" asked Caitlin.

"We just started," said Carrie. "You won't be too far behind."

Nick looked at the game and saw his sisters' pieces halfway around the board. "Let me get a drink first."

Nick drank several glasses of water and ate a bag of pretzels. He was barely past the Gingerbread Plum Tree when Carrie won. Afterwards they all went out to the yard and played baseball until supper time. Nick did the dishes, his regular chore, while his mom put the girls to bed. His dad came home just as Nick was finishing up.

"Hello, kiddo! What's for supper?"

"Hey, Dad. Mom left some meatloaf in the microwave."

As his father washed up, Nick heated the plate.

"I talked to the guys about the Blue Marauders. They're all psyched."

"Good."

"But where are we going to practice? I mean, they'll need the elementary school field for rec league, and I don't guess we can use the high school field."

"Not a problem. I talked with Heidi before signing the team up. You can use Dan's field."

Nick knew Heidi. She was the director of the town's sports programs, and one of her jobs was figuring out who got to use the town facilities. But Nick didn't know who Dan was or which field his dad was referring to.

"Dan?"

"Dan Caton. You know, Caton's Garage, across from the Village Store."

Caton's Garage was a filling station near a tiny cluster of stores on the far side of Lancaster Hill. The area, which Lancaster residents called the "Village," included a convenience store, a pizzeria, a realtor, and a barbershop. But Nick didn't remember any playing fields there, and he said so to his father.

"Sure, you've seen it. A nice flat field behind Dan's place."

Nick felt cheated. He thought he knew where his father meant. "That's not a soccer field. That's a forest."

"No siree. I checked it out before I signed the team up. It's a nice flat field. Dan's been haying it until a couple of years ago, so it's all grass, just needs a mow."

"Dad!"

Nick saw the humiliation immediately. The Blue Marauders would be playing on a rinky-dink, uneven field covered with rocks and mud. Nick imagined the established teams laughing at them, maybe even refusing to play. Then Nick thought of what he'd tell his teammates. No way Erik would think Dan's hayfield was a substitute for the manicured fields the Thunder played on.

"Nothing that you and the boys can't fix up. Do a little work for a change, instead of all the pointless running around. You boys provide the labor, and Tim Thomas will donate the turf to resod it. Pat Cooper's been looking at what chemicals we'll need, and he says the field checks out nice and flat." Pat Cooper was Will's father, and he worked for Tim Thomas's landscaping business.

"You already talked to him about it?"

"Sure. It's no secret."

Nick began to recalculate. "How long will it take to clear?"

"Two days, maybe three. Got to get the rocks and tree stumps out."

"Dad, it'll never work!"

"Sure it will. That's why Heidi's supporting the team; she wants that field cleared. If you do that, she'll buy goals. She might even throw in some bleachers and a port-a-potty."

Nick saw that his dad was enjoying his consternation. His dad loved to spring unpleasant surprises to see how Nick would react. On the other hand, his dad seemed to have worked out the angles, and if he said it was flat, it'd be flat.

"We'll need some equipment."

His dad smiled to see him rising to the challenge. "Yep. That's where Dan comes in. He wants the field cleared too, and he likes the idea of some free labor. Dan'll rent what's needed from Tim. A mower and a tiller, for sure. A roller and a grader, too, I expect."

Nick sighed. This was not going to be easy. And he'd have to think about how to sell the others on it. But maybe it would work.

Nick's dad looked at his watch. "If I were you, I'd give Dan a call before he goes to bed."

ABBEY ARRIVED HOME and went right up to her room. She put in her ear buds and lay on her bed. She was alone in the house. Her older sisters were at sleep-away camp and her mother, a radiologist in the VA hospital in Forsberg, did not get home until shortly after six. Her dad's schedule was less predictable. He was a consultant on environmental compliance, whatever that meant, and his hours depended on the job. But he had been late every day this week. Abbey turned the volume on her ear buds to max.

"It's not like I even want to play on the Blue Marauders," she told herself. "I'll play with the Thunder and play real soccer."

Abbey's bedroom got hot in the summer. The sun shone in through the large, south-facing windows and made it feel like a sauna. But her mom and dad, annoyingly environmentally correct, laughed at her request for air conditioning. She closed her eyes, listened to her music, and sweated.

CHAPTER 2

Field of Dreams

Nick woke up ready to go. He threw on a pair of Adidas shorts and an old L.A. Galaxy shirt and raced downstairs, hoping to catch a ride to Dan Caton's field with his dad. He wanted to see what they were facing before he spoke to Erik.

Nick's sisters were playing dog in the living room and he stopped to scratch each of them behind their ears. They barked at him as he went into the kitchen.

"Hey Mom, where's Dad?"

"He had to leave early for a job down south. He left a package for you next to the toaster."

Nick poured himself a huge bowl of Cheerios and opened the pack-age. It was a thick manila envelope from the Tri-State League: player registrations, rules, directions, and contact information. He frowned. There were a lot of forms to fill out. Flipping through the papers again he found a schedule. The first game was on the Saturday before school started, against the Kilby Titans. At home. At Caton Field. That was just eight days away. And the registration forms were due four days before that. Nick felt an uncharacteristic moment of panic. He leaned his head back, closed his eyes, and moaned.

"What's wrong, Nicky?"

"Nothing, Mom. There's just a ton of stuff to get ready for the season."

"I can help you tonight if you want."

"That'd be really great. By the way, can you drop me at Caton's Garage when you take the girls to day care?"

"As long as you're ready to go in two minutes."

Nick hurriedly packed a bag and loaded his bike into the station wagon. Ignoring his mother's disapproving stare, he carried his bowl of cereal to the car and finished eating it on the way to Caton's, leaving the empty bowl on the passenger seat when he got out. His mother's voice called after him, "You have to be home this afternoon for your sisters. Don't forget!"

Nick waved as his mother drove off and then turned around to look at Caton's Garage. He had driven past the garage thousands of times and visited it, too. His parents had taken their old Pontiac there before it died. Their new cars were under warranty, and they had stopped using Caton's as much.

Mr. Caton was an old-time resident of Lancaster. He'd been the volunteer fire chief for twenty years when he was younger, and now, in his eighties, he was always around at town events, town meetings, elections, the Rhubarb Festival, shaking hands and greeting old friends. His son, Tony Caton, had been a classmate of Nick's dad at school and had taken over running the garage for a while. But some argument had caused Tony to move down state and start his own shop. Dan kept the old place open with the help of his daughter and her husband.

Screwing up his courage, Nick walked into the little garage office. A bell tinkled overhead. Behind the desk was a large woman in sweatpants, Dan's daughter. Nick thought her name was Steffie but wasn't sure.

"Is Dan around?"

"He's out back somewhere. What do you need him for?"

"I'm Nick McCoy. My dad talked to him about using the field behind the garage for soccer."

"I'll get him." The woman pushed herself up and bustled through a swing door into the back of the garage, calling "Dan! Dan!"

Eventually Dan came out, a thin man in grey coveralls. His face was deeply lined and framed by the last few strands of wild grey hair. Age had caused him to become bent over, and he had to stretch his neck upwards to look straight in front of him.

"So you're Charlie's kid. I remember you from this high," he said, holding his hand down by his knees.

"Yes, sir." Putting up with this sort of remark was the price of living in a small town.

"Want to see the field?"

"Yes, sir."

"Come out back."

Dan led Nick through the back door of the garage and out to a fenced-in back yard filled with rusting car parts. There was a hole in the fence which opened onto a large space surrounded by majestic pines trees. There was enough land for several soccer fields, but it was wildly overgrown with grass and brambles up to Nick's waist.

"What do you think, son?"

Nick hesitated. He thought it was a hopeless mess. He said, "Needs some work."

"Yep, that it does. But it's a fine field."

"A bit overgrown."

"Just needs a mow. Good drainage."

"Dad said there'd be rocks and stumps to remove."

"Your dad's a kidder. There may be a couple of rocks, but nothing too big." Nick didn't say anything and Dan continued. "You know, it was the main field for the high school back in Tony's day."

"It was?"

"Sure. Old high school was across the road. Well, there's no space on that side for fields 'cause the land goes straight up behind. So the field was over here."

"I didn't know."

"It's overgrown now, but it's a good field. There won't be no stumps. Those pines are trying to move in. But I've kept 'em back. Always wanted to have a real playing field here again."

Nick brightened. "Still, it will take more than a regular lawn mower."

"Yep, that it will. But you let me know when you boys can come over. I'll talk to Tim Thomas, and we'll get the machinery over here."

"Our first game is in eight days."

"Better get to it then, hadn't we?"

"What if we start tomorrow morning?"

"I'm here. I'll call Tim tonight and work it out. You just get the boys here."

"Thanks, Mr. Caton."

"Dan."

"Thanks, Dan."

AFTER LEAVING THE garage, Nick had an idea. He crossed the road, entered the Village Store, and asked for Rory Patenaude, the owner. Charlene, a high school student with a brother in sixth grade, a year behind Nick, sat behind the counter.

"He's in back. But you better grab him quick. He's heading up to the store in Willsboro."

"Thanks, Charlene." Nick knocked briefly and headed through the doors marked "Authorized Personnel Only," which led to the store's small office and storage room. Squeezed behind the desk, fiddling with a drawer, Nick saw Rory's familiar bulk.

Anyone who frequented the Village Store was familiar with the ins and outs of Rory's long and losing battle against an expanding waistline. Rory Patenaude was an institution in Lancaster. The Village Store, a small convenience store with a post office attached, had been owned by his father and grandfather before him. Everyone in town passed through one way or another, when they didn't want to make the drive to the supermarket, on their way to the dump, to pick up a paper, or just to swap town news.

Some people complained that the store had lost its character since Rory had taken over. Rory had bought three other stores in the surrounding villages and he'd added a host of new-fangled items, including bakery bread, imported cheese, and grind-your-own gourmet coffee. Rory was also a town selectman and had made some enemies pushing changes to the zoning laws that limited development. This particularly hit old-time residents, many of whom were cash-poor farmers and needed to sell land to stay afloat.

Still, most people in Lancaster had a fond spot in their heart for Rory. Stuffed into a T-shirt and baggy shorts, even through much of winter, he cut a familiar figure in town. While he didn't suffer fools and had a temper when provoked, his generosity was widely acknowledged. He visited shut-ins, drove elderly residents to their doctor appointments, and spent many hours at Polly's Café, treating friends and acquaintances to coffee and donuts. Last year, when the Robinsons lost their home to fire, Rory had led the effort to raise money to have it rebuilt and, it was rumored, had donated most of it himself. Before that, Rory had helped Will's parents out, loaning them money for their daughter's school, and forgiving the loan when Pat's wife died.

"Hey, Mr. Patenaude."

Rory responded without looking up. "Howdy, Nicholas, how's tricks?"

"Uh, you know we're going to make a playing field out behind Caton's Garage?"

"Sure do. Dan's been wanting to do that for a while. Ah, here it is!" Rory held up the accordion folder he'd been looking for.

"You know why we're doing it?"

"What is this, twenty questions? What do you want? I'm off to Willsboro in five minutes."

"Well, we're starting a soccer team. In the Tri-State League. We're going to play on the field."

"So?"

"Well, some of the teams in the leagues have sponsors that help pay for their uniforms and stuff and I was wondering . . ."

"If I'd sponsor you?"

"Yeah. We'll have games down here. People'll come from out of town. They'll come in and buy drinks and snacks and things."

"Got it! Good sales job, kid. How much are the uniforms?"

"Oh. I don't know."

"Nicholas, Nicholas! You gotta know that before you come in. I'll tell you what: Go home and figure out what you need. Uniforms gotta include 'The Village Store' across the front. Gotta look nice. You tell me how much it'll cost, and we'll discuss sponsorship. No promises, but I want a nice-looking proposal. All the questions answered."

"Okay!"

"You should ask Georgi, too. He's soccer mad, and he might want to get in on this."

Georgi owned Georgi's House of Pizza next to the Village Store. It was just a bunch of plastic tables and chairs on one side of a counter with a pizza oven, a grill, and a Coke machine on the other. As one of only two restaurants in town, it did its share of business, particularly with the school kids, but that did not make Georgi anyone's favorite person. He was burly, sweaty, and disagreeable. When he was not yelling at his customers for taking too much time to order, he was yelling at his burly, sweaty sons or his burly, sweaty wife. The family didn't stop arguing just because a customer asked for service. They kept right on yelling at each other as they took orders and handed out the plates.

On top of being generally unpleasant, Georgi spoke a heavily accented English that was hard to understand. And when you misheard him or misunderstood him, he got furious. All this flashed through Nick's mind as he said to Rory, "I wasn't planning to talk to Georgi."

"No, you should. Definitely. Maybe we'll split a sponsorship. I'll be in most of next week. Now I gotta get outta here."

With that, Rory called out to Charlene that he'd be back in three hours, and he had his cell phone if she needed anything. Then he was gone.

FORTUNATELY, THE HOUSE of Pizza didn't open until noon, so Nick could put off talking to Georgi. And as he biked up to Erik's house, Nick felt pleased with the morning's work.

Erik was in the back yard practicing lacrosse. Nick grabbed a stick and the boys threw the ball around for a while before Nick asked, "Did you talk to your dad about coaching?"

"Yes. He'll do it, although he'd still like to find someone else. What about the field?"

"We're set with that. I think I got us a sponsor too."

"Who?"

"The Village Store. It's not definite yet. Rory said I had to find out how much the shirts would cost and come back with a proposal."

"Cool. We can call Intersports and find out what they would charge. But when are we going to use the field? I can't figure it out. After school starts it'll be all rec league."

"We've got a new field. Behind Caton's Garage."

"There's no field there."

"That's what I thought, but I went to look at it this morning. It's totally flat and, uh, drains well. It just needs cleaning up. And Heidi's agreed to buy us goals and bleachers."

"You're kidding, right?"

"No, man."

"Nick, it's a hayfield!"

"It'll be good, I promise. Dan said it used to be the old high school field back in my dad's day. And Dad and Pat Cooper will do the resodding once it gets cleared. All we have to do is provide the manpower."

"We who?"

"The Blue Marauders. We've got to start work tomorrow so the field is ready for the first game. You know it's in eight days?"

"How are we going to play a game in eight days? We don't even have a team!" Erik caught Nick's last toss and threw his lacrosse stick down disgustedly. "C'mon, let's go up to my room."

Up in his room, Erik dragged the full story of the field from Nick. At first, Erik felt they should just give up on the whole thing and play with the Thunder. But once Nick finally convinced him to give it a chance, Erik figured they had to act fast. He turned on his computer and sent an e-mail asking the rest of the team to meet at Caton's Garage the next morning.

Then he turned back to Nick. "Now we just need a full team. Who we got?"

"Jamie in goal," Nick replied. "You, Dylan, and Leon up front. Me and Will in midfield. Gabe and Parker on D."

"Parker?"

"Yeah."

"Okay, so let's figure we need at least two subs. That means five more players."

"Yeah."

"We'll never find that many."

"What about that guy Matty from Forsberg?"

Matty Hall's parents were friends with Erik's mother and father. Matty was a good three-sport athlete and anchored most of Forsberg's teams. Nick remembered he wore glasses and had long hair, which he wore in a ponytail. He also remembered that Matty was the only good thing about Forsberg soccer.

"He's playing Thunder."

"Yeah, well so were you. Forsberg's further away from Milford than Lancaster. Call him and see if he wants to play with us instead."

"Okay, it's a chance. But remember, his parents work in Milford. They won't think of the commute as a big deal."

Erik wrote Matty an e-mail while Nick hovered over his shoulder.

"Tell him we only have twelve players," Nick suggested, "and he'll get a ton of playing time."

Erik nodded. "Who else can we ask? What about Liam in sixth grade? He's pretty good."

"Can't touch the sixth graders. My dad said that was part of the deal with Heidi. She didn't want to hurt the rec program."

"Well, what about Jackson, then? He's in eighth grade, but he's younger than I am."

Jackson had played rec league with Erik and Nick when he was in sixth grade and they were in fifth. He was tall and thin, even taller than Gabe. He looked gangly and uncoordinated, but he was an effective defender, usually managing to get a head or foot on the ball.

"He's not bad," Nick said. "I think he played Thunder B last year. We should call him." Erik found Jackson's number in the phone book and left a message.

In the end, they identified three other kids as likely candidates and left texts, e-mails, or phone messages for each of them. The messages dangled the hope of additional playing time, always an issue on the over-subscribed Thunder teams.

"It's still not enough," Erik said. "Most of these kids are playing Thunder and won't want to come over to the Blue Marauders."

"Let's have try-outs. We can make a poster like Gabe suggested."

"We could put a message on the Central Valley Soccer Facebook page."

"I'm not on Facebook," said Nick.

"I know, and it's a pain. But I'm a member of the group. Let me post a quick message."

Erik's fingers hurried over the keyboard. He typed:

> **Blue Marauders** (Lancaster). U-13 team in Tri-State A League. Seek players w/ *skill*. Try-outs Monday (8/24) – 12:30 pm at Lancaster Elementary School. Questions? E-mail erikst@cvnet.com.

"What do you think?"

"Fine, I guess," said Nick. "Shouldn't it say 'soccer' somewhere?"

"It's a soccer board, idiot. Everyone will know that."

"Well, maybe we should do a poster too. It'll make Gabe happy, and his dad can put 'em up for us."

Erik and Nick spent the next hour designing the poster. They downloaded a great picture of Cristiano Ronaldo laying out for an aerial volley. On the top they added text: "TRY OUT FOR THE BLUE MARAUDERS." On the bottom, the same text that Erik had put in his Facebook post. They printed out ten copies and figured it was time for lunch.

After ham and cheese sandwiches, Erik said, "Should we do the shirts now?"

"Oh, God! No! Let's go to the Pond."

"Look, why don't you let me do the shirts, okay? Jamie and I can design something and we'll see how much it costs at Intersports?" Erik suspected that, left to Nick, the team shirts would never be ordered.

"Sure," said Nick happily. "Once you get some prices, we can go talk to Rory and Georgi."

"Georgi?"

"Yeah. Didn't I tell you? Rory thought he might want to get in on the sponsorship too."

"That should be fun." Erik tried to imagine asking Georgi for money.

Nick shrugged. "I think Rory wants to make us jump through hoops. It'll be fine. Can we go to the Pond now?"

BY NINE O'CLOCK Friday morning, five Blue Marauders were out behind Caton's Garage wondering what to do. There were two ferocious machines on loan from Tim Thomas, but no one who knew how to use them.

Gabe climbed onto a tractor and said, "Let's just start."

Nick nodded.

"We should wait for Mr. Caton," said Erik.

"How hard can it be to cut grass?" Gabe replied. He turned a key, and the machine started up with a huge growl and bucked forward toward Leon, who dove out of the way. Almost at once, the machine came to a halt with a grinding and coughing of steel rubbing against steel.

As Leon got up and dusted himself off, Will walked up. "Thank God you're here, Will," Erik said. "Maybe you can prevent Gabe from ruining a couple hundred thousand dollars of equipment."

"That thing's a monster," said Gabe jumping down.

Will smiled his engaging smile, and everyone relaxed. "Sure. I don't think we want to start with the tiller though."

"Then what's the plan?" Nick asked. As he spoke, Jamie's parents' ancient Subaru pulled up, followed by Dan Caton's truck. Jamie's parents had agreed to release Jamie from his morning chores so he could help with the field.

"I guess we should ask Dan," Will said.

While they were waiting for Dan, Nick asked if anyone knew if Parker was going to show up.

Erik said, "He came by the Pond yesterday after you left. But he was pretty vague."

"No way he's going to show up," Dylan said. "He's hanging out with all the headbangers from the high school. Did you see his outfit yesterday? It was like ninety degrees and he was wearing black jeans, a hoodie, and a ski hat."

"But he's going to play, right?" Nick said. "We need his defense."

Gabe shrugged. "He said he would. Just don't count on him before noon. I don't think he's gotten up before noon all summer."

Dan ambled up and said, "Nice of you boys to show up so early. It'll be good having a playing field back here again."

"How do you want us to get started, Mr. Caton?" Erik asked.

"Call me Dan. Now, you see them markers?" The boys looked around and noticed the little red flags waving in the grass. "Pat Cooper put those in to show where the field'll be. First off, we need to mow the whole area and get the grass down. Now I was told some of you boys have experience with these machines. Is that right?"

Will and Jamie raised their hands. Jamie had grown up helping on his parents' farm, and Will just understood machines, seemingly having absorbed the magic touch from his father. It was always a mystery to Will and Jamie that Nick was such a klutz with machines. After all, Charlie McCoy was a whiz with them. He worked with super high-tech construction equipment, massive cranes and space-age diggers. But somehow the knowledge had never transferred to Nick. Perhaps it was because Nick never saw much point to things unless there was a ball and a game to play.

Dan assigned Will and Jamie the task of mowing and put the other boys to work clearing junk from a path on the east side of the garage that would become the new driveway. The path was littered with old tires and dead car parts. Dan told the boys to load everything into his pick-up.

After the field was mowed, Will moved on to tilling, turning up fresh, black dirt and rocks where the grass had been, while Jamie drove a tractor behind him. The other boys followed Jamie, looking for any large rocks and throwing them in the tractor's bucket loader. "We'll dump 'em over by the trees," Dan told them. "If you come across anything too big to move, just mark it, and we'll see what Pat and Charlie can do tomorrow."

After a hard morning, the boys were delighted when Dan brought pizza and soda over from Georgi's for lunch. As they ate, they filled out the league registration forms that Nick's mother had put in his backpack.

Soon the boys were back at work. Will was finished tilling, but the rock picking took forever. Parker arrived around two o'clock. He was dressed in the same black jeans and hoodie as yesterday. Silently, without excuses, he joined the others.

"Hey man," said Nick. "Nice of you to show up."

"Nickster," said Parker in a mild tone, unfazed by Nick's sarcasm. He gave a vague smile and a thumbs-up sign. "Wouldn't miss it."

"Yeah, but are you playing for us?"

Parker asked a little about the team and what to expect. Nick said they needed him to play fullback. There were fourteen games and practices maybe four times a week. Parker said he'd have to think about that sort of commitment. Nick told Parker that the team was counting on him to play right back.

A little after three, as the boys' strength was beginning to flag, Charlie McCoy and Pat Cooper showed up along with Hector Juarez, Leon's father, and Marty Farrell, Jamie's father, to lend a hand. Pat had brought Angie with him, and she sat with Dan and watched the men and boys work. They lasted for another two hours before Charlie called a halt for the day. Pat brought out some lemonade and pretzels.

As they sat around eating their snack and complaining about their sore backs and aching feet, Dan went over to his shed and came back dragging a faded wooden sign with the words "Caton's Field" carved into it. He smiled. "We'll give it a paint job and put it out front when you're done."

ON SATURDAY, THE boys were at Dan's by eight in the morning. Nick's dad, who was coordinating the work over the weekend, had insisted on an early start. To the boys it seemed as if Mr. McCoy, unnaturally chipper and cheerful for the hour, took pleasure in rousting them out of bed at an ungodly hour and denying them time to eat breakfast.

The boys perked up, however, when they got to the field and Mr. McCoy broke out cider and donuts. Also, it was reassuring to see several new people on hand to help out. In addition to the boys' fathers who had worked yesterday afternoon, Leon's mother was there, as were Heidi and her husband, Dan Caton's daughter, some co-workers of Pat Cooper, and several high school students.

Pat got the tractor ready for grading, and Charlie McCoy organized the kids to go through the field picking rocks. The boys groaned.

"We did that yesterday," said Nick.

"Yep. And now we have to do it again."

The field was picked clean, and the rest of the long morning was spent unloading sod from Tim Thomas' trucks.

At lunch, Pat cooked hamburgers and hot dogs on a grill loaded onto the bed of his truck, and the boys complained about their sore muscles. Afterward, some of the boys helped Pat fertilize and water the field, while others worked with Charlie McCoy to distribute heavy rolls of sod around the field so they would be ready to lay the next day.

ON SUNDAY, IN deference to those attending church, Mr. McCoy told the boys to meet at Caton's at noon. Leon and Gabe went to Catholic mass at a large contemporary church located just north of Lancaster on the highway that cut between the Cayuga River and the town. Will and Dylan went to the Church of Christ service at the Lancaster Parish, the old white colonial church at the top of

Lancaster Hill. The McCoys also went to Lancaster Parish when they went to church, but that was usually just on Easter and Christmas.

Erik's family was Jewish, but non-observant, and he didn't attend any services. Jamie didn't go to church either. A few years ago, Jamie's parents had started to attend Friends meetings in the Community Center. They had tried half-heartedly to convince Jamie to join them, pointing out that Abbey and her parents attended meetings, but they were never successful, and they didn't believe in imposing their beliefs on their child. Instead, Erik and Jamie arranged to meet to pick out the team jerseys.

They met at Jamie's house, a ramshackle ex-commune that his parents had purchased in the 1970s. As the other inhabitants moved out, his parents had gradually cleared the title and transformed it into a workable little organic farm. They didn't make a lot of money, but they spent even less. Their lives were focused on the farm and on a series of obscure political causes that Jamie never quite understood.

Jamie's room was an island of cleanliness in the mess that overwhelmed the rest of the house, which his parents treated as a mere extension of the barn. Stockpiles of grain and fertilizer and pieces of farm equipment littered the downstairs. Two years ago, Jamie had starting insisting that his parents take off their shoes before they came into his room. They rolled their eyes at the request, but complied whenever they remembered.

By the time Erik arrived, Jamie had already searched the Intersports website and chosen the three shirts he liked best. They were all blue: one with a white pointy collar and yellow trim, one with shimmering light and dark blue stripes, and a third that was a replica of the classic Italian Azzuri shirts. Jamie went through the website again with Erik and they found a fourth possibility, a royal blue shirt with red trim around the neck and sleeves. All the designs, with custom lettering, ran about thirty dollars a shirt.

Erik said they'd need white shirts too, in case the other team wore blue.

Jamie hit his forehead with his hand, "Oh, crap! You mean home and away. Yeah, of course. That'll add to the price a ton. Sixty dollars."

"And if we want Rory and Georgi to pay for them, we'd be asking for, like, eight hundred bucks. I wonder if that's too much."

"Hey, how about this?" said Jamie.

As they were talking, Jamie had taken over clicking through the website and had stopped at a plain navy blue shirt with white trim on a rounded collar. The distinguishing feature was that it was reversible to a white shirt with blue trim.

Eric grimaced. "I guess we better price it."

After this somewhat depressing decision was made, they got down to designing a logo and came up with a target-like circle saying "The Village Store" around the top and "Georgi's" around the bottom.

As they were finishing up Jamie said, "Hey, how sure are we that Abbey can't play?"

Erik smiled at the apparent casualness of the question. Everyone knew that Jamie adored Abbey.

Abbey's family lived up the hill from Jamie's parents' farm, and the two of them had grown up together, attending the same preschools and summer camps. As toddlers, they were best buddies. Their lives became less intertwined as they progressed through elementary school, but they still went to all the same birthday parties and took the same music lessons and art classes. Jamie was devoted to Abbey and open about it. When other boys tried to tease him, he would look at them with his serious face and respond calmly, "I just think she's really cool." If she was there, he'd turn to her and say, "I just think you're cool. Right?" At which Abbey would smile fondly and say, "Right."

It was no use teasing Abbey either. If Erik made a crack about Jamie being in love with her, Abbey would shoot right back, "Like you aren't, Steiner!" Or if someone like Gabe tried a joke, she'd say, "Maybe when he's mature like you, he'll realize girls really do have cooties."

So Erik considered Jamie's question seriously. The main problem facing the Blue Marauders was whether they'd have enough players. The second problem was whether they'd have enough good players. Abbey would help on both counts. "Nick said girls can't play in the boys' league," he said at last.

"Yeah, I guess. But don't you think we should check it out?"

Erik brought up the league website. With Jamie looking over his shoulder, he clicked through several links but couldn't find anything definitive. There were girls' leagues and boys' leagues, but there was nothing on the site about girls playing in the boys' league.

"So?" said Jamie.

"Well, maybe. I'll ask my dad to check. He's really good at this stuff. But look, let's not say anything to anyone about this yet."

"Right. It may not come to anything."

"Not to Abbey but not to Nick either. Okay?"

"If you think so," said Jamie mildly.

"I do," Erik said firmly. "Look, it's noon already. We should grab lunch and head to Caton's."

WHEN JAMIE'S MOM dropped them off, it was almost two o'clock and the rest of the team was already hard at work. More than a quarter of the turf was down, and large swathes of luscious green sod stood out against the black of the freshly tilled soil.

Nick and Dylan, shirtless and sweating, carried a heavy patch of sod between them and yelled out, "Nice of you two to show up at last."

It was five in the afternoon by the time the new sod was fully laid, and Dan came out from the garage to inspect the work.

"Looks fine," he said. "One of you boys want to take the sign home and paint it?"

The boys looked at Jamie, who volunteered. He was widely recognized as the best artist in his grade.

"You'll just need to water it for the next couple of weeks, morning and afternoon," Pat Cooper said.

"Will do," said Dan.

"If everyone stays off it, the field should be ready to go in fifteen days."

"Fifteen days?" Nick said, his voice rising to a squeak. "But our first home game's on Friday. We need to practice!"

"Oh, not on this field," Pat said. "Sod won't take unless it sits for at least fifteen days. A lot of people say three weeks. I never had a problem cutting it down a bit, but I won't allow less than two weeks."

Nick was boiling. His dad said this would work so, of course, it didn't. Another typical screw-up by his father, he thought. He wanted to protest, but it was hardly Mr. Cooper's fault, and besides, no matter how kind and generous he was to his children, Will's dad could be a little intimidating. He was a wiry man with an angular, weathered face and a physique like a welterweight boxer. He was a man of few words, and hard, skeptical looks. Nick looked around for his dad instead, but Charlie McCoy had gone to return the roller and grader to Tim Thomas.

Most of the kids didn't seem worried. They figured Nick, or maybe Erik, would work things out sooner or later. But Nick noticed Erik roll his eyes, obviously thinking that this sort of thing would never happen with the Thunder.

Dan was concerned about not waiting long enough. "You sure fifteen days is enough? Be a shame to waste all this."

"Nah, fifteen days is plenty. If it gets enough water."

Just then, Charlie McCoy returned. "Well, lads, it looks good."

"Dad, Pat said we can't play on it for fifteen days," Nick said with an edge in his voice.

"Sounds about right. I thought it was longer."

"Dad, *you* said five days. Eight at the most."

"Pat?"

"As I said, fifteen days."

"Dad, our first game is on Friday. It's a home game. Didn't you look at the schedule?" Nick was almost shouting now.

His father ignored the tone. "Well, we'll have to call and see if we can change it. You got yourselves a nice field. Look how flat it is."

"We have to practice, too. Where will we do that, Mr. McCoy?" Erik asked.

"The elementary school never starts their program until the second week of school. I'm sure Heidi will have no problem with you practicing there for now."

Nick swallowed hard. His dad never took any of his problems seriously. He did not see that it wasn't just a matter of the first game. Nick had told his team they would have a field, and they didn't. Despite the fact they had agreed to spend the whole weekend working. He could tell that Erik was already sore, and the others were going to be mad, too, if they couldn't find a field.

Gritting his teeth, Nick said, "Okay, Dad. Will you talk to Heidi about practicing? Maybe we can play the game at the elementary school field too."

The moment of tension passed, but it had drained away the atmosphere of triumph. The boys, and the men, were tired. While the kids gathered their things and began to disperse, Erik reminded everyone about practice Monday at noon. "It's try-outs, so bring your friends who might want to play. We need everyone there."

CHAPTER 3

Try-Outs

Nick headed to Erik's house early the next day. The first thing Erik told him was that his dad was not going to make it to practice. He had some meeting in Boston trying to find money for his struggling software start-up. Nick thought that was okay. He and Erik could run the try-outs.

After a lengthy discussion of who might show, Erik said, "Remember we thought that Abbey couldn't play?"

"Yeah?"

"Well, my dad looked up the league rules, and there are no rules against girls playing. All the rules just say 'players.'"

"Even the girls' league?"

"Dad looked at that too. Their rules specifically say 'girls,' so no boys can play, but Abbey could play with us."

Nick thought about it. Abbey was a great player, but Nick had never heard about a girl playing for the boys' Thunder. "Do you think we should ask her?"

"You mean, is she good enough?"

"Well, yeah, that too. But also, wouldn't it be weird?" Then Nick answered his own question before Erik could respond. "If we win, no one'll say it's weird."

"Yeah, and Abbey would help with that. She really would. She never makes a mistake."

"Do you think she'll want to play? I mean, she was going to be a big thing on the Lady Thunder, or whatever the team is called."

"We can always ask. She's coming to practice today."

"She is?"

"I called and told her to come."

"Was she still mad?"

"Yeah, I think so. But I told her what my dad found out, and I told her she could play and that we really need her." Erik waited but Nick didn't say anything. "At least we'll have a chance to talk her into it."

Nick smiled. He bet he could talk her into it. He loved talking people into things, and after all, why wouldn't she want to play with them?

WHEN THEY REACHED the elementary school field, there were two people they'd never seen before. A tall kid with curly blond hair and a bunch of Adidas gear was juggling neatly. An older man, with sunglasses, khakis, and a blue jacket was sitting in the grandstand talking into a cell phone.

"He looks pretty good," Nick whispered, pointing to the new kid.

Erik grunted agreement as the man with the cell phone approached them. "Kids, is this the Marauders' practice?"

"Yes, sir," Erik answered.

"When will the coach be here?"

"Uh, the coach won't be here today. That's my dad, and he couldn't make it."

"So who's running practice?"

"We are, I guess," Erik said.

"But you're having try-outs."

"That's right."

The man scowled and turned away. "Well, this is one god-damned way to run a team." Then he yelled to the blonde boy, "Kenny, come over here."

The boy loped gently over and smirked at Erik and Nick.

"Kenny, there's no coach here. These two say they're running the try-outs."

"Really?"

"Yeah. What do you want to do?"

"Can't you call Coach Scruggs again?"

"Listen, Kenny, I've talked to him twice already. He has a bug up his butt about missing the deadline."

"But it's not like I didn't play the last two years!"

"Well, you know Scruggs. He likes to show he's in charge."

"Why can't I play for Bedford? They'll be good this year."

"You know we talked with them, too. You'd have to start in the player pool and work your way up. I don't want you to waste a month scrimmaging with second raters. It makes you weak."

Kenny looked around sardonically. His father followed Kenny's gaze and nodded. Then he pulled Kenny toward him and put his arm around his shoulder. "Look, Slugger," he said in a whisper, clearly intended to be private, but loud enough for Erik and Nick to hear, "This may be good for you. You'll have a chance to exercise leadership. You'll have strong opposition, and you'll have to carry the team. It'll be a learning opportunity."

Then he let Kenny go and said more loudly, "So what do you say, Kenny? Let's stay and see how the try-outs go. If it doesn't work out, we can do something else."

"Okay Dad, I'll give it a try."

"Great." The man turned to Nick and Erik as if they had not been there for the whole prior conversation. "Boys, this is Kenny Garrity. I'm Mr. Garrity. What are your names?"

"Nick McCoy," Nick said through gritted teeth.

"Erik Steiner," said Erik, trying harder to be polite.

"Well, listen, boys. You tell your coach that Kenny played Thunder A the last two years, but we missed the deadline for filing this year because we were in France and my secretary forgot to send in the papers."

Kenny tossed his head.

"So we're looking for a good alternative, and we saw your notice. Kenny will stay and practice with you today, but ask the coach to call me so we can see if this will be a good situation for him."

"Yeah, right," Nick said.

Mr. Garrity held up a finger, not noticing Nick's tone. "Hold on." And then, into the phone, "Yeah, yeah, I'm just dropping Kenny off. I'll be with you in a moment. You're in L.A.? I'll call you back." He hung up, "What was that, kid?"

Erik jumped in, "That's fine, Mr. Garrity. We should be done at two o'clock. And I'll tell our coach."

"Good. Kenny, I want you to practice with your left foot today. Take the time to work on some of your weaker skills. I'll see you in a couple of hours." With that, Mr. Garrity walked off, leaving the three boys looking at each other awkwardly.

Before anyone said anything, a car horn sounded in the parking lot, and Dylan, Jamie, and Leon piled out of Leon's mother's car, along with a fourth boy that neither Nick nor Erik recognized. Leon's mother was barking angrily after them in Spanish, probably about not honking the horn.

Kenny took his ball and went off to juggle by himself. Nick looked at Erik and mouthed, "What a jerk!"

Erik shrugged in acknowledgment and said in a quiet voice, "Go pass with him."

"You go!" replied Nick, pushing him in Kenny's direction.

When Kenny saw Erik coming, he trapped the ball he was juggling and hit him a hard square pass. Under Kenny's scrutiny, Erik allowed the ball to roll up his instep, flicked it in the air, and headed it twice before letting it drop, catching it on his foot, and knocking it back to him. Erik smiled. That would give the kid something to think about.

"Hey, man," said Leon, "I am soooo sore."

"Me too," said Dylan, "how 'bout you, McCoy?"

"Nah," Nick said, pulling back his sleeve and making a bicep, "muscles of steel, buddy."

Dylan took the bait immediately. He whipped off his shirt and flexed, showing off a beautifully cut torso. "I'll test my guns against yours any time, McCoy."

Nick laughed. "Steroids are illegal, Dyl. Hey, who's your friend?"

The new boy, hanging a little behind the others, had sat down to put on his cleats. Leon motioned to him saying, "Mario, come meet Nick."

Mario stood up and walked over in his socks. He spoke shyly and with a noticeable accent.

"Where you from?" asked Nick.

"Guilford."

"You don't sound like you're from Guilford."

"Via Peru," said Leon. "Your family moved here in, what, March?"

"May."

"His dad works at the hospital, and he's looking for a team. You played in Peru, right?"

Mario smiled. "Yes, lots of soccer."

They kicked the ball around awhile, waiting for the others to arrive. Nick saw at once that Mario was a limited player. Decent but limited. He could do some nice tricks but he always kept his head down when he did them.

WILL, PARKER, AND Matty Hall–Erik's friend from Forsberg–were the next to show up. Will and Matty joined Erik and Kenny, while Parker, looking startlingly pale and thin in black shorts and a black T-shirt, jogged a slow warm-up lap around the field.

Gabe arrived with another boy about his size, but with red hair and freckles. They sat down to put their cleats on, and Gabe's voice boomed out, "Hey, dudes, come meet Terry."

Nick went over to introduce himself. "Hey, Terry, I'm Nick."

"Yeah, Nick is the team prima donna," Gabe explained helpfully. "He thinks the sun shines out his ass."

Nick responded by mooning Gabe. "Better get your sunscreen on, Gabe."

Gabe laughed. "Terry's dad is a cop in Warrick. Terry was the QB of the football team there."

"But they canceled the program," said Terry. "Because they couldn't get insurance. Wusses."

Nick smiled. "You play a lot of soccer?"

"Some pick-up. At least it's exercise."

Gabe chimed in, "Terry's a great athlete. I've seen him play, and man can he whale on the ball."

Based on the conversation, Nick figured Terry would be pretty useless, but he just said, "Great, well, welcome aboard."

"Hey, who are the other newbies?" Gabe asked.

"Leon brought a friend, Mario, from Peru."

Gabe nodded sagely at Terry. "Probably illegal."

"His dad works at the hospital, Gabe. Give it a break. Anyway, the other kid is Kenny Garrity, and the sun really does shine out of his ass." Gabe blinked. He never knew when Nick was kidding. "Also, the kid with the pony tail is Matty Hall. He played for Forsberg the last couple of years, so you may recognize him."

Just then, Jackson approached with Will. "Hey, Jackson," Gabe said, "are you playing?"

Jackson looked at Gabe with calm indifference. "Currently I am walking to the field, holding my bag. No playing is going on."

Gabe leaned over to Terry and fake whispered, "He's an idiot."

Jackson was about Gabe's height, but much thinner, built more like Parker than Gabe. His family ran a local cement company. Two of Jackson's older brothers had already graduated from high school and joined their parents' business. And everyone expected Jackson and his other brother, Thomas, to join them in time.

Jackson's schoolmates used to kid him about it, because the idea of Jackson pouring cement seemed like such an incongruous idea. Jackson was good in school and always held himself out as something of an intellectual. He was often silent, but when he spoke it was usually to say cutting remarks in a grandiloquent manner. But if he was asked about his future, he would invariably answer, "I already have a place reserved at Cement U."

ERIK CAME OVER and said to Nick, "We should get started. You want to do a crossing drill before we scrimmage?"

"Sure."

Just then, Nick noticed Abbey watching from the far end of the field, near the path that led to the town green. He ran over.

"Hey, Abbey, what's up?"

"Hey."

"C'mon. It's awesome you can play."

"Right."

"I mean it. I never wanted you not to. I just assumed you weren't allowed to play in the boys' league."

"I know."

"No harm, no foul?"

Abbey turned to look at him. "No harm. But I still don't know whether I should play."

"Erik isn't so wild about giving up the Thunder either."

"Yeah, but some time I'm going to have to start playing in the girls' league. I mean, that's how it works, right? Girls and boys."

Nick shrugged. "Yeah, I guess. It sucks. But also it doesn't. And, anyhow, you don't have to decide your whole future now. Play with us this year, and next year, who knows?"

"One of the Thunder coaches told me I'm already late getting my name out there. For all-star teams and college scholarships and stuff."

Abbey often thought about where soccer would get her. Abbey, or her parents, hoped it would get her into an Ivy League college, or a free ride at some big state university. She was that good. But that stuff didn't mean anything to Nick. He didn't even know if he was going to college.

"Abbey, you're a great player. They'll come to you. They will. If you want to play with the Thunder, that's cool. But don't let anyone scare you into it."

Abbey smiled. What Abbey loved about Nick, what everybody loved about him, was that he wasn't afraid of tomorrow. And somehow you always felt a little braver in his company.

Abbey said, "I looked at the schedules, Nicky. Girls' Thunder and the Marauders. There are only three games that conflict. There's a couple where I'd have to race to make it, but I asked Mom, and she said we could manage."

"You mean play both?"

"Yeah, what do you think?"

Nick did not like it. He thought Abbey should be a Blue Marauder. He could not conceive of dual loyalties. He said, "You'd miss practice, wouldn't you?"

"Yeah, mostly. I'd have to go to the Thunder practices."

Nick knew he should tell Abbey that it would be cool if she played on both teams. He tried to summon up a smile and tell her just that. But somewhere, the smile died. He did not want her to be a sometimes player, only making it to the games, and not even all of them. She wouldn't be part of the team. It wouldn't be like the last couple of years. It would, basically, suck.

Abbey saw Nick's hesitation. "So it's all or nothing for you, right? It's not enough that I talk my parents into driving me all over the state. If I can't make it to every damn practice, you think I have no right to play. Well, figure it out, do you want me or not? Erik thought it was cool."

Abbey stomped off, leaving Nick speechless. But she stomped off in the direction of the field.

THE CROSSING DRILL Erik set up called for three players with Jamie in goal. The center forward made a long pass down one of the wings. The winger had to collect the ball and hit a cross into the box as the center forward and the other winger ran to the goal.

The drill turned serious when Gabe was added as a defenseman. Gabe tried to muscle the attackers off the ball, and he was mostly successful until Kenny leaped high above him and sent a header into the lower right corner of the net. Kenny whipped around and pumped his fist. Abbey, the first to react, whistled and gave Kenny a high five. "Beautiful goal," she said.

"He climbed on my back," Gabe protested.

"No, he out-jumped you," said Abbey.

"Looked like a foul to me," Nick said.

"No way, man," Kenny said. "That's called high-quality soccer. Hey, let me be on defense. I'll give five dollars to anyone who scores."

Everyone hesitated. It was an odd challenge. But Dylan, at least, saw no downside to taking up the offer. "I'll take your money, man."

Erik suggested they should start the scrimmage but Gabe shouted him down. "Give us a chance to take some money off this turkey."

Erik looked to Nick for help but Nick just stared back. "Let him play defense."

So they kept going, with Kenny as defender. When no one scored after several tries, Erik said, "That's it. Let's move on."

Nick, who was waiting next in line, said, "No, give me a chance. I've only crossed it so far."

"Okay, but after this we play."

Nick nodded to Leon on his left and Will on his right. He looked at Kenny. "Ready?"

"Whenever."

Nick hit the ball to Will down the right wing and then crossed positions with Leon, sending Leon to the near post. Will took the ball to the corner, turned neatly and hit a low cross, belt high across the middle. With Leon too close to the goal to make a play, and with Nick behind him, Kenny was confident that he could clear it away harmlessly. Even when Nick closed faster than expected, Kenny remained confident. All he had to do was keep his body between Nick and the ball. Kenny shifted to block Nick out, but Nick had somehow snaked further forward than seemed possible, and now he dove for the ball, his body fully extended. Falling on the ground, Nick took Kenny's elbow hard in the chest, but his head had met the ball before Kenny's foot, sending it careening, hard and low to the far post. It hit the back of the net before Jamie even had a chance to move.

There was a stunned silence. Then Nick hopped up and rubbed his thumb and fingers together to indicate that a payment was owed. Everyone waited for Kenny's reaction.

"You win some, you lose some," he said casually. "You want your money now?"

"Nah," said Nick. "Let's scrimmage."

THE PLAYERS DIVIDED up, with Kenny and Nick on different teams. At first, they ignored each other, but after Kenny's first goal, Nick concentrated on man-marking Kenny, denying him touches whenever his team had the ball. Frustrated, Kenny retaliated by man-marking Nick. This was a harder task than Kenny anticipated, as Nick's boundless energy and his sudden changes in direction made him hard to follow. Nevertheless, Kenny's pursuit made it harder for Nick to control the tempo of his team's play. The beneficiaries of Nick and Kenny marking each other out of the game were Erik, who scored five goals, and Will, who took up the slack for Nick's team.

When the scrimmage was over, Nick felt exhilarated, and he gave Kenny a hearty high five. "Great game. We're going to make an awesome team."

Kenny was confused. He thought Nick disliked him, and the feeling was mutual. But he wanted to be gracious, "You did all right."

Nick's ears perked up at that. "All right? I dominated you," he thought. But Nick didn't say it out loud. Besides, Abbey was walking over, and he had unfinished business with her.

Abbey was still red faced from the scrimmage. Her skin glowed a deep pink and her blond ponytail was dark from sweat. But instead of coming over to Nick, she went first to Kenny.

"You were great," she told Kenny.

Kenny accepted the compliment. "You too. Are you playing for the girls' Thunder?"

"Yeah, and the Blue Marauders. They begged me. So we'll be teammates."

NICK HANDED OUT registration forms to Jackson and Terry. Mario hung back until Nick approached him directly. "Aren't you going to register, Mario?"

"Did I make the team?"

"Yeah, you made the team. Everyone makes the team. But we're glad to have you."

"What about me, McCoy?"

Nick turned and saw Abbey holding her hand out. He bowed and held out a form. "Sointanly, Ms. Stephens. We here at the Blue

Marauders are honored to have you grace us with your presence."

"Cut it out," said Abbey. "Kenny's going to be a great addition, hunh? You guys went at it today. He'll really help the team." As she spoke, she looked over at Kenny, who was standing off by himself talking into a cell phone.

Nick now saw what he had not seen before. Kenny was tall, handsome, blond, and probably rich. Nick laughed at himself. He was never jealous of other kids. He never had been, and he wasn't about to start now. "Let's just hope he agrees to play. I'm not sure he thinks we're good enough for him."

"Well, you better talk him into it if you want to compete with the big teams."

"Thanks for the confidence, girl. We'll do fine. But you're right, he'll help. And so will you. So fill out that form."

"Yes, captain," Abbey said.

Erik, meanwhile, had gone up to Kenny as Kenny was putting his phone away. "Hey, good practice today. I hope you'll join us."

"That was my dad. We decided I'd play here for the fall. He thinks it'll probably do the least damage to my long-term prospects."

Erik paused for a second to remind himself how desperately the Marauders needed players. "Cool. You can get a form from Nick."

"Is the girl really going to play?"

"Yeah. She's good, isn't she?"

Kenny smirked. "You know the Tri-State League isn't like rec soccer."

Erik held up his hand. "Okay, man. Just don't let her hear you say that. We need a team."

"You sure do."

NICK AND ERIK arranged to meet Rory before practice on Wednesday. When they entered the Village Store, Rory was at the cash register talking to some of his regulars.

"I'll be with you in a minute, boys. Why don't you go over and see Georgi, and I'll swing by in ten minutes."

Erik and Nick nodded, a little taken aback. They had hoped to run the proposal by Rory before talking with Georgi. In the ideal world, Rory would have talked to Georgi for them. But now there was little choice but to head next door to the House of Pizza.

Georgi's was closed before noon and, as usual, the door was locked and the windows dark. The boys knocked tentatively on the window in case Georgi, or one of his family members, was in back.

At first, there was no answer, and the boys hoped that the meeting would have to be delayed. Then Georgi himself appeared in the front window. He looked hot and bothered. His wild black and grey hair was barely contained under a hair net. He wore a white tank top that revealed his thick, hairy arms and chest. He bellowed through the window, "We're closed. Open at twelve. Read the sign!"

"We don't want pizza!" Nick yelled, in order to be heard through the window.

"Then go away!"

"We have a favor to ask," Erik shouted.

It's unlikely that Georgi would have opened the door if Rory hadn't showed up. "Not a favor," said Rory. "A business deal."

Seeing Rory, Georgi shrugged and unlocked the door. Rory pushed in, followed by Nick and Erik.

"Here, let's sit," Rory said to everyone.

After everyone took a seat, Rory said, "So what's the deal?"

"Ah, Mr. Patenaude, Mr. . . . , Georgi," Erik started, before realizing that he did not know Georgi's last name. "Good morning."

Georgi looked at Rory, who just shrugged.

Nick took over from Erik, "As you know, or as Rory knows, we're forming a soccer team to play in the Tri-State League. We're going to play in the A league against teams like the Thunder, the

Bedford Red Demons, and a bunch of the other big towns."

Nick paused, and Erik broke in. "We're playing over at Caton's Field. Behind Dan's garage. And we expect to draw some crowds."

"Yeah," Nick said. "There'll be a lot of local people coming to watch us, and also visitors. When I went to a Thunder game last year, there were, like, a hundred spectators. And we figure they'll all need snacks and pizza after the game. Or at halftime."

"Okay, you got your sell, boys," Rory said. "Now make the ask. What do you want?"

"Well, we're looking for someone to sponsor the team," Erik said. "We were hoping that you might be willing to do that in return for some free advertising."

"Not free if we're paying for it," Georgi muttered.

"What a lot of other teams do is have local businesses sponsor them and buy their jerseys," Nick said. "So we wondered if you wanted to sponsor us by paying for our jerseys, and in return we would put your names on them. Go on, Erik, show them the design."

Erik took out a piece of cardboard where he had drawn an enlarged version of the team's blue jerseys. It showed the circular target design with "The Village Store" making up the top of the circle and "Georgi's" making the bottom.

Rory nodded appreciatively. "Pretty nice. So what's the cost for this free advertising?"

"Well, the coolest jerseys are $30 apiece, and we were hoping to get maybe fifteen blue jerseys and another fifteen white jerseys for away games."

"Nine hundred dollars?" Georgi said immediately. "Are you nuts?"

"Well . . . ," began Erik.

"Seems a little steep, boys," Rory said. "Try again."

Erik looked at Nick. Nick said, "Well, as Erik said, those are for the home and away jerseys. We can get reversible shirts, with a blue side and a white side, for $20 each. We have fourteen people signed up right now, but we want to buy fifteen in case someone else joins. That would be . . . "

"Three hundred dollars," Georgi grunted.

"Now, that's a more reasonable figure," Rory said. "And there's a logo on both the blue side and the white side?"

"Yeah," Erik said.

"Front or back?"

"Uh, front, the number is on the back."

"Why should I pay for a logo on an away shirt?" asked Georgi. "No one will come to my pizzeria when you are playing in Bedford."

Nick and Erik looked at him, first trying to make sense of the question and then not knowing how to answer it.

"Ah, now, Georgi. Let's not nickel and dime the boys. What do you think? A good investment in the community?"

"Uunh," Georgi shrugged.

"Bring some life down here."

"You see my place empty?"

"But this will bring more families and children. You know the kids. Lots of impulse purchases. High-margin items."

"Too many kids already."

"Nah, not really. I know you could sell more pizza. Twice as much. You can hire someone else. Besides, you love soccer."

"Hunh, yah football! Hellas. Not kids!"

"Well, so they're not the Greek team. But it's a start. Everyone's got to start."

Nick cut in, "We're pretty good, Mr. Georgi, for seventh grade."

Suddenly, Georgi looked serious. "You, Rory? You put up money?"

"Yeah, I will. I'll put up $200 if you put up the rest."

"One hundred bucks? That's a lot. The profit on twenty-five pizzas."

"You'll sell 'em. To the kids, if nothing else."

"I'll sell 'em if I don't put up the money too."

"That's true enough, Georgi. So it's your choice. But it's a neighborly thing to do."

Georgi leaned over and took Erik's drawing from him. He looked at it carefully. Erik said, "That's a drawing of the more expensive shirts. With the collars. The reversible shirts just have crew necks."

"My name in front?"

"Along with 'The Village Store.'"

"How many games?" Georgi asked Nick.

"Fourteen. Oh, seven home games. More if we make the playoffs and get a home game. Which we will."

"Rory, you come here, you cost me money."

"It'll be good to have some more life passing through here."

Georgi hesitated one more second. Then he said, "Okay, I sponsor." Immediately he got up and went into the back office and came back with five twenty-dollar bills. He slapped them on the table. "Take 'em quick before I change my mind."

Nick darted his hand out to take the bills, but Rory beat him to it. "I'll hold this. Have the shirt people send me a bill."

"Okay, yes sir!" Erik said. "I'll order the shirts tonight."

"Thanks very much," Nick added.

"Good job, boys. Now get along. Georgi and I have other matters to discuss."

NICK WAS SURPRISED to see Abbey at Wednesday's practice. She said her Thunder practice wasn't until late afternoon, so she figured she could do both. Kenny was there too, dropped off by a woman who was presumably his mother. He sat alone putting on his cleats and then went off to juggle by himself while the others were shooting on Jamie. Abbey gave Nick a look that said, "Don't be so useless," and she went over to talk to Kenny.

Erik's dad blew his whistle and brought the kids into the center circle. He began by introducing himself.

"I'm Erik's dad. You can call me Mr. Steiner or just plain Larry. Either works. I know most of you already, and for the newcomers, I look forward to working together.

"We have our first game on Friday, so we don't have much time to prepare. I'll announce the starting line-up before the game. In the Tri-State League there is no requirement for equal playing time, but it's a tradition on our Lancaster teams, and I think it makes sense to keep it up. Another Lancaster tradition that we must all remember is sportsmanship. We play hard, but we play fairly, and we always behave with decorum. I don't want to see violent tackles, and I do not want anyone yelling at the referees."

Nick tried hard not to fidget. He liked Mr. Steiner, and he was glad Mr. Steiner was coaching the team, but Mr. Steiner liked to talk. Practices had lots less running, and lots more listening, with him as coach.

"The game on Friday starts at five o'clock, so we need everyone to arrive no later than four thirty. And don't forget to bring shin guards. It's a league rule, and you will not be allowed to play without them. Now to some administrative matters."

Mr. Steiner passed out rosters, schedules, phone numbers, and a complete set of league rules. Then it was time for calisthenics, followed by a long series of passing and dribbling drills, and finally a short scrimmage.

Gabe's father showed up while the team was scrimmaging. He was still in his policeman's pants but without the jacket and cap. Russell, or Russ, was a barrel-chested man with a crew cut and red face. He stood next to Mr. Steiner to watch the boys play. The two men offered differing advice. Erik's father emphasized looking for teammates and playing positions. Gabe's dad called for more speed and effort.

"It's good of you to do this again, Larry," said Russ. "I'm happy to help out as time allows."

"Well, Russ, your help is always welcome."

"You figured out a starting line-up yet?"

"Erik and I discussed it last night. Only tentative, but you can have a look. Here."

Mr. Steiner opened the notebook he was carrying and showed it to Russ. Russ nodded in satisfaction seeing his son written in as sweeper. "With Gabe, Nick, and Erik up the middle, they should be in good shape. I always say soccer is like baseball. You've gotta be strong up the middle."

Mr. Steiner nodded.

"Who's the blond kid?"

"Kenny Garrity."

"Looks good. He's tall. Nice complement to Gabe."

"Yes."

Mr. Steiner found that it was generally best to agree with Russ, at least when nothing was at stake. Several years ago, they had found themselves on opposite sides of a town budget issue. Russ had urged the hiring of a third full-time policeman, and Larry had been against it. This made relations frosty for a little while, but with the amount of time their children spent together, they had to find ways to accommodate each other. In the interest of peace, Larry had decided to support Russ's call to buy a new police car even though he doubted the necessity of it. The gesture had left Larry with something of a bad conscience, but it had improved relations between the two men.

"What about Terry?" said Russ. "He's a big, strong boy. Maybe we should have him start for Abbey and get her coming off the bench."

"That's possible, but Terry's new to the team and Erik tells me he doesn't have the soccer skills Abbey has. She's very good at passing the ball up to the midfielders."

"If she can stand her ground. The boys at this level are much more physical."

"We'll see," Mr. Steiner said blandly.

"Sure. I'll be at the game on Friday if you need any help. And let me know if you can't make practice. I can always step in for an afternoon."

"Thanks, Russ. I know I can rely on you."

When practice was over, Russ Drybzyck marched off to collect his son, content that all was well. As the players dispersed, a handsome blond woman approached Mr. Steiner with her hand out.

"Mrs. Garrity," she said in a bright, firm voice.

"Pleased to meet you. I'm Larry Steiner. Erik's father."

"I understand you're the coach."

"That seems to be my role."

"Wonderful. We are so pleased that Kenny could still find an A league team this late in the year."

"We're pleased to have him."

"I imagine so. It's not often a team gets a center midfielder like Kenny."

"Uh, he certainly seems a fine boy."

"Oh, more than that, I think. It's important you know what you have in Kenny. He's been a team captain and a State All-Star selection. We'd like him to keep growing in that direction."

Erik's dad was nonplussed. "I can see that."

"No doubt he'll rejoin the Thunder next season, but we must think about this season, too. It's never good to fall behind your peer group."

"Oh, no."

"It's wonderful to see you out here. It's so important for parents to take an interest in their children's lives. Mr. Garrity and I are very concerned about Kenny spending his time productively. He needs to be challenged, and he needs to exercise leadership. He'd make a fine captain for your team."

"I hadn't thought about naming captains."

"Perhaps you might consider it. The Thunder teams always name a captain. Do you mind if I ask about your coaching experience?"

"No real experience. I've coached these boys since they were in kindergarten, but I'm not much of a soccer person. I was a swimmer in college."

"Oh," said Mrs. Garrity, seeming at a loss for words. "Well, that's a shame. I had thought the Tri-State League would have certain requirements for this sort of thing. Still, one can do wonders with good help. We'll have to see what we can do about that, won't we?"

Mrs. Garrity smiled warmly at Mr. Steiner and walked away before he could be sure what she meant. He watched as she disappeared into her car. It seemed that coaching the Blue Marauders was going to be a little different than coaching the rec league team.

CHAPTER 4

First Game Jitters

The point was made to him again that evening at dinnertime. He and his wife, Lisa, were just putting the plates on the table when the phone rang.

As usual, Erik's sister got to it first. "Steiners," she said, "Elena speaking." Disgustedly, she handed the phone to her father. "It's for you. Someone who sounds very grumpy."

"Yes, this is Larry Steiner," said Mr. Steiner.

"Coach Steiner, what the hell do you think you're doing?"

Mr. Steiner looked apologetically at his wife and went into the study.

"Who is calling, please?"

"This is Mac Scruggs. I want to know what the hell you're trying to pull."

"Do I know you, Mr. Scruggs?"

An exasperated snort sounded through the phone. "Head of Thunder soccer. I got the roster for this blue whatever team today. It looks like you've been poaching players."

"You mean Erik?"

"Yeah, Erik Steiner, Nick McCoy, Matty Hall. They were all signed up with our Thunder A group, and now they're suddenly signed up with you. Then there's a bunch of players from our B team."

"Well . . . "

"I haven't heard boo from these kids. No one told me they're not playing Thunder, and I'm gonna assume they are. You also have a girl signed up. Abbey Stephens. I'm not sure what that's about, but this is a boys' league. The young woman in question is committed to playing Thunder Girls, and I assure you Steve Hartmann is furious."

"Steve Hartmann?"

"What is this? Amateur hour? Steve Hartmann is the coach of the Thunder Girls and he's been Youth Coach of the Year three times. Maybe you should know that."

"I believe Abbey intends to play for the Thunder Girls and the boy's team."

"Unprecedented. No girl in a boys' league. And you can't play for two teams in one league."

"My understanding is they're not the same league. And I did call the Tri-State Soccer Association. They said there was no rule preventing girls from participating in the boys' league."

"Listen, Steiner, the Stephens girl has a future. Some of those other kids might too. But not if you mess it up. The only real soccer in this area is Thunder soccer and they're not playing Thunder if they play for you."

Larry Steiner breathed deeply. "Look, Mr. . . . . Scruggs?"

"Mac Scruggs."

"First of all, Mr. Scruggs, I did not poach anyone. The boys decided of their own free will to form a local team in Lancaster, and that option was very attractive."

"They're making a big mistake."

"Second, you are correct that the boys should have informed you of their decision not to play Thunder. I will talk to them about their carelessness."

"You better do more than that. I'm not taking the boys back when your team goes belly-up. And poor Ms. Stephens will be truly up the creek."

"Mr. Scruggs! It's one thing to call up during the dinner hour to threaten *me* on the basis of unsubstantiated accusations. But how dare you threaten a group of thirteen year olds who simply decided they would like to play for a team near their home rather than commute forty-five minutes to play with kids they don't even know!"

Mac Scruggs spoke more calmly. "I'm not threatening anyone. I'm just saying it like it is. Your boys need to know that Thunder doesn't cater to kids who can't keep their commitments. As for the girl, you tell her that if she plans to play in your game on Friday against Kilby, she can forget about showing up to Thunder on Saturday."

Larry Steiner was gripping the phone so tightly that his knuckles were turning white.

Mac Scruggs continued, "Another thing, Coach. You don't seem to know much about soccer on this level, so let me tell you a few things. You've only got fourteen kids. Most teams have twenty or more. They'll run you into the ground. On top of which, you've only got three or four legitimate A league players. Other than Garrity, who's trouble in his own way, all your kids are raw. Without coaching, they'll likely never develop real skills. The rest of the team are thugs and toe-kickers. It's embarrassing and pathetic. You're going get your ass handed to you again and again. This league is for competitive soccer. It's not fair to make quality teams travel to play meaningless games in the middle of a hay field against some amateur-hour, small-town hick boys and girls just to satisfy your own damned ego.

"Listen, I'm not unreasonable. I'll take the boys back if you withdraw your registration in twenty-four hours." With that, Mac Scruggs hung up, leaving Erik's father staring at the phone with no outlet for his fury.

"What's up?" Erik called from the kitchen.

Mr. Steiner struggled to regain his composure. "That was Mr. Mac Scruggs."

"He ran try-outs," Erik said. "He's like the guru of Thunder Soccer. He was going to coach Nick's team."

"Yes, and it appears he is rather upset because none of you boys thought to tell him that you aren't playing Thunder soccer this year."

"Oh," Erik said. "It all happened so fast. I guess we forgot."

"Seriously, Erik, you should be aware that he has threatened to make it very hard for anyone who plays for the Blue Marauders to play Thunder soccer next year."

"That's ridiculous!" said Mrs. Steiner. "Surely he's not serious."

"You'd think not, but he sounded quite upset on the phone."

Erik's immediate reaction was to capitulate to Scruggs's demands. Sure, Erik was willing to try the Marauders, but not at the cost of *never* being able to play Thunder. That was too much to ask. But he looked at his father and found himself saying, "It doesn't matter, Dad. I'm playing for the Blue Marauders."

"Good," Mr. Steiner said. "Honestly, now that I've talked with Mac Scruggs, I'm not sure I would even want you to play on the Thunder. Let's just make sure we beat the pants off of them."

Mr. Steiner's wife looked at him oddly. This was a side of her husband she had not seen before.

MR. STEINER CALLED the parents of his team members the next day to let them know of the threats made by Mac Scruggs. He felt that the kids who chose to play for the Marauders, and their parents, should be conscious of the potential risk they took of closing off other avenues.

He started with Abbey's parents, because the threat to Abbey was the most immediate. Abbey's mother expressed concern. "She's really been looking forward to playing with the Thunder," she said. "We'll have to discuss this and get back to you. I'll try to reach Coach Hartmann."

He called Kenny's parents next and received a very different response. "Thank you for calling, Coach Steiner," Kenny's mother had said, "but I am fairly certain that Coach Scruggs did not mean to include Kenny in the group. You see, when we missed the deadline, it was he who let us know that a new team based out of Lancaster had registered and recommended that Kenny try to get a position there. He said that, as long as Kenny played A league somewhere, he would take him back on the Thunder team next season. Of course, one can see that he might be annoyed with the children who failed to inform him of their change in plans."

Leon's mother found it hard to even understand the threat. "What does he mean?" Maria Juarez asked. "What does he mean when he says that they won't play for the Thunder? They are playing for your Blue team, no?"

"Well, I think he means next year."

"Next year? I don't even know if Leon will want to play soccer next year."

"But if he wants to."

"Well, he would play for you."

"Yes, but if we don't play again next year."

"Why should that be?"

Gabe's father understood Mac Scruggs's threat immediately.

"Let me tell you, that bastard better never be speeding through Lancaster."

"Now, Russ."

"He'll get his ass handed to him on a plate."

"I just wanted to let you know, in case it changed anything for Gabe."

"No siree! We'll settle that with the Thunder kids on the field. There'll be no objection from me if Gabe takes a couple of 'em out."

Charlie McCoy also understood the threat and could not stop laughing about it. "I can't believe he really said that. What a jackass!"

Larry also told him what Scruggs had said about the inability of the Blue Marauders to compete with the rest of the teams in the league. Charlie assured him it was a bluff.

"He doesn't know our kids. We'll do fine."

"I hope you're right," said Larry, but he was not much comforted.

THE NEXT MORNING, Mr. Steiner finalized his line-up for the first game, penciling Abbey in at left back. The line-up looked like this:

Goalie: Jamie

Sweeper: Gabe

Left Back: Abbey   *Right Back:* Jackson

Stopper: Will

Left Mid: Kenny   *Cent. Mid:* Nick   *Right Mid:* Matty

Left Wing: Leon   *Cent. Forward:* Erik   *Right Wing:* Dylan

Subs: Parker, Terry, and Mario

Mr. Steiner was pleased with the line-up, but he still had plenty of concerns. He hadn't heard back from Abbey's parents, and he worried about whether she would play. Reflecting on Mac Scruggs's comments, he worried whether Erik, Nick, and Will would find themselves overmatched on this new level, and whether the other players would be able contribute anything at all.

He also worried if the elementary school field would be ready on time. Charlie McCoy and Pat Cooper said they would paint the lines and put up the nets on Thursday evening. But they had not managed to do so because Charlie got stuck on a project in Putney with the paint in the back of his truck.

"No problem," Charlie had said. "We can do it Friday afternoon. I should get there by 2:30. That will give us plenty of time."

But Charlie was not perfectly reliable with respect to deadlines. So Mr. Steiner worried.

ERIK WAS ALSO worried about the game. Erik was always tense before a game. He liked to be alone and listen to music on his headphones. He would imagine traps and turns, passes and shots. He would review step-by-step in his mind's eye the dribble moves he planned to use that day. He always avoided Nick for the last couple of hours before a game. Nick claimed he never got nervous. But he did get excited, which showed itself in an exaggerated playfulness. He'd dance around, draping his arms over anyone around, telling jokes, teasing, laughing, and, from Erik's point of view, generally making a pain of himself.

But on Friday, Erik found himself unable to focus on the upcoming game. He kept thinking about the Blue Marauder uniforms. They didn't have any. Intersports needed eight or nine days to turn an order around. If there were no delays they should have the shirts for the second game. In the meantime, they had to play in whatever they could scrounge up. Erik had called everyone to ask them to remember to bring a blue shirt, but he kept thinking about how unprofessional the team would look with a bunch of mismatched blue shirts.

ABBEY WAS NOT so much worried as confused. Her parents had called Coach Hartmann after her mother's conversation with Mr. Steiner, and he had been very nice. He had discussed Abbey's future in glowing terms and expressed the strong desire that she play for the Thunder Girls. He said that he was not aware of a rule that specifically prohibited a person playing in both the girls' league and the boys' league, but he discouraged it. He cited the importance of kids having activities outside of soccer and the fact that she would not be able to give her all to either team. He discussed the potential for injury from overplaying, particularly ACL and tendon injuries. "Also, boys this age can be fairly aggressive," he had said. "They are beginning to get their strength, but haven't learned how to control their bodies yet."

All of this was pretty persuasive to Abbey's parents. They thought she should play for one team, and that team should be the Thunder Girls team. "It just doesn't make sense to risk your health," her mother had said. "Coach Hartmann sounds like he'll be a wonderful teacher," her father had added. After a long sulk, Abbey had agreed with them. She would play Thunder soccer exclusively. But she still didn't know how she would break the news to Erik and Nick. The thing was, she still wanted to play for the Marauders, despite all of the good arguments against it.

So Abbey and her parents were going up to watch the game and cheer. But after going through her wardrobe a couple of times, Abbey found herself dressing to play. Just in case. Then, not wanting to answer too many questions from her mother and father, she put sweats on to hide her soccer gear. And stuffed her cleats and her shin guards into her backpack when no one was looking.

KENNY WASN'T NERVOUS, he was just angry. He was angry at Coach Scruggs, who had thought a stupid deadline was more important than Kenny playing Thunder soccer. He was angry at his buddies who had shaken their heads in disbelief when they learned that Kenny was going to play for a team in Lancaster. He was angry at his parents because they had not found a way to fix things. And he was still angry at Nick for managing to score off of Will's cross at the try-outs. As his mother drove him to Lancaster for his first game, he steamed.

OF ALL THE Blue Marauders, Parker was perhaps the only one completely calm. Parker was calm because he had actually forgotten all about the game. On Friday afternoon, he was in Warren with some of his older friends, eating pizza and setting up for a gig they were playing that night at a party organized by some of Warren's incoming high school seniors. He had run into his buddy

Reno on Thursday night, who told him about the gig. The band's regular drummer was sick and they were looking for a replacement. Parker had spent all morning practicing the set list and had never given a single thought to soccer.

WHEN MR. STEINER and Erik arrived at the elementary school half an hour before kickoff, they were relieved to find the field was ready, with freshly painted lines, corner flags, and nets in the goals.

The Kilby kids, at least twenty of them, were already there, running drills in precise formation. They wore flashy orange shirts with thick blue vertical stripes up the sides and large blue collars.

A league referee and two linesmen, dressed in the traditional black and white, stood at the center circle of the field, passing a ball back and forth, laughing and talking.

At the other end of the field, the Marauder kids and some of their brothers and sisters shot balls on Nick, who saved just about everything on target. Other siblings and parents milled around the spectators' benches.

Mr. Steiner walked over to where Charlie McCoy and Pat Cooper were standing. "I'm glad you were able to get the field ready," he said.

Charlie explained that he and Nick had shown up a little earlier to find Pat Cooper and Will already hard at work. By the time they arrived, there wasn't much to do. Then he grinned and pointed at the Kilby team. "See how many kids they have? They showed up in three separate minivans, and the kids just kept pouring out of them. It was like watching clown cars unload."

"Lot of coaches too," Pat Cooper said.

"The guys you see running the drills?" said Charlie, nodding toward the Kilby team where three young men, dressed entirely in Adidas, were leading the warm-ups. "They're only the assistants."

As Mr. Steiner looked across the field, an older man, tall and fit, with tidy, steel grey hair, and also dressed entirely in Adidas sweats, approached them and thrust his hand out.

"Coach Steiner?" he asked.

"Yes," Mr. Steiner said, grabbing the offered hand.

"Coach Beaufort. Looks like we'll have some nice weather for the game."

"That's something."

"Our kids are looking forward to getting the new season started. I'm sure yours are too."

"Absolutely."

"One thing. It's an away game for us, so we have our orange and blue uniforms. Home team always wears white, of course." Larry looked at him, not understanding. "I only mention it because everyone on your team seems to be wearing blue shirts."

"Pretty different blues," said Charlie McCoy. "And no orange."

Coach Beaufort smiled at him indulgently. "Similar enough if you have to make split-second decisions. Home team wears white. I'm sure Coach Steiner agrees."

"Don't we have some yellow pinneys in Dan's shed," Pat Cooper said.

"Not sure yellow will help," Coach Beaufort said. "Too similar to orange."

"Are you sure the shirts will cause a problem?" Mr. Steiner asked.

"Just talking with the refs about it, and rules are rules. We don't want the first game to be a forfeit, do we? Of course, your boys could play a friendly scrimmage in the blue shirts."

"No, no. I'm sure we'll be able to manage," Mr. Steiner said.

"Well, good luck," Coach Beaufort said, grabbing Mr. Steiner's hand again before walking away.

The three Lancaster men stood looking at each other. "Can you beat that?" Charlie McCoy said. "Scared to play us, I guess."

"Will you two go see who has white shirts with them?" said Larry. "Then we'll see what we can scrounge up from kids on the sidelines."

In the end, they were still three shirts short, and Mr. Steiner sent Erik sprinting home to dig up whatever he could find. "Raid your sister's closet, if necessary," said Mr. Steiner, and he went off to sit on the players' bench to collect himself.

SO FAR ONLY eleven Blue Marauders had showed up. Parker, Terry, and Abbey were still missing. Gabe's dad said he'd had a call from Terry's mother and they were running late. No one knew where Parker was. That left Abbey. Mr. Steiner thought he'd seen Abbey's mother, so surely Abbey was around. He scanned the spectators, looking for Abbey's parents. He found them and hurried over.

"Hello Doug, Jean."

"Hi, Larry."

"Where's Abbey?"

"Oh, I'm so sorry we didn't call," her mother said. "After talking with you, we called Coach Hartmann and decided it was best to just play in one league."

"Well, I understand that, I just wish I had known sooner. It looks like we're going to be a little short-handed."

As if by magic, Abbey appeared next to her father. "Did you say you were short-handed, Mr. Steiner?"

"Well, Parker and Terry aren't here."

"I've got my stuff," Abbey said. "I even have a white shirt in my bag. I guess I should play," she said to her parents, removing her sweatpants. "After all," she said, grabbing her backpack and taking off across the field, "it wouldn't be fair to leave the boys short-handed. With no notice."

"But you don't have your cleats!" her mother said, trying to get something out before her daughter was out of earshot.

"Yes I do," Abbey called back, "They're in my bag. Shin guards too."

"What about the Thunder?" her dad asked, yelling so as to be heard.

"Oh, I'm sure they won't mind. One game. Just to help out." Abbey gave a quick wave and then ran the rest of the way across the field to join the rest of the team.

Abbey's mother said, "We had agreed she was going to just play for the Thunder. Coach Hartmann thought she could get hurt playing two leagues."

Larry looked thoughtful. "Well, I can't say it wouldn't help to have her. But I won't let her play if you don't want her to."

Doug Stephens turned to his wife. They tried to do their best for their children. They treated them like adults and talked through important decisions. In the end, they generally found that their children made good choices. They had talked with Abbey about whether she should play with the Marauders as well as the Thunder. Certainly, Doug and Jean had shared their opinions, but they had left the final decision to Abbey. Once she had made the choice, however, they were not at all pleased about her changing her mind on a whim.

On the other hand, they weren't sure how to stop her without causing a scene. And as Larry had said, her friends did seem to need her.

"I guess it'll be all right for this one game," said Doug.

"Did you see her pack her soccer gear?" asked Jean, still mystified and a little miffed.

Her husband just shook his head.

WITH THE GAME due to begin, the league referee looked at his watch. Mr. Steiner called his team in and quickly went over the line-up. Mrs. Garrity had told him that her son was a *center* midfielder, so he had to ignore the black look from Kenny when he announced Kenny would be playing on the left.

The referee blew his whistle. The Kilby kids gave a hearty yell, "KILBY!" and took the field.

"One second boys," said Mr. Steiner.

As he said this, Terry came rushing in to the group, "I'm here coach! Where am I playing?"

"You start on the bench, Terry. That'll give you time to get ready."

"Coach, I'm ready! Cleats on! Mouth guard!" Terry gave a smile showing nothing but blue plastic.

"Good, but you'll start out." For that, Mr. Steiner received another black look.

The referee blew his whistle again, but Mr. Steiner held his team back. "Three things," he said. "Play as a team. Play hard. Play fair. And now . . . " Just then the ref blew his whistle a third time, and the boys, looking apologetic, took off for the field before Mr. Steiner could finish his thought.

AS THE BLUE Marauders waited for the whistle to begin their first game, it cannot be said that they were undaunted. Altogether they were just twelve boys and a girl dressed in a ragged mix of ill-fitting white and off-white T-shirts, and they stood against twenty-one confident competitors, clad from head to toe in matching orange and blue.

Erik was, frankly, embarrassed. He cursed Nick for talking him into this. It was not made better by the referee who motioned him into the circle for the kickoff and condescendingly reminded him that the ball had to move forward before it could be passed back. "He thinks we have no idea what we're doing," Erik thought.

Kenny shared Erik's embarrassment and cursed under his breath. The white shirt he had borrowed from Erik was too small, both too short and too tight around the shoulders, and he felt he looked ridiculous. He searched for his mother in the crowd, and shot her an appealing look, "Do I have to be here?" But Mrs. Garrity was talking on her cell phone, giving an outraged blow-by-blow to her husband, and could only wave distractedly when she noticed Kenny looking at her.

Even Nick, whose confidence was generally boundless, felt uncertain. He told himself firmly that uniforms and numbers didn't matter, but as he looked over at the Kilby team, even he felt a twinge of doubt.

The dynamic changed almost immediately when the whistle blew. As the Blue Marauders stood ready to kick off, Erik noticed the Kilby goalie at the edge of his 18-yard box, exchanging words with his central defenders. Without raising his hand, Erik gave Nick a brief nod to direct his attention to the fact. Nick nodded back. The whistle blew and Erik tipped the ball to Nick, who now stepped up and slammed the ball as hard as he could toward the Kilby goal. It took only a split second for the goalie to realize that the ball could sail over his head into the goal. He started sprinting backward, almost tripping over his own legs. For a few seconds everyone else on the field stood motionless in anticipation. Even the fans quieted and watched as the ball followed its long arc toward the goal.

But the shot was slightly under hit, and the Kilby goalie had reacted quickly enough. He was able to get a hand on it before it fell into the goal and bat it down in front of him in the six-yard box. Grateful and relieved, the goalie gracelessly fell on the ball as a roar went up from the sidelines. The crowd thought they might see a competitive game after all.

Unfortunately, that was the best moment of the day for the Blue Marauders. Kilby quickly took control as their wingers started to make effective runs and good crosses into the middle. Most of the balls were batted away by Gabe and Will, and sometimes by Nick, who came back to help. But one cross, one of the few that came from the winger on Abbey's side, got through and landed right in front of the Kilby center forward, who had no problem slotting it into the back of the net with just ten minutes gone in the first half.

"Tighten up," Kenny yelled at his teammates, ignoring the fact that the Kilby winger had only beaten Abbey because she'd been forced to cover his midfield position when he was caught up on the attack.

Meanwhile, Erik, Dylan, and Leon asserted little pressure on attack. Leon was beaten to several passes and Kenny stopped looking for him. Dylan had some effective runs down the wing, but tended to take the ball too far and get caught by the defense out by the corner flag, ahead of his teammates and unable to make a cross. Erik could not get on track. Kilby's central defenders were fast and smart, and every time Erik received the ball, they double-teamed him and poked it away before he could make any moves.

Nick was everywhere on the field but couldn't get enough touches. When Kilby had the ball, they passed quickly so the ball was already away when Nick tried to tackle. When the Marauders had possession, they hit long balls forward rather than working it through the midfield. Matty kept looking for Dylan and Erik up front. Kenny seemed to look for anyone other than Nick.

Still, it was only 1–0 at halftime, and when Mr. Steiner called his squad in, they were not overly discouraged about their performance. Anything could happen at 1–0.

"We need to attack through the middle more," Nick said, "and we need to stop letting them get such good passes to their wingers."

"We need more help on defense," said Gabe. "Will and I are getting bombarded."

"You have to stay in position," Kenny said to Nick.

Nick was about to give an angry response but Erik spoke first. "I sucked, but we can beat these guys up the middle."

Will said, "We have to slow it down. Work the ball up more."

"I can beat their defenders," said Dylan, "but the through balls are going too wide."

Several parents who were standing over the boys offered their own prescriptions. Charlie McCoy told Nick, "You can take these kids, son. Don't be too ready to pass."

Russ Drybzyck said to anyone who would listen, "You gotta get a body on 'em. Hit 'em in the mouth, and they'll back off." When he said this to Abbey he added, "It's a contact game, honey. No tea parties out there."

Mr. Steiner was unsure which advice was sound. He settled for saying, "Good job so far. We're only one goal down and we're doing fine. Let's get some more shots on goal."

The second half started out well. There was a clever move by Nick leading to a good chance for Erik, and a nice pass over the defense from Abbey to Kenny, who got off a shot that required a diving save from the Kilby goalkeeper. But after fifteen minutes, with Will on the bench, one of the Kilby central defenders came forward and received the ball with only Terry in front of him. He beat Terry in the penalty box and hit a rocket of a shot at Jamie. It was the type of shot that haunts goalies. It was hit hard, from close range, and right at his face. Jamie had to duck not to save it. But he couldn't get his hands up in time and he wasn't quite committed enough to take the ball on his nose.

After the second goal, the tired Marauder team slowed down while the fresh Kilby subs kept running at them. The Blue Marauders slipped further and further back on defense and the rest of the game was played within thirty yards of the Marauders' goal. Finally, Kilby poked in a third goal after a confused scramble in the penalty box.

When the whistle blew, Mr. Steiner offered his dejected players some final words of encouragement. "Guys, it was a good first game. We'll only get better. So be proud of what you did, and don't forget practice on Monday at 3:30."

After handshakes with the Kilby team, everyone filtered slowly home. Abbey found Kenny changing out of his cleats by himself, his white shirt discarded in a pile on the ground next to him.

"You were great," she said.

He nodded, then added belatedly, "You looked good out there, too. Their wingers were pretty fast, huh?"

"It could have been worse."

"I doubt it. Kilby's the worst team in the league. Every year. If you lose to them, you'll get killed by the other teams."

"Really?"

"And now I'm stuck. Once you play with a team, you can't play with anyone else."

"The team isn't as bad as it played today. Nick's better, and I've never seen Erik lose the ball like that."

Kenny looked at her skeptically. "The Will guy is okay." Then he smiled, "And you're cool."

"Give 'em a chance. I'll be rooting for all of you."

"Rooting?"

"This was a one off. I'm playing Thunder Girls."

"Well, that makes sense. You'll be a great player in that league."

Abbey held up her hand for a high five. "I've gotta go. See you around?"

Kenny slapped her hand, "Yeah, sure."

CHAPTER 5

The Beginning of School

Sunday was the seventh-grade picnic at the Pond to celebrate, if that's the right word, the first day of school. Erik was visiting his grandparents, but everyone else was there.

The parents grilled hamburgers and hot dogs and chatted about their summers and the coming year. Older siblings mostly stayed away, but younger brothers and sisters were everywhere, mostly playing ball or tag and making sandcastles.

The seventh graders avoided both their parents and their siblings. The girls sunbathed out at the raft, while the boys played horseshoes in a pit set back in a clearing in the woods around the point from the main beach. Having been together, in most cases, since kindergarten, the kids knew each other well and held little mystery or terror for each other.

After a little while, Abbey, Yvonne, and Tabitha swam in to join the boys. Tabitha was Abbey's best friend. She was a big girl, taller and wider than Abbey. She played center for the basketball team and split the pitching duties for the softball team with Abbey. Abbey had always wanted her to play soccer, but Tabitha said that if she ever played a sport in the fall, she'd play football.

But what drew Abbey to Tabitha was her personality. Tabitha

was confident, loud and brassy. Her family ran the last working dairy farm in Lancaster and they'd been there for generations. It seemed like she was related to half the residents in town by blood or marriage. Parker was a cousin, Nick a third cousin, and Jackson was a cousin by marriage. Rory Patenaude was a godfather.

The dairy farm struggled and Tabitha went on and off the school lunch program, but none of that dampened her confidence. Abbey had never seen her scared of anyone. The boys wavered between being impressed and intimidated by her repertoire of dirty jokes and off-color comments.

For Abbey, the clean-cut, all-American girl with clean-cut, all-American parents, hanging out with Tabitha was a relief. Mostly Abbey just listened while Tabitha talked a mile a minute, about school and work and boys, about the town and vacations and farming, and anything else that came into her head. Tabitha said things that Abbey would never dare to say—the kind of things that no one in her family even thought—and Abbey admired her for it. She didn't want to be like Tabitha, but it was wonderful to know that the possibility existed.

Yvonne, a relative newcomer to the school, was another thing entirely. She had transferred to the school in sixth grade when her parents moved to Lancaster from Connecticut. Immediately, half the boys had fallen in love with her. This was partly because she was new, but also because she was cute. Short and already curvy, Yvonne had big brown eyes, curly brown hair, and a sly smile that would flash suddenly when she was talking with someone she liked (usually a boy).

In many ways, Abbey had more in common than Yvonne than with Tabitha. Yvonne's father was a county supervisor in the school system and her mother taught English at Milford High, and they set the same high academic standards for Yvonne that Abbey's parents set for her. Abbey and Yvonne worked on the same projects at school; they took piano lessons from the same teacher; and liked many of the same books. It was just that Abbey never felt really comfortable around Yvonne. She felt she had to be perfect and smart, and that Yvonne judged her for any failure.

The boys were happy to make room for the girls in their game of horseshoes and a battle of the sexes was quickly set up. The boys chose Dylan, Nick, and Jamie to play for them, and the rest of the seventh-grade girls swam in from the raft to watch. The winners, it was agreed, could choose one of the losing team to bury in sand. They played first to reach 20 points. The girls took an early lead, on good throws by Tabitha and Abbey, but they were still at a disadvantage. Jamie had a horseshoe ring at his parents' farm and was the best player by a long shot. He kept the boys in the game until Nick and Dylan, who were also solid players, hit ringers in two consecutive innings to put the game on ice.

To no one's surprise, the boys chose Yvonne to bury. Jamie said it was because she was the smallest so she'd be the easiest to bury. Tabitha raised an eyebrow. "Good thinking, Jamie! You wouldn't want to have to pat down a girl's body any longer than absolutely necessary."

The crowd laughed, and Jamie blushed.

Nick said, "Yeah, it's a painful task, but someone's got to do it. Let's go."

Nick liked Yvonne a lot. When she moved to Lancaster, she moved into a house about half a mile from Nick. They became friends riding the bus home together in winter, on days Nick could not ride his bike. Nick told her everything she needed to know about the school, the town, and the other kids. Earlier that summer, they had gone with a bunch of their friends to a free concert offered by Hereford College on the Milford Green. When they had walked into town together to get some waters and sodas for the group, Yvonne had reached out to hold his hand. Nick was so surprised at first that he almost snatched his hand away. He didn't though, and it was nice. They had held hands all the way to the store. On the way back, they were both carrying grocery bags so there was no more chance to hold hands. But just before they had reached their friends, Yvonne had looked at him and given him one of her best smiles.

All the kids, boys and girls, as well as some of the younger siblings, helped bury Yvonne. Quickly she was fully covered, with just her head and a few brown curls poking out of the sand. Most of the kids began drifting away, but Yvonne stayed buried for a while longer and Nick and couple of his other classmates sat with her. Nick fed her potato chips while some other boys took turns holding up a can of soda so she could suck at it through a straw.

Several of the girls started playing volleyball, and slowly everyone, including Yvonne, joined in. As the sun faded over the pond, parents began to pull their kids out of the game, reminding them that they had school tomorrow, and the picnic wound to a close.

ONE PERSON WHO did not attend the Sunday picnic was the new seventh-grade teacher, who had begged off to visit a sick mother. Last year's teacher, Ms. Burris, had moved to Pittsburgh when her husband was transferred there. Nick had gotten to know her pretty well because, in addition to being the seventh-grade homeroom teacher, she taught mathematics to kids needing extra help. She had a way of explaining things that Nick found easy to understand, and he was disappointed when he discovered that she was leaving.

As a result, the kids did not know what to expect when they piled into the classroom on the first day of school. They were greeted by a short, round man with neatly combed, shoulder-length black hair and small, black-framed glasses. He wore a blue blazer, khakis, a pale green collared shirt, and a dark blue tie.

He stood at the door, smiling in welcome, and offering instructions, "Put your backpacks away and choose a seat. Quickly, now! Quickly!"

Once everyone was seated, he called the class to order and, as the talking subsided, he introduced himself.

"Good morning, class!" He waited for a response that did not come. "First things first. I am Mr. DeMille. Yes, before you ask, my first name is Cecil. But I am no relation." He paused again, but was rewarded only by blank stares.

"As most of you are aware, the celebrated Ms. Burris has moved on to better things in Pittsburgh, and I am your new seventh-grade homeroom teacher. I will also teach you science, math, language arts and social studies. We will get to know each other very well this year, and you will discover that I have extremely high expectations of you. This is not only because I have a great confidence in your abilities, both individually and as a group, but also because seventh grade is an important turning point in your education.

"It's a shame, in my opinion, that considerations of space require that Lancaster's seventh-grade classroom be located here in the elementary school, as it may leave you with a delusion of seniority and august standing in the community. Housed with the eighth graders and high school students, you would quickly realize that you are, instead, low men on the totem pole with much to learn. Despite the location of this classroom, you are in middle school now, and must quickly begin to prepare yourselves for high school, where more will be asked and more will be expected. My job is to be sure that you are fully prepared for the experience.

"There are several things I am particularly excited about this semester. First, is the math curriculum. After reviewing and extending your study of fractions and percentages, we will be broadening your knowledge of algebra, and I hope we have a chance to study arithmetical operations in different bases. This is tricky material, but absolutely vital.

"I am also looking forward to the social science curriculum. We are studying first cultures; in Egypt, Mesopotamia, China, India, and, above all, Greece. This is a fascinating time period, and you will have a challenging assignment. You will have to write your first extended research paper. It's a difficult task, but one that you all can excel at."

Mr. DeMille continued on, talking about classroom procedures (strict) and homework expectations (high), but Nick tuned him out. He had already made up his mind that Mr. DeMille was everything he hated in a teacher—a pompous, self-important windbag. Nick looked for someone to roll his eyes at. But Erik, Dylan, Abbey, and Yvonne were up in front and they were not looking around. Nick had to satisfy himself with rolling his eyes at Gabe. Gabe nodded back and, when Mr. DeMille's back was turned, pantomimed shooting himself in the head.

Nevertheless, it was the first day of school, so very little happened. There were lots of books and papers and folders to be handed out. There were bus routes to be discussed, and school rules to be reminded of. Only in math class, toward the end of the day, did Mr. DeMille finally offer some substance. Before school ended, he gave a brief half-hour review of everything they should know about fractions coming into seventh grade. Trying to follow the lecture, many of the students felt their heads spin as Mr. DeMille raced through the material. Nick's head did not spin because he stopped listening. He assumed the lecture would be repeated later more slowly.

Besides, Nick's thoughts had already turned to soccer. Very soon the team would gather at the elementary school field. Abbey would not make it because she was rushing off to Milford with her mom for her first practice with the Thunder Girls. But everyone else would be there.

Nick was trying to plan the drills for the team to recommend to Mr. Steiner. He thought back to the game against Kilby and decided that the main problem was in trapping and marking. He wondered how they could work on that. Maybe he and Erik could search for some good drills on the Internet.

Suddenly Nick remembered that Erik had told him that morning that his father could not make practice, and that Mr. Steiner had arranged for Gabe's dad to take his place. Nick groaned.

"Ah, a contribution from, Mr., uh, McCoy is it?" Mr. DeMille approached Nick's desk. "Something about factoring displeases you?"

Nick looked up and gauged the situation. Factoring? Yes, it rang a bell. Yes, it probably displeased him. But wisest not to say so at the moment. Keeping one's head down was the best policy. "No, sir. Just . . . clearing my throat."

"I see. Well, how would you factor 15 divided by 20?"

Nick looked around the room and considered. He looked at the blackboard, filled with numbers. What did he know about fractions? Not much, but he felt pretty calm. "Bottom of the ninth," he said to himself, "a high hard one right at the head."

Out loud, he said, "They're divisible by 5?"

Mr. DeMille looked at him. "So?"

"Uh, so it's like, maybe, three fourths?"

"Precisely! Very good, Mr. McCoy." He looked at Nick suspiciously for a moment, then added just as the bell for the end of school rang, "Full points."

Nick resisted the urge to raise his fists in the air. "The crowd goes wild," he thought, changing his metaphor, "as Nicky McCoy sends a buzzer-beating three pointer to win the game."

As they walked out of school, Erik gave him grief. "You had no idea what DeMille was talking about, did you?"

"Au contraire, mon frère." The boys had started French in fifth grade, and this had become one of Nick's stock phrases.

"No way, Nickster," Dylan added. "I saw your math homework last year."

Yvonne, overhearing the conversation, came to Nick's defense. "I thought it was wonderful. Mr. DeMille was so surprised."

Abbey also overheard and grimaced. "Look, it's just a math problem. Not a very hard one."

"Not for you, maybe," Dylan said. "But Nick's slow."

"Leave off, Dylan," Yvonne said.

"Don't worry. Dylan can't bother me," Nick said. "Abbey, when you're done with practice, scout out the Thunder Boys for us, would you. We play one of their teams next Saturday."

WHEN THE BOYS got out to the field for practice, Russ Drybzyck was waiting for them impatiently. Terry, Mario, and Kenny were already there. Kenny was at the far goal practicing his juggling.

"Come on, everyone," Mr. Drybzyck bellowed, "let's get changed. Hurry, hurry."

Erik had his cleats on first and began to get out some balls to kick around, but Mr. Drybzyck stopped him. "No balls yet, Erik. Conditioning first." Then Mr. Drybzyck noticed Kenny at the other end of the field. "You, boy! Come on in and put the ball away. Work before pleasure!" Kenny resignedly shuffled toward the other boys, hitting the ball back and forth between his feet.

When the team was ready, Mr. Drybzyck had everyone stand around the center circle. "Right," he barked when everyone was in position, giving a powerful hand clap. "Let's start to work. I saw the game on Friday and I won't say you played badly, but you faded in the last quarter because of conditioning. Now, I know they had more people than you, but that's no excuse. You have to be the fittest, strongest team around. Jumping jacks!"

And Mr. Drybzyck proceeded to lead them through a long workout that he called his "Marine Corps" drill. They did multiple sets of jumping jacks, squats, squat thrusts, sit-ups, arm circles, and push-ups.

The rest of practice consisted of just two drills, both of which required only one ball. The first was a slide tackle drill, where a boy with a ball was given a five-yard head start to dribble to the goal and shoot. The defender was meant to catch up and slide tackle the ball carrier before he got his shot off. This resulted in frequent collisions, which Mr. Drybzyck cheered on.

The second drill consisted of a game like "5,000." One boy hit a long goal kick, and the remaining boys tried to be the first to reach it (headers were worth 500 points, and other first touches, 100 points) or control it (the boy who managed to kick the ball back toward the goal also received 500 points). Again, this resulted in a lot of hard physical challenges. "You gotta want the ball!" Mr. Drybzyck told them. "The winner will always be the person who wants it more."

Practice ended with eight of Mr. Drybzyck's infamous "super sprints," which were wind sprints interrupted by the kids throwing themselves on the ground at every whistle.

When the practice was over, the kids just lay on the ground panting, some of them barely suppressing tears of exhaustion. Mr. Drybzyck looked around satisfied. "Good practice, boys. We'll make Marines of you yet."

BUT THE PLAYERS were in grim moods. They packed their bags and made their way homeward with a minimal of chatter. Erik walked with Leon and Mario, who were headed to the high school library to meet Leon's mom, and in Leon's case, probably browse the science fiction section. Erik's house was about halfway between the elementary school and the high school. After a few minutes of silence, Leon said, "Man, that sucked!"

"Yeah," Erik agreed.

"I hate it when he runs practice. Tell me your dad isn't going to miss a lot of practices?"

"He better not. I can't take any more of that." Erik turned to Mario. "What did you think of Officer Drybzyck's practice?"

Mario felt shy. He also felt guilty because he had only done one "super sprint" before coming up with a cramp. Mr. Drybzyck had yelled at him, but he refused to continue, and for a moment he considered giving up on the Blue Marauders. He thought the American idea of soccer was loco.

"Mario was the smart one," Leon said. "I wish I had thought to fake a cramp."

"I wasn't faking," Mario said.

"We know that," Erik said. "Don't take it too hard. Drybzyck's a jerk. He doesn't know anything about soccer. He just likes making all of us miserable."

Leon said, "Hey, Mario, that was a great move you put on Dylan in the one-on-one."

"Yeah, that was sweet. Like one of those Ronaldinho thingies." Erik dropped a ball on the ground and in slow motion flicked it minimally out to the right with the outside of his right foot, and then pulled the ball back inside with the inside of the same foot. "I have never been able to get that move."

"The Elastico," said Mario. "Lots of Peruvians can do it because it was a signature of Teòfilo Cubillas, one of our greatest players."

"Can you show us how to do it?"

"Sure."

For the next ten minutes, Mario walked them through the Elastico until the boys understood what their feet should be doing. Erik even managed it once at semi-full speed.

FORTUNATELY, MR. STEINER was at practice the rest of the week, and things calmed down. He had thought a lot about the Kilby match and didn't think that the kids were overmatched athletically. Instead, he thought that the Marauders were not used to playing 11 v. 11 and needed work on maintaining and understanding their positions. Accordingly, Mr. Steiner began each practice with a little chalkboard talk where he reviewed the roles and responsibilities of each position, mostly cribbed from articles he'd found in an online soccer encyclopedia. After describing the positions, he had the team play out a series of scenarios, moving the ball up the field without opposition while Mr. Steiner provided a running commentary about what to do next.

"Okay, now Matty has received the ball from Gabe on the left side of the midfield. Where should Nick be?"

"Running back for the square pass," Nick said, bored but dutiful.

"And you, Dylan?"

"Breaking up the wing."

"That's one option. Dylan can break up the wing, in which case Erik should cut toward Matty. Or, he can cut back and outside to offer Matty another short pass. Kenny, where should you be?"

"Covering the middle," Kenny said, thinking that really he should be playing center midfield and making Nick's cut.

"Good! Let's all do that, and see where Matty passes the ball."

And so it went. It all seemed so brainy and so different from just playing soccer that the boys, even Kenny and Nick, were pretty impressed by it. Nick thought that this would shut Erik up about quality coaching—Mr. Steiner was coming through with a pretty serious coaching effort, even if it was boring as sin. Still, Nick figured that soccer was just like everything else—the more serious you got, the more talking there was.

Erik was less impressed. He appreciated his dad's efforts—he saw him on the computer for hours in the evening looking for coaching material—and much of what his dad told them sounded like really good advice. But he hated all the standing around.

AT THURSDAY'S PRACTICE Erik had another disappointment. He had expected to have the shirts from Intersports ready to hand out for Saturday's game against the Thunder Green, but they hadn't been delivered yet, and Mr. Steiner had to remind everyone to bring their own blue T-shirts to the game. There was some discussion about making sure everyone brought the same shade of blue shirt, and wore blue shorts, so they could look more like a team. But as this seemed to raise more problems than it solved, Mr. Steiner cut the conversation off. "Any blue shirt will do. And bring a white one too, just in case."

He made everyone repeat what shirts they were going to bring several times, haunted by a possible replay of the start of the last game.

"The game is at two o'clock Saturday at the Thunder field in Milford. I want everyone there at least a half hour early. One thirty at the latest. We had good practices this week. I think if we all play in our positions, we'll do fine."

Kenny sniggered. Mr. Steiner looked at him, "You know the Thunder players. Is there any insight you can offer?"

Kenny rolled his eyes and smirked. "This Thunder team is the best in the league. Kilby doesn't hold a candle to them. They'll destroy a team like this. I'd just say that the center midfield needs to hold up better than it did in the last game." Kenny looked at Nick.

"You just don't screw up your position too badly, and we'll take care of the rest, Garrity," Nick said.

"Now, boys," Mr. Steiner said sternly. "Remember, we have to work as a team. I am expecting you to support each other, just the way we've worked on." Nick and Kenny glowered at each other but said nothing.

THERE WAS NO practice Friday afternoon. That morning Nick learned he'd failed his first math quiz of the year. School was moving way too fast. Mr. DeMille had announced himself pleased with the review of last year's material and was already starting to introduce new concepts. The homework sets were massive. Even Leon, Erik, and Abbey said they were barely keeping up.

Will failed the Friday quiz too, and Mr. DeMille held him and Nick in during lunch to discuss their results.

"It won't do to get behind so early in the year," he said. "I want to give you another chance to show me what you can do. There will be a make-up on Monday, but I need each of you to put your nose to the grindstone and cut out the goofing off."

Will hung his head and blushed, but Nick looked daggers at Mr. DeMille. He hated it when teachers assumed academic problems were really attitude or behavior problems. It was just a way teachers excused themselves for being lousy teachers. Nick might slack off sometimes, but he was no worse than a bunch of other kids, like Gabe and Tabitha, who did fine on the quiz. And it was totally unfair to put Will in this category. Will always worked hard.

Nick and Will got together to study after school on Friday at Will's house, but it turned out to be a mistake. They found that their shared ignorance and lack of understanding were mutually reinforcing. Nick thought he understood division until Will started asking him questions about it. And Will totally confused Nick about reducing fractions. Eventually, every time one of them started an explanation, the other began to crack up, knowing that it would just lead in circles. With tears in his eyes from laughing at Will's attempt to divide 34/100 by 17/25, Nick suggested they call Erik.

"We can't," Will said. "He's at the Thunder Girls' game watching Abbey. His sister has a U-15 game right after."

"Okay, who then? Leon knows this stuff, but he can never explain it. It comes too easy for him."

"Dylan?"

Will dialed Dylan's number, but it was busy.

"How about Yvonne?" Nick suggested.

Will laughed. "Okay, you give her a call."

AS IT HAPPENED, much to her own surprise and indignation, Abbey was not playing soccer for the Thunder Girls. Instead, she was sitting next to Erik in the grandstand watching the game. They did not talk because Abbey was furious. She was so mad that she couldn't talk without crying. And she refused to cry.

Abbey had practiced with the Thunder Girls team all week and really enjoyed it. Some of the girls on the team were pretty good, but none of them could or would head the ball properly. They closed their eyes and flinched as the ball came to them. So Abbey, playing central defense or center midfield, was dominant in her own half and even better coming up on attack.

Abbey was also one of the fastest on the team. She got a tremendous kick out of turning on a burst of speed to win the race to a through ball or catch up with someone who had dribbled through the other defenders. Abbey knew just how to throw a hip or shoulder to muscle an attacker off the ball, and she had the poise to collect the ball afterward and find the best pass back up to her midfield.

All week, the coach praised her and took her aside for special instruction. The other girls realized how good she was and competed to play with her. It was fun, and Abbey was looking forward to her first game. The Thunder Girls were going to win big.

But waiting in the huddle before the game, Abbey learned she was not on the starting team. Then, after announcing the line-up, Coach Hartmann took her aside and explained that the Thunder coaches had decided that she should not play in any league games this year.

"Why?" Abbey asked, shocked.

"We understand that you played a game for the Blue Marauders last week."

"So what?"

"So, you were asked not to. First, that's insubordination. Second, the league rules say that a person may only play for one team at a time."

Abbey was speechless and breathing hard. Tears welled in her eyes. "You never said I couldn't play! My dad just said you didn't recommend it!"

"I think the intent was clear. I don't know what your father chose to hear."

"But it's unfair! The boys and girls are in separate leagues anyway." Abbey almost shrieked.

Coach Hartmann, who had been in a half crouch in order to look Abbey in the eye, stood up. "Hysterics won't help. Quite unusually, because of your talent and potential, a decision has been made that we are willing to keep you on the team. You can't play this season, but if you continue to practice with us, there's no reason for this to impact your status in future seasons."

Abbey's parents noticed the commotion and came over.

"Is something wrong?" her father asked.

"I'm just discussing with your daughter a decision made by the Thunder Soccer Club that she will not be eligible to play Thunder Girls this year because of her appearance in a boys' league game."

Abbey's parents were as stunned as Abbey. "When was this decided? Why weren't we informed?" her father asked.

Abbey interrupted Coach Hartmann's answer by yelling at the top of her lungs, "IT DOESN'T MATTER. I WOULDN'T PLAY FOR YOU IF THIS WAS THE LAST TEAM ON EARTH!" Then she sprinted away to escape the attention she had drawn.

Her mother followed her while her father stayed talking to Coach Hartmann. "This is absolutely appalling behavior," her father said.

"Well, seventh graders can be emotional," Coach Hartmann said in a soothing tone.

"NOT HERS, YOURS!" Doug Stephens roared. "I cannot believe that you wait until minutes before a game to tell her this. I don't understand the decision at all. No one ever said that she wouldn't be allowed to play."

Coach Hartmann cut him off. "I believe that is precisely what Mac Scruggs told the Marauder coach. A player cannot play for two teams in the same league. Which is, in effect, the same thing I told you. Your girl has talent, but she needs coaching and discipline. If she can get over herself, she's welcome to practice with the Thunder Girls. She'd be able to play next season. In the meantime, I have a game to coach."

Mr. Stephens controlled himself with difficulty. He took a deep breath and counted to ten. As the game began, Mr. and Mrs. Stephens looked all over for Abbey. They couldn't find her, but they were not overly worried. The Milford soccer fields were located in a large open park, with trails leading off into the woods in many directions. The area, the whole town in fact, was very safe. As angry as Abbey was, her parents knew she had a good head on her shoulders and wouldn't do anything too crazy.

IT WAS ERIK who found Abbey. She was sitting on a log in the woods, a few feet off one of the trails that led away from the soccer fields. She was behind a bush so that she could see people coming and hide if she wanted to avoid them. She did not hide from Erik.

"Hey," Erik said.

"Hey," said Abbey. Her eyes were red, and she sniffed.

"I think your parents are kind of worried."

"I know. I just want to be alone for a while."

"You want me to leave?"

"No. Just, let's not talk, okay?"

"Okay." Erik sat on the log next to her.

After a little while, Abbey said. "They won't let me play in Thunder games."

Erik shook his head. "I heard."

"Can I still play with the Marauders?"

"Of course."

Abbey half smiled. "That's what I'm going to do."

After a while, Erik was dispatched to pick up Abbey's things so she could put her sweats back on, and they snuck back to the small grandstand on the visitors' side of the field to watch the game.

They did not talk much, except to comment on the play.

"That was a good move," Erik said, seeing a clever dribble, or a nice pass.

"That was sucky," Abbey said, seeing a missed tackle or shot.

"You know the next game's tomorrow? It's here, against the Thunder."

Abbey nodded, and Erik continued, "We can probably give you a ride if your parents are busy."

"That would be nice, thanks!"

THAT EVENING, ERIK called Nick to let him know that Abbey was going to play with the Marauders full time.

"That's great," Nick said. "We really have to get it going against the Thunder."

"Well, it's not like we can do worse than we did against Kilby," Erik said, not knowing how wrong he would be.

CHAPTER 6

Thunder Green and Other Setbacks

The shirts arrived on Saturday. Erik called Abbey to ask if she could be dropped off early, so they would have time to pick them up before the game. Intersports was in the shopping district on the far side of Milford, so Mr. Steiner drove on the bypass to get there. The shirts were in a cardboard box on the check-out counter, ready to be picked up when they arrived.

Erik and Abbey opened up the box and found that the shirts looked fine. They were not as snazzy as the Kilby uniforms, but they had they had the fresh, hopeful smell of new clothes. Erik selected number 11. Abbey picked number 3, Paolo Maldini's number. He was retired, but she had a poster of him in her room.

The only slight disappointment was how heavy they were, because of the double layers needed to make the reversible sides. Erik worried it might slow them down on hot days.

"The weather will turn cold soon enough," said his father.

They reached the Thunder fields at a quarter past one. Nick was already there, juggling a soccer ball and clowning with anyone he could find. Erik went off to the far side of the field and put his ear buds in. He needed a half hour of calm before the game.

Abbey brought the box of shirts over to one of the benches

while Mr. Steiner stood nearby going over his starting line-up. He had not been sure whether Abbey would play again, and he had penciled in Terry as the starter. He still thought this might be the right move, because, in his eyes, she had seemed to struggle trying to defend the faster Kilby wingers. But given the unpleasantness with the Lady Thunder, he decided to start her at least for the day.

He looked around nervously for the opposing coach. The awful Mac Scruggs coached one of the Thunder teams, Thunder Red, but thankfully not this one. This was the Thunder Green team, coached by someone called Charles Courtland.

Finally, a man in a blazer and khakis approached, "Coach Steiner?"

"You must be Coach Courtland?"

"No. Randy Garrity. Kenny's father."

"Oh, yes, Mr. Garrity. Nice to meet you."

"Likewise. I hear you've run some good practices. I hope to get up there myself next week if the travel schedule allows."

"Fine."

"I heard about last week. Pretty bad showing against Kilby. My wife said the boys looked confused."

"Well, the first game. It was a step up for everyone."

"Not for everyone. Kenny has a lot of experience playing at this level, and he's got a good head on his shoulders."

"I certainly do appreciate his work and effort."

"Let's be honest, Coach," Mr. Garrity said. "You've got some driftwood here. There are kids on this team that couldn't start in the B league. So maybe you can't expect to beat teams like the Thunder, but you can still have a productive season. Kenny needs leadership experience, and he wants to help out. Move him to center midfield, make him a captain. He'll make everyone better and maybe have a chance to learn a bit of grace under fire, if you know what I mean."

"We don't have captains," said Mr. Steiner.

"Then perhaps you should. That's what's so great about sports in this country. It's the one area where you can still focus on excellence, not just teach to the middle. Just think about it, Coach." Mr. Steiner said nothing. "Now on a separate topic. I understand you have a nice little software company looking to make the leap."

"Yes, Iliad Software," Mr. Steiner said, confused by the change of subject.

"I know all about you. Ten years developing some pretty nice self-programming smartware in the operations field. A small but loyal customer base. Hot new product idea, and you think you can jump into the big leagues with $5,000,000 or so in development money. Not going well, though. The money guys are skeptical of your ability to handle such a big project."

"How did you hear about us?"

Randy Garrity gave a broad smile and pulled out a business card. "Principal Director, Cayman Capital. We should talk. And think about what I said about Kenny."

"Uhh, thank you," Mr. Steiner said, accepting the card. "Will do."

It was only after Mr. Garrity walked away that Larry Steiner had time to reflect on what had been said. Had he just been offered a chance at a five-million-dollar investment if he moved Kenny to center midfield and made him captain? Surely he'd misunderstood. "I hate coaching soccer," he thought, before having his attention drawn to the sound of boys yelling at each other.

"Let go of the shirt. I'm always number 6!" Kenny was tugging at the hem of a shirt held by Nick.

"I got it first. You let go."

Kenny tugged harder, almost pulling Nick over.

"What's going on?" Mr. Steiner shouted.

"He's taking my shirt," said Nick.

"But it's my number."

"I got it first."

"Did not."

"Did too."

Thankfully, Mr. Steiner interrupted the repartee. "How old are you people? For God's sake."

"All right, take it, already." Nick tossed the shirt at Kenny. He didn't care about what number he wore, he just was not going to let Kenny bully him.

Kenny pulled on the shirt, looking pleased with himself. Nick took one of the last remaining shirts out of the box, number 13. He looked at it with disgust and put it on.

"Everyone come in!" Mr. Steiner said loudly. "No more of this childish behavior. We have a game to play, and we have to play as a team." He gestured to the field, where a team of twenty kids, dressed in immaculate white uniforms with green trim, were confidently passing around brand new white and green Nike balls in well-ordered 3 v. 1 triangles. "Now go out and warm up!"

As the Blue Marauders took shots on Jamie, Nick and Erik watched the Thunder Green warm-up. They looked dazzling as they moved quickly through a series of complicated drills. Both boys were aware that this would have been Erik's team if it were not for the Marauders.

"What do you think, Steiner?" Nick asked.

"I wish we had matching shorts and socks." Erik had meant it as a joke, but it didn't come out that way. He pointed to a tall, solid kid with pale skin and thick black hair wearing number 7. "Remember that guy from the try-outs? I still can't believe he's U-13."

"He's okay," Nick said, but he knew what Erik meant. The kid was ungodly fast and had awesome control.

"So what's our strategy?" Erik asked.

"I'll get the ball to you, and you score."

Erik laughed. "Yeah, but do you want me to score with my left foot or right foot? And which corner should I shoot for?"

"Left foot, right corner."

"Okay." Erik looked around at the crowd. "There's must be 200 people here."

Nick shrugged. "I guess the Thunder is big news in Milford. That's what happens when you win three Tri-States in five years."

IN THE HUDDLE before the game, Mr. Steiner announced the same starting line-up as for the last game. "And I want us to think about what we learned last week. Play your positions. Look for passes." Then he asked Kenny if he had any tips about their opponents.

"Watch out for Jimmy, he's number 7," Kenny said. "He has a rocket shot, and he'll come in from midfield and take crosses in the box. Also Martin, number 9, on the wing, is really fast."

"We can play with these guys," Nick told his team as the huddle broke up.

But if the Marauders could play with them, it was not immediately obvious how. The Thunder Green pushed the ball relentlessly at the Marauders with speed and control. Kenny was right that number 9 was fast. Just five minutes into the game, they discovered how fast.

Jimmy, the number 7, won a 50-50 ball from Nick in midfield and sent a long pass behind the defense. Martin accelerated to the ball, leaving Jackson in his dust. With Gabe and Will slow to cover, he had an open shot from the edge of the six-yard box, which he slammed into the net.

Nick held up his hand, "My bad. I gotta win those challenges."

The second goal came fifteen minutes later and was arguably Nick's fault again. Jimmy found space when he and his center forward crossed paths, and both Nick and Will followed the center forward. Momentarily unmarked, Jimmy pressed up to the penalty area and cracked a ferocious line drive inside the left post, where Jamie once again had no chance to save it.

Will and Nick glared at each other for a moment, but both backed off when they saw the look of accusation in the other's face.

"Sorry," Will said, "I thought you had him."

"Nah, my bad," Nick replied. "But I'll stick with him from now on."

And from then on he did. For the rest of the first half, Nick limited his game to making sure Jimmy did not beat them. He stuck to Jimmy like a barnacle, denying him the ball, and letting the rest of the game take care of itself. It was effective. Jimmy was bigger and stronger, but Nick was more dogged and quicker. He beat Jimmy to every pass. Finally, Jimmy grew frustrated and threw an elbow as they went up together for a head ball. Nothing was called, but it didn't matter. The Thunder Green had lost its dominance in midfield.

However, the team from Milford had players other than Jimmy, and they continued to work the ball up the wings, putting pressure on the Marauder defense and forcing them into mistakes. The Thunder Green scored two more goals before halftime.

"Look, you're playing well," Mr. Steiner said to his team as they filed in for their halftime pep talk. He saw disbelief in the faces around him. "No, you're holding up against the best team in the league."

Mr. Steiner sensed Mr. Garrity and Mr. Drybzyck hovering outside the circle of players, looking unhappy. He had to think of something to give his team confidence fast. He had seen how Nick had been beaten on the first two goals, and it was obvious that Kenny was a better match for Jimmy physically. Maybe getting Nick out of the middle might even help their attack.

"Let's try something," Mr. Steiner said. "Kenny, you move to center midfield. Nick, go to left. Maybe you can help push the ball forward if we get number 7 off your back."

"But I've finally got him under control," Nick started to say. Then he stopped. He was sure that it was a bad decision, but he'd just sound like a whiner trying to explain why.

Instead he said, "Erik, Dyl, Leon. Get ready. The ball's coming to you. And Dyl, move inside more."

Erik looked at Nick, surprised. He had seen the Thunder Green attack lose its power when Nick started man-marking Jimmy. Changing now seemed dangerous, "Are you sure, Nicky?"

Nick shrugged. Kenny smirked. Gabe said, "Good idea, Mr. Steiner. We gotta get a body on that guy. No offense to the great Nicky McCoy, but he's a wee little fellow."

As the players went running onto the field, Mr. Steiner heard someone say, "Great job, coach!" But he was unsure who said it.

Kenny did not intend to let his chance at center midfield pass by and slip away. He looked tall and confident with his blond hair waving in the breeze that had begun to pick up. He knew it had just been a matter of time before the Marauders were his team. He shouted instructions and encouragement at his teammates. "Focus, Mario. Move a little left." "Parker, closer to me." "Terry, stay back and give me room." "Erik, anticipate the through balls." He didn't notice that most of his teammates' eyes were on Nick, now lurking on the left side of the field, wondering what he would do next.

Still, Kenny wasn't stupid, and he was a good soccer player. He'd seen what Nick's tough marking had done to Jimmy after the second goal, and he vowed he'd do the same, but better, because he knew all of Jimmy's moves. For a while, Kenny covered Jimmy just as well as Nick, and the Marauder defense improved generally. There was no longer a hole on the left side, because Nick was there. And there was no hole on the right because Abbey moved over to that side when Terry, who was left footed, came in the game. She couldn't beat Martin in a foot race, but she anticipated passes down the wing and cut them off before there was any danger.

Even the Marauder attack came to life. Kenny did indeed put a couple of balls through, and more threateningly, Nick found space to work on the left side. He pushed the ball easily past his opposing midfielder and forced the defenders to move up on him. He hit Dylan down one wing. He hit Mario down the other. And he would have hit Erik in the middle, except that the Thunder Green defense had taken Erik's measure and sandwiched him constantly between two defenders. And when Nick tried to dribble closer to the goal himself, the defenders swarmed him before he could find an open man. Once when Nick lost the ball to Jimmy, helping out on defense, it led to a dangerous counterattack by the Thunder Green.

Kenny screamed at Nick, "You're out of position. Play your zone!"

"Move your ass and give me someone to pass to!" Nick screamed back, after which Mr. Steiner decided to give Nick a rest.

He sent Will in to play left midfield and while Nick was off, Thunder Green scored their fifth goal. When Erik and Kenny sat down, the Thunder Green scored their sixth goal.

When Erik came back in, Nick went up to Erik, "Man, this sucks."

"Get it to me. I'm going to score," Erik said flatly.

"Fine, but move out of the middle so their defenders aren't all over you."

The last ten minutes finally gave the Marauders some reason to hope. Nick and Erik stopped playing the static positions coached by Mr. Steiner. Nick roamed all over the field, calling for the ball, providing an outlet to his teammates and ignoring Kenny yelling, "Stay out of the middle!" Erik wove all over the attacking half, sending Mario and Leon across the field to get out of his way when he strayed into their territory.

With five minutes to go, Nick found Erik with space on the right wing, and Erik cut hard to the goal, slipping easily around the first two defenders who came to stop him. As the last defender gunned toward him, Erik feinted right, moving the ball in that direction with the outside of his right foot. Then, just as the defender committed, Erik's right foot extended further out, wrapped around the ball, and whipped it back to the left, leaving the defender on the ground behind him. A perfect Elastico. Erik took one more touch to set the ball up for his shot and smashed it into the upper right corner of the goal.

Mario stood clapping for the successful Elastico even before the shot went in. Erik's Marauder teammates engulfed him. It was their first goal in the Tri-State League. Maybe this had broken the drought. The whistle blew a few minutes later, and the Marauders cheered loudly before lining up to shake hands.

At 6–1, the game was lost, and badly. But there was no despair in the air. Kenny had found his position. Abbey had found her team. Nick knew he could play with anyone in the league. And Erik had mastered the Elastico.

THE MARAUDERS WERE pretty upbeat going into practice the following week. At school on Monday morning everyone was talking about the Elastico. Also, Will had word from his dad that Caton Field would be ready for practice on Tuesday. The first home game there would be that coming Saturday. Jamie spent art class designing a poster, hoping to draw some fans.

The only down note was Nick's fraction make-up. Comparing notes with Will after the test, he realized that he'd forgotten to switch denominators and numerators when he changed from division to multiplication.

"Never mind, Nickster," Will said. "That's just one mistake. It sounds like you did okay on the rest."

But Nick was fairly certain it wasn't going to be all right. Something about Mr. DeMille struck him as vengeful. And he hated the fact that none of his friends saw it. Abbey, Erik, and Dylan all thought he was great. So did Yvonne.

"Hey, Nick," Yvonne said, flashing her smile. "How'd you do?"

"Okay, I guess." Yvonne would think he was an idiot if he failed the test again after she spent an hour explaining things to him and Will.

"You know I'm having a party, right? October third. The invitations should go out this week, and everyone's invited."

"Cool."

"We're going to set up the stereo system in the barn so we can dance. My dad and I are going to teach everyone how to swing dance. Make sure you're there, okay?"

"Sounds great."

Nick's dad was a fiddle player and he'd been organizing contra dances at the school since Nick was in first grade. So the seventh graders were used to dancing together. But a dance at Yvonne's house, with real music, was a different matter. Also, October third was the night after the game at Kilby. It would be sweet to celebrate a victory by dancing with Yvonne. And maybe Abbey, too.

MONDAY'S PRACTICE WAS a relaxed affair, but several of the other parents showed up to watch Tuesday's practice because it was the first at Caton's Field. Mr. Juarez was there, talking to Officer Drybzyck. Pat Cooper walked the field with Charlie McCoy, admiring their work. Dan Caton, his face shaded by an engineer's cap, sat watching in a portable lawn chair.

Randy Garrity was also there, accompanied by a muscular young man in shorts, a T-shirt, and Adidas soccer slippers.

When Larry Steiner arrived, Mr. Garrity and the young man caught up with him first. "You made a class move there last weekend. I think the team gained a lot of confidence with Kenny in the middle. You should think about what I said about naming a captain."

"Uh, Mr. Garrity, I really don't . . . ."

"Just think about it. Look, I want to introduce you to Tad."

"Really pleased to meet you, Coach Steiner," the young man said, looking truly pleased. Tad looked like a cross between a gorilla and a J-Crew model. He was not tall, but he was solid, with thickly muscled shoulders and thighs that bulged out of his shirts and shorts. He had a clear, innocent face and unruly straw-colored hair.

"Tad here is a senior co-captain of the Hereford team. Academic All-American and headed to Wall Street next year. UBS, right?"

"Yes sir, Mr. Garrity."

"The point is, Larry, I've asked him to help you. I know that you aren't a soccer player, so I figured it would help to have someone around who knows the ins and outs."

"That's great. The kids'll get a real kick out of it."

"Now Tad is available just on Tuesdays and Thursdays. I figured it made sense to make those the days that the more advanced kids could focus on their technical training."

"Well, I think everyone may need help with their technique."

"Sure, sure. We want to help everyone. But Tad would be wasted on kids still learning to make a square pass. Try it out and see how it works, that's all I'm saying."

"Okay, we'll see how it goes. Welcome aboard, Tad."

Tad was a help. He kept the kids moving through their drills and gave them useful tips on shooting and passing. Mr. Steiner noticed that a vast majority of his tips went to Kenny, Erik, and Will. Still, the kids seemed to really enjoy working with him, and he was, on the whole, an asset.

Toward the end of practice, Erik noticed Georgi standing on the sidelines. Georgi was scowling, but then again, he was always scowling. Erik and Nick went over to him.

"Hey, Mr. Georgi," Erik said. "We want to thank you for the shirts. They came out looking really sharp."

"Our first game on the field is Saturday," Nick added. "You'll see how good they look."

"Seven home games you said!"

"That's right. One against each team."

"But not seven on this field!"

The boys looked at each other without comprehension.

"Not seven games here, next to my restaurant with a chance to sell pizzas."

Understanding dawned on Erik slowly. "We had to play our first game up at the elementary school because the field wasn't ready."

"So only six games here. One game short. You owe me!" Georgi turned on his heel and stomped away.

Erik and Nick looked at each other, shaken but also trying to hold in their laughter.

"Wait 'til he's gone," Erik whispered desperately. When Georgi rounded the corner of the garage, the two of them collapsed into giggles.

"If he's serious, we would owe him about fifteen bucks," Erik said, finally. "What should we do?"

"Let's wait and see what happens."

WEDNESDAY MORNING, MR. DeMille described the research paper that was expected of the seventh grade that fall. They were to write a history paper using at least four different sources on some aspect of Egyptian culture. They needed to produce a bibliography to be approved by Mr. DeMille in two weeks, and the final paper, between three and five typed pages, by Monday, October 19th.

In response, the class let out a collective groan. It was the most difficult assignment they had received in all their years of schooling, and it seemed an impossible amount of work. Mr. DeMille smiled at their discomfort.

"You will find, dear pupils, that this is nothing compared to what is expected of you in high school. I suggest you start early and give yourselves plenty of time. One of the most important lessons to learn is how to pace your work. This is *not* an assignment that can be completed at the last minute. I would be happy to meet with any of you to discuss a schedule if you are having trouble getting started."

"How do we know what to write about?" asked Dylan.

"We have already started reading about Egypt, and will continue to do so over the next month. Take a subject that interests you and explore it in greater depth."

"What if nothing interests you?" Tabitha asked.

"In that case, pretend you are interested in something, Ms. Williams."

The whole class laughed, and Mr. DeMille launched into a presentation that no one paid much attention to about the difference between using a source correctly and plagiarizing.

At morning recess, Nick was held in to discuss the results of his fractions make-up test. He had failed miserably, getting only 8 out of 25 points.

"I have to say that I am disappointed, Mr. McCoy. I've recommended remedial tutoring with Ms. Basquiat. You should meet with her at the end of the day to arrange schedules. The rest of the class is moving ahead, and we do not have time to keep going over the basics in class."

Nick heard the message loud and clear. "You are stupid and you will never amount to anything." Nick knew that already. He just wished Mr. DeMille would shut up and stop telling him how dumb he was.

"I hear you're a soccer player," Mr. DeMille said.

"Yes, sir."

"Well, you won't win a scholarship if you can't learn simple fractions."

Nick did not say anything. He didn't play soccer for scholarships. He played for now. Because he loved it.

"I want to see how you do in your other classes. If you can't keep up I may have to recommend to your parents that you cut back on your extra-curriculars. Soccer is all very well, but your education is what's important."

Nick pricked up his ears. None of his other teachers had ever threatened his soccer before. Nick felt his pulse increase and his breathing begin to get ragged. He fought to calm himself. He would not let DeMille get to him.

But Mr. DeMille had seen the reaction and gave a satisfied grunt. "I recommend you get to work on your research paper," he said, before waving his hand to dismiss Nick.

MEETING WITH MS. Basquiat made Nick a little late to practice. He biked down Lancaster Hill furiously, pulling up to Caton's Garage just as Jamie, who had forgotten his cleats and had to go home before practice to get them, was being dropped off by his mother.

"You don't look so good," Jamie said.

"Nothing some soccer won't cure," Nick said. "I've got to get over a case of school."

"I know what you mean. DeMille is really piling on the work."

"He's a jerk."

"He's not that bad. He just wants to see what we can do. High school will be much worse."

"Says who? De Pill?"

Jamie let it drop. "Did you see the weather for Saturday? It's supposed to get cold and thunder and rain all day."

"That's okay."

"For you maybe. But it sucks when you're a goalie. And no way my parents will come if it's raining. They'll remember some errand five minutes before kickoff."

"Georgi won't like it either; if there are no spectators." Nick explained how Georgi had complained about being cheated out of a game's worth of revenue.

Jamie laughed. "He can't complain about the rain, can he?"

"We'll see."

The rest of the Marauders were still waiting for Mr. Steiner to arrive. Erik was passing with Leon, Will, and Mario. The others were gathered around Kenny on the sideline. They all burst into laughter just as Nick sat down to put on his cleats.

Dylan said, "Oh, Nick. You've got to hear Kenny's story about scuba diving in, where was it?"

"Mauritius."

"Yeah, Mauritius. He almost got the bends trying to avoid a shark."

"So, man, you took a holiday to Mauritius even though you were living in France?" Gabe asked

"We go sailing there every year. Best scuba diving in the world."

"That's like a holiday on a holiday."

"France is cool. But Greece is better. The girls at the topless beaches there are amazing," Kenny said.

"No way!" Terry said. "You went to a topless beach?"

"It's no big deal. In Mauritius, the beaches are all clothing optional."

"Like National Geographic," Gabe said. "Hey, Abbey, wanna go to Mauritius?"

"Not with you, Gabe. It's painful enough seeing you shirtless at the Pond."

Kenny said. "Do you sail, Nick?"

"Yeah, a bit, on Lake Fors."

Kenny laughed. "You mean in, like, a Sunfish? No, I mean real sailing. On a J-Class or above. You have not lived until you've seen the sunrise from a boat in the middle of the ocean with no land in sight. It's spectacular."

Nick said nothing. He had nothing to compete with Kenny's la-di-da stories about sailing around the world. His friends were eating the nonsense up. But he bet he could beat Kenny in a race around Lake Fors in a Sunfish.

Kenny turned to Abbey. "You sail, don't you? You told me you go to the Caribbean over spring break."

"When did she tell him that?" Nick wondered. But Kenny and Abbey had gone out on the field to kick around a ball.

"That's the life I want to live," Gabe said admiringly. "Beaches, yachts, travel."

"That's just money!" Nick said. "It's not life."

"Close enough," said Dylan. "He went to the World Cup final. Come on, now. *That* would be cool!"

Nick was never jealous of people. And he really was not jealous of Kenny. Sure, it would be nice to see a World Cup match live. So would a lot of things he did not have—like passing grades in math. He'd always rather be Nick, thank you. Even so, as he passed the ball around with Jamie and Dylan, he found himself aware of Kenny's voice, still telling stories to Abbey.

AS PROMISED, TAD showed up for the practice on Thursday. He talked briefly with Mr. Steiner, proposing a number of warm-up drills and suggesting they work on set pieces, like corner kicks and free kicks. Mr. Steiner was content to follow his advice. Tad knew what he was doing, and the kids had responded well to him on Tuesday.

Tad blew a whistle and called the team together. Dylan was last to the circle.

"Ten push-ups," Tad said.

Dylan jumped down, and ripped off ten perfect push-ups.

"Good. Now, listen to the whistle and don't be the last one in. We're going to practice set pieces today. We'll do some corners and then we'll do some free kicks. Jamie's in goal. You three," Tad pointed at Gabe, Will, and Jackson, "on defense. Kenny, you take the corners."

"Tad?" Nick interrupted. "Erik always takes the corners. He's got, like, laser sighting."

"Call me *Coach*. Anyone coaching you is Coach, got it?"

Nick rolled his eyes. "Yes, *Coach*."

"You'll all get a chance, but I want to see what Kenny can do. Now go!"

Tad selected three attackers and showed them runs to make while Kenny took a series of corners. After demonstrating several options, Tad selected some of the weaker players and turned to Mr. Steiner. "Can you try the same thing with this group at the other goal? Just run the plays with two defenders and three attackers, and without a goalie."

As Mr. Steiner's group walked to the other side, Tad turned to his players. "All right, let's switch sides. Kenny, switch sides."

"I thought we were all going to get a chance?" Nick asked.

"When I'm ready. For now, we'll switch up offense and defense. Kenny, get to the corner."

The attackers and defenders switched roles, and Kenny hit a couple of lousy corners. Tad went over to talk with him, repositioned the ball, and adjusted Kenny's run up, and the next few were better.

"Great job!" Tad said. "Okay, let's move on to free kicks. Defenders make a wall. Attackers, I want you to set up on either side of the wall. Kenny will take the kicks."

Nick shook his head, but it was Erik who said something. "I think it's someone else's turn, Tad."

"*Coach,*" Tad said darkly. "Look, Kenny'll probably take the kicks in a game situation, so it makes sense to work with him first."

"Why would Kenny take 'em?" Nick asked. "Erik is the best shot on the field. And I'm the second best."

"Hey, I know you think you're a big star, but I'm trying to get a team ready for competitive soccer. Who takes the kicks is a coach's decision. It's not a popularity contest. Got it?"

"Yeah, I GOT IT!" Nick said, walking away from the wall. The others looked around uncomfortably as Nick went to sit on the sideline.

Tad ignored Nick, and led the rest of the kids through the drill, practicing different free kick strategies. He left Kenny taking the free kicks as he went to explain the drill to Mr. Steiner's kids.

As he returned, he stopped at center field, blew his whistle, and called the kids in. "We gotta move on if we're going to have time to scrimmage." Everyone ran toward him. Everyone except Nick. Nick got up slowly from the sideline and walked very slowly back into the huddle.

"Last one in gives me ten push-ups," Tad said.

Nick just looked at him.

Tad said again, "I want ten!"

Nick did not move. Tad looked at Mr. Steiner.

"I think we can dispense with that rule for the moment," said Mr. Steiner gently.

"Okay," Tad said gruffly, "let's move on. We're going to scrimmage." He counted the players. "We're one short," he said, looking at Mr. Steiner.

"Yes. Mario's father called me. He had car trouble."

"Okay, I'll play for him. Jamie, Leon, Jackson, Terry, Abbey, Dylan, and Nick, will be pinneys. I'll be shirts with Erik, Will, Kenny, Matty, Parker, and Gabe."

They started with a game of one touch, which went badly since the kids had never played a one-touch scrimmage before. Mr. Steiner, who was refereeing, blew the whistle a lot for double touches, and after a while the game degenerated into a lot of mindless booting.

Tad stopped play. "We have twenty more minutes of practice. We'll play normal rules, but keep looking for your teammates." He kicked the ball to the pinneys to start the new game.

The game was lopsided, with Tad's team controlling the ball and scoring several goals and missing several more. Nick's team didn't even threaten. Every time Leon or Dylan got the ball anywhere near the goal, Tad took it away with such ease that he appeared not to be moving at all.

The scrimmage was almost over when Nick received a pass in midfield and took off on his own. He shrugged around a lazy challenge from Kenny before Parker and Gabe converged on him. Nick faked to Parker's side before cutting back hard around the outside of Gabe. The two defenders collided, leaving Nick alone with the ball. Dylan was on his left, covered by Will, and Leon was on his right, with just Tad between Nick and the goal. For a split second they locked eyes.

"Better make the pass," said Tad. "You're not coming through."

Nick slowed his dribble and waved to Leon, showing him where to run. But as he did so, Tad closed with frightening speed. He lunged at Nick, with one massive leg blocking the pass to Leon and the aiming for Nick's ankles. It was a textbook aggressive tackle, the sort of tackle Tad had used to stop some of the best forwards in the college game—but somehow it did not stop Nick.

In the moment between Tad pouncing and Nick losing his legs, Nick had slipped a toe under the ball and flicked it up in the air and forward. Somehow, the ball found the hole between Tad's knees where his legs bowed out slightly, and squeaked through. And somehow, Nick had stopped his momentum and spun full circle away from Tad's tackle, back in the direction of the goal. Nick had tipped but kept his balance, and collected the ball, only to see Will racing in from the wing to try to block his path to the goal.

Meanwhile, Tad had not given up. Like an enraged bull that had missed its target, Tad was momentarily confused by the sudden disappearance of his victim. Shaking his head clear and looking around, he spotted Nick again and reacted with startling agility. His forward momentum was converted to turning torque and in the blink of an eye he was accelerating back the way he came, closing on Nick from behind.

Nick held the ball a second longer, until both bodies charging at him were absolutely committed, and then he delicately played the ball off to Leon, coming in unguarded from the right. The ball rolled smoothly, hitting Leon in stride just a few feet from the goal, and it was the easiest thing in the world for Leon to turn his foot and knock it securely into the net.

Nick, however, didn't see the goal. While Will had slid in front of Nick, missing him entirely, Tad had driven right through him from behind with his cleats up. It was not a practice tackle. It was not even a legal tackle. It was a tackle to break legs, a tackle to punish or eliminate an opponent. It was a red card tackle. And Nick went down hard.

Tad bounced up, red faced, and stood over him. "NEVER EMBARRASS ME AGAIN!"

Except for Nick's moans, the field was suddenly silent. Mr. Steiner ran over and motioned to Tad to move away. Tad hesitated for a moment. Then he turned and actually ran to the sidelines. He collected his gear and then kept going, all the way to the parking area. A moment later, the kids heard Tad's car start up, pull backward sharply out of its parking space, and screech away.

Mr. Steiner knelt down at Nick's side and looked at his leg. A long cut along one calf that bleeding. Mr. Steiner cleaned up Nick's cut and called an end to practice. He asked Terry and Gabe to help carry Nick over to his car, while Erik loaded Nick's bike in the back.

By the time Mr. Steiner and Erik had driven Nick back home, Nick was looking more himself, and he even insisted on limping from the car to his house. Mr. Steiner breathed a sigh of relief as he explained what happened to Beth McCoy.

When Erik and Mr. Steiner got home, Mrs. Steiner said that there was a message from Mr. Garrity to please call as soon as possible. Mr. Steiner gritted his teeth, breathed deeply, and took the telephone into his study.

"Garrity," a gruff voice barked through the phone after one ring. "Oh, Coach Steiner, it's you," Mr. Garrity said, noticing his caller

ID. "I just had a message from Tad that he can't coach any more. No explanation, nothing. What the hell is going on there?"

"He mauled one of the kids at practice."

"What?"

"During a scrimmage, he made an exceptionally hard tackle on one of the boys. I would say he almost broke the boy's leg. He left a deep gouge in his calf."

"That's not like Tad."

"He lost his temper."

"Which boy was it?" Mr. Garrity said.

"I don't think that really matters," Mr. Steiner said. "Tad left immediately afterward. To tell the truth, I think he was ashamed of himself."

"Well, it's all one heck of a mess. You've got a sinking ship up there."

"I think you may be exaggerating."

"No, Larry," Mr. Garrity continued, "you've got some top talent on that team, but they need a leader. A leader takes care of his people. I'll be watching on Saturday."

Mr. Steiner opened his mouth to reply, but Mr. Garrity had already hung up. He went back to his kitchen, handed the phone to his wife, and said, "God, I can't wait until the season is over."

CHAPTER 7

Crash and Burn

On Saturday morning, Nick's mother put a clean bandage on his leg and wrapped it carefully. "Really, Nick, the slightest knock might open your cut again."

"Mom, it's okay. It's just soccer."

"And you should wear something under your jersey. It's going to be cold today."

"Let him be, Beth," Charlie said. "He'll be fine."

Mrs. McCoy frowned and went to get the girls dressed, making sure they had their raincoats, rain pants, and rubber boots. Nick's sisters loved attending his games anyway, but the wet weather that morning made it doubly exciting. There should be lots of fresh puddles for them to stomp in.

Nick and his family were among the first to arrive at Caton Field. Rain drops began to appear on the windshield as they pulled up. Dan was standing on the side of the field in full rain gear.

Nick went over to greet him. "Hey, Dan. Our first home game."

"Sure." It was a neutral comment, but Dan sounded proud.

"Shame about the weather."

"Can't always be sunny."

The game was set to start at ten o'clock. But five minutes before game time, the rain began to come down hard and there was still no sign of the Winchester team. The Blue Marauders were running around trying to stay warm, while most of the fans had retreated to their cars. Mr. Steiner sat next to Charlie McCoy on the home team bench, feeling like a drowned rat.

"They'd be smart not to show up," said Mr. Steiner.

"Refs said they have until 10:15 to show."

"You want to check up at the elementary school field? Make sure there was no confusion?"

"Sure." But as Charlie stood up, a yellow school bus pulled into the field. The Blue Marauders cheered, but Mr. Steiner's heart sank. One more hour standing around in a cold rain.

A man from the bus came up to Mr. Steiner. "Sorry we're late. Took a wrong turn in Windsor."

"No problem," Mr. Steiner said, looking over the Winchester team as it made its way to the field. Winchester was an industrial center about an hour and forty-five minutes southeast of Lancaster. Its main industry was plastics, but it also had some chemical plants and furniture manufacturers. It was not a pretty town by any means, but it had almost 300,000 residents. It was a big town and the boys were big too. Several were as tall as Mr. Steiner himself.

After much thought, Mr. Steiner had decided to leave Kenny at center midfield and Nick at left. As he had explained to his wife, "I'm not doing it because of Garrity. It worked better last game. It makes sense to have the bigger boy in the middle. And it frees Nick to be more attacking."

His wife had said she was sure he was doing what he thought best.

"Of course I am!" Larry had said.

"Don't be angry at me," Lisa had said. "I'm on your side."

He made another decision at game time to start Terry for Abbey. He felt that the team might need Terry's strength. Mr. Steiner felt Abbey's surprised look when he announced the starters, and he added quickly, "Remember, everyone plays the same amount so it doesn't matter who starts." The team was silent, but Mr. Steiner guessed what they were thinking. "If it didn't matter who starts, why make the change?" Mr. Steiner had no answer to that question so, instead of responding, he hurried the kids onto the field.

THE GAME PROVED as ugly as the day. The Winchester team was not subtle. They played English-style soccer at its worst. Every time a Winchester defender touched the ball, he pounded it into the Marauders' half. Once across midfield, the Winchester players lofted the ball into the Marauders' penalty box and charged the goal. There was no art to the tactics but, in the driving rain, they were effective.

The first goal was typical. Jamie was bumped by one of the Winchester players as he went up to snatch a cross out of the air. The wet ball slid through his rain-soaked gloves and fell on the goal line. There was a mad scramble and then the ball was in the net. No one knew who actually knocked it in.

Winchester added a second goal, and the game looked completely lost until Will caught the Winchester defense moving up and hit a long ball to Dylan racing down the wing. Dylan's first touch knocked the ball in the direction of the goal, but his second touch was too far in front of him. The goalie came out and would have cleared it if he hadn't slipped in the mud. Dylan took the opportunity to knock the ball around the goalie and score on an empty net. It was not much of a goal, but it was better than nothing. The fans of the Marauders, mostly now sitting in their cars with the heaters on, watching the game though foggy windshields, gave a muted cheer. Someone honked a horn.

But Winchester put in three more muddy, artless goals in the second half while the Marauders had none. Nick limped around for fifteen minutes until Mr. Steiner took him out and sat him on the bench for the rest of the game. The rest of the team, weighed down by their heavy cotton jerseys soaked with rain, and battered and bruised by the Winchester players, were generally ready to go home. They hit the ball wherever they could and yelled at their teammates for not being there.

5–1 was a generous score. It could have been worse. This was not a loss like the one against the Thunder, where everyone felt good at the end. Instead everyone—almost everyone, Dylan was delighted to have scored—felt terrible.

BY MONDAY, THE field had dried up, but the weather was still cool. Mr. Steiner decided to return to his emphasis on positioning. The kids had responded better to that approach than the alternatives.

But the team was in no mood for standing around. When Mario let a ball roll under his foot out of bounds, Kenny turned to Gabe and said, "You see, that's why I don't pass it to him. He's useless."

"And he never passes it back, anyway," Gabe said.

"Now boys . . . ," Mr. Steiner began.

"Yeah," said Nick, "put Gabe on the wing. 'Cause he flubbed, like, six clearances in the last game. Get him out of defense where he can't make boneheaded mistakes."

"At least he played the whole last game and didn't punk out in the second half," Kenny said.

"You know, Kenny," Leon said, "we'd just be happy if you passed it to *anyone* on the team."

"If you want the ball," Gabe suggested, "go get it. Don't duck and run every time a defender comes near you."

"I've never seen Leon or Mario head the ball," Terry said, quite complacently for someone who had just started playing soccer, and still had trouble with a square pass.

"That's enough," said Mr. Steiner.

But later, when Terry was bending down to pick up a ball, Leon poked his toe in and kicked it away. Terry stood up and slammed his hand into Leon's chest. Mario stepped in behind Terry and cleated him in the leg. Nick grabbed Mario and pulled him back, while Dylan and Will jumped in front of Terry to stop him from throwing himself at Mario. Kenny and Gabe stepped up on either side of Leon, before Erik and Parker stepped up to push them away. Only Jackson, who looked on the whole thing as seventh-grade silliness, and Abbey, who thought it was just idiotic boys, stood apart.

The boys stared at each other for a few tense seconds until Mr. Steiner stepped in again and said, "That's it, I'm canceling practice. We'll try again tomorrow. And I expect you all to be more mature."

WILL AND NICK, who had biked to practice, went to get their bikes together.

"Man, that sucks," Nick said.

"Sure," Will said, "but did you notice the field? It was still in pretty good shape. It held up to our game on Saturday."

Nick grinned and slapped Will on the back. "I'm glad you are keeping your eye on what's important."

TUESDAY'S PRACTICE WAS better. Officer Drybzyck and Mrs. Juarez were both there to watch. No one wanted to get in a fight with Officer Drybzyck around. He was liable to wade in and break it up with a night stick. And Gabe didn't want to argue with Leon in front of Mrs. Juarez. The Juarez family lived near the Drybzycks and went to the same church. They weren't close friends, but they pretended to be. So Mrs. Juarez could make an awful lot of trouble for Gabe if she tried.

The boys ran through their drills sullenly and then played a low-energy scrimmage. Nick's leg was still sore so he took it easy. But the few times he tried to go full out, the calf held up pretty well. At the end of practice, Mr. Steiner reminded everyone that they had a game the next day at 4:30 p.m. He expected them to play as a team.

THE WEATHER HAD warmed by Wednesday, promising a beautiful Indian summer evening, and there was a good group of fans for the game. In addition to the usual mix of parents and siblings, several of the sixth and seventh graders had come down to Caton's Field to watch.

Erik's father had arrived early to put the corner flags up and have a little think about the team. As he prepared the flag, he saw Rory and Georgi walking slowly toward him.

"I haven't had a chance to thank you for sponsoring the team," Mr. Steiner said. "It's made a real difference for the kids."

Georgi grunted. Rory said, "Pleasure to do it. But I admit that the results have been a little disappointing so far."

"I haven't seen you at the games."

"No wins. Three losses. The Tri-State website has the standings. Blue Marauders are bottom of the league."

Larry Steiner offered a polite smile. "It's our first year. And, the season is young yet. Are you watching us today?"

"Sure. Good to check up on the investment every now and then. How about you, Georgi?" Rory asked.

"Mmmmeh. I have pizzas to make. I see ten minutes maybe."

The Bedford team arrived in twos and threes. They were known as the Red Demons and had gleaming scarlet uniforms. Bedford, two hours south of Lancaster, was a well-off community that boasted a liberal arts college, an art colony, and a host of magnificent homes belonging to the town's summer residents. Bedford had a long tradition of quality soccer, and they had won the U-13 Tri-State Championship five times. This was mostly due to Benjamin Rush, a Boston transplant who had moved to Bedford forty years ago, fresh from captaining the Harvard team. He started as the high school coach and had since taken charge of all of the youth soccer programming in the area.

When he arrived at Caton Field, Mr. Rush sought out Mr. Steiner and went over to introduce himself. Mr. Rush was a tall thin man with neat grey hair, combed in a careful part. Instead of the usual soccer sweats, he was dressed in a suit and tie.

"Mr. Steiner?" he said, holding out a hand, "I'm Benjamin Rush. Please call me Benjamin."

"Nice to meet you Benjamin, I'm Larry."

"It's wonderful to have a new team in the league. First new one in five years, I believe. Please don't hesitate to let me know if I can make the transition to the league easier for you."

"Thank you, I appreciate the offer," Mr. Steiner said. It occurred to him that, in four matches, these were the first kind words he had heard.

"I see your team is straggling in a little late."

"Well, they do that sometimes."

"Oh, I quite understand. Home games are the worst. The boys live five minutes away so they don't leave their houses until six minutes before game time. I usually have to bench latecomers for at least a half to get the message through."

"Well, I'll have to consider that," Mr. Steiner said smiling. "But we only have fourteen players, so it's a little difficult."

"I hear you have a filly on the team."

"You mean . . . ?" Mr. Steiner began.

"Yes, a girl. Good show! A blow for women's rights! I'll make sure my boys don't treat her too roughly."

"Oh, I don't think that will be necessary."

"Not at all. Not at all. Happy to do it. Anyway, very nice to meet you, Larry. Best of luck today."

"Thank you. Likewise," Mr. Steiner said.

The Blue Marauders, except for Jackson and Leon, all made it to the field before kickoff. Erik, who came with his mother, was one of the last to arrive. He jumped out of the car and sprinted into the huddle where his father had gathered the team.

"Erik, where were you?"

"Sorry, Dad. Mom and I lost track of time."

"Does anyone know where Jackson and Leon are?"

"Leon had a cold," Gabe said. "He was out of school on Friday. I guess he's still sick."

"And Jackson?"

"He has an orthodontist appointment," Erik said. "He asked me to tell you, but I forgot. The orthodontist said that if he didn't have the appointment today, there was no room for another six months. His mom insisted. Sorry, Dad."

Mr. Steiner sighed in exasperation. "Well, we have a full team. Parker, you start at right defender."

Parker looked up and Mr. Steiner saw dark rings under his eyes. "Are you okay, Parker?"

"Yeah, just tired. Late night last night."

"Terry, you start at right back. Parker, rest for ten minutes and then you'll go in. Mario, you're at left wing. What I want to see is two things. First, everyone playing position. Second," and here Mr. Steiner looked meaningfully at Kenny, "everyone passing to everyone else. And I will *not* have anyone yelling at their teammates. Understood?"

He received a small chorus of "yeses" and sent his team onto the field.

Erik said to Nick, "At least they're smaller than Winchester." Indeed, the Red Demons, if anything, were a little shorter on average than the Blue Marauders.

"They're quick though," Nick said. "Did you see their passing drills?"

"Yeah, they looked good. I wish we could do more of that."

"Really? I'm figuring we should do less. We have to be like Kenny. Pass less and impose our wills on the game."

"Maybe," Erik said.

"Well, that's what I'm going to do. When I get the ball, go to the box and get open. I'll find you."

Soon after the opening whistle, Nick put his new scheme into action. When he won the ball off a clearance from the Red Demon defense and looked around, he saw Kenny calling for a square pass and Dylan offside down the left wing. But he also saw some space through the midfield, and, all things considered, he decided the ball was best at his feet.

"Anyway," he told himself, "I won the ball, so it's mine to lose."

Nick drove the ball down the middle, beating one Red Demon and then another. Finally, as three defenders converged on him just twenty-five yards away from the goal, Nick found a gap and angled a sharp pass across the penalty box to Erik. Unmarked and with time, Erik easily beat the goalie. 1–0 Marauders.

It was a beautiful goal, but it probably sealed the Marauders' fate, because it convinced Nick that he'd found the answer to their problems: himself. For the rest of the game, Nick dribbled and dribbled every time he touched the ball. Kenny, Erik, and the other attackers soon followed suit. Will and Abbey kept hitting crisp passes to their forwards, only to watch their teammates lose possession trying to take on the whole Red Demon team.

If anything, the Marauder's defense was even worse than its attack. Some of the players, like Matty and Terry, took Mr. Steiner's emphasis on position too much to heart, and would not follow the ball beyond what they perceived to be their proper zone. Others, including Nick, decided that they needed to be where the action was and completely abandoned positional play. The result was a lot of open space, and the Red Demons made the most of it. They played an attractive style of soccer and moved the ball around quickly.

"That's it!" Mr. Rush called from the sidelines incessantly. "Let the ball do the work."

Bedford's central midfielder was particularly good, switching directions as he received the ball and constantly changing the direction of attack from one side of the field to the other. As he did so, the Red Demons made darting attacks up the sides, catching the Blue Marauders out of position again and again. Jamie made a number of good saves, but the Red Demons nevertheless scored three fairly quick goals before halftime, mostly driving up Nick's side of the field. Perhaps only Benjamin Rush noticed, but the Marauder defense actually improved when Nick came out with ten minutes to go in the half. Still, it was 4–1 by the time the halftime whistle blew.

The Blue Marauders made their way to the sideline morosely. The Marauders were exhausted from chasing the Red Demons, and they had no idea how to stop them, let alone how to score themselves. Parents, friends, and schoolmates were watching. They were representing the honor of the town. And yet the game seemed hopeless. They were embarrassed and didn't know how to end the embarrassment.

"Nick's got to cut out the showboating," Kenny said angrily, as he came into the huddle. "Pass the damn ball and play your position!"

"Like you're doing any better!" Nick yelled back angrily. "You give their center middie so much room that he can do what he wants!"

"We have to stop chasing them," Will said. "I'm so exhausted I could puke." Everyone looked at him. Will was never tired.

"And the forwards have to come back," Jackson said. "Their defenders are coming up and there is no one covering them."

"I think Jackson's right," Mr. Steiner said. "I want everyone coming back more. Let's leave Erik up as the lone forward. Everyone else, let's try to pack it in and keep it close."

Nick was about to say, "That's a loser's strategy," when he remembered that he shouldn't say that kind of thing to Erik's dad. He was doing his best.

At the start of the second half, Kenny was sitting out, and Nick and Abbey walked onto the field together. "Man, can you believe what a creep Kenny is?" Nick said.

Abbey looked at him sharply. "No. He's right. I don't know what's wrong with you. You're running around like a chicken with its head cut off. You haven't passed the ball to anyone."

Nick looked at Abbey, shocked and then angry. "Oh, that's right. I forgot you're on his side. You're going to meet up and go sailing in the Caribbean."

"Don't be stupid," Abbey said.

"I bet you wish you were playing for the Thunder. You'd fit right in!"

"Idiot!"

The whistle blew for the second half, and the game grew more lopsided. The Blue Marauders were exhausted and their legs gave out on them. The Red Demons ran and passed and shot and there was little the Marauders could do to stop them. The only break came about halfway through the second half, with Kenny back in at center midfield. Abbey won the ball on defense and hit a high ball up the middle, where Kenny and Erik were waiting. Kenny out-jumped two Red Demon defenders and flicked the ball backward into the open space behind the defense. Erik outraced the Red Demon defense to the ball and sprinted to the goal. The quick Red Demon defenders ran after him, but Erik was almost as fast with the ball as without it, and they could not catch him. From the 18-yard line, he curled a shot just inside the right-hand post for the Marauder's second goal.

Erik's goal made it 7–2, where it stayed for the rest of the game. Afterward, Mr. Rush came to shake hands with Mr. Steiner.

"Good game, Larry. Eased off the throttle at the end there. No need to show anyone up."

"Thanks," Mr. Steiner said, unsure of the etiquette.

"The gal played well. She's an asset."

"We think so."

"But you may have lost control of the rest of your team somewhat."

"Well, I . . . ." Mr. Steiner was not sure what to say.

"Well, back to basics, I always say. Look," he put his hand in his jacket pocket and pulled out a card. "I run a camp for coaches. Just contact me if you're interested. I think you may find it very helpful."

"Thank you," Mr. Steiner said, not knowing what else to say.

"As I say, I like to see the new teams succeed."

More dispirited than ever, Mr. Steiner called his team together. "Next practice is tomorrow," he said, woodenly. "We have another game Friday. Away at Dover at five o'clock. I will pass out directions tomorrow. Make sure you get in touch if you don't have a ride. And . . . ." He had a hard time thinking of any encouraging remarks. "And get some sleep tonight."

NICK AND ABBEY avoided each other at school the next day. Unfortunately, Tabitha was behind them and noticed them ignoring each other, and on the way out to recess she asked loudly enough for everyone to hear. "What's the problem? Lovers' tiff?"

There was an uncomfortable silence, which Tabitha enjoyed. Quips about Nick and Abbey always drew a lot of attention, because at least half the girls were in love with Nick and most of the boys were in love with Abbey.

When no one else responded, Erik said, "Disagreement over soccer."

"That is why I never play that sport. Lots of passes, too little scoring," Tabitha said. "Seriously, what happened?"

"Drop it, Tabby," Nick said.

"C'mon, cuz," Tabitha said, "dish the dirt."

Neither Nick nor Abbey responded then, but Tabitha followed Abbey to the swings, sure that she could get the story out of her there. Most of the other girls followed them.

Nick headed to the basketball court along with most of the seventh-grade boys. He shot baskets, watching the girls out of the corner of his eye, until Dylan threw him a pass that slipped through his fingers and hit him in the head.

"C'mon, Nickster. Quit yer mooning," Dylan said.

Without answering, Nick walked away and went to sit at the picnic table. Erik, Jamie, Dylan, and Will followed him.

"What the hell is wrong with our team?" Nick said. "Why can't we win?"

"Because we suck?" Dylan suggested.

Nick looked at him. "These guys aren't better than us."

"The Bedford kids were really good," Will said.

"We don't play smart," Erik said.

"And everyone fights the whole time," Jamie said. "It sucks."

"I only fight with Kenny because he's a total jerk. He picks on Mario, and he never passes. He just sits around and talks about his travels and his yachts and his money. And Gabe and Terry and Abbey fall all over him."

Dylan laughed. "Abbey, too? I thought it was just Gabe and Terry."

"Does Abbey like him?" Jamie asked.

"I think we'd be better without him," Nick said.

"No way," Erik said. "He's a jerk, but we'd suck without him. And he's not the only one who didn't pass Wednesday."

"You mean me?" Nick said.

"Yes, you! You were a total prima donna out there. Like Kenny said, pass the damn ball and play your damn position!" Erik stomped off.

Nick looked around at his other friends. Will said, "It wasn't your best game, Nick."

"Hold on," Jamie said. "What's up with Abbey and Kenny?"

Dylan laughed. "Don't worry your head about it, short stuff. Abbey just noticed there was new blood in the neighborhood, and it's tall and blond. It won't last, 'cause he is a jerk."

NICK CAUGHT UP with Erik at lunch. He waited as Erik loaded his tray, and then guided him to the end of an empty table.

"I'm sorry," Nick said once they sat down.

"For what?"

"I sucked on Wednesday."

"We all did."

"Yeah, but I'm sorry for everything else, too. You know. The whole Blue Marauder thing. I mean, I know you wanted to play Thunder. And I bet you wish you did now. You'd be on the Thunder Green. You'd be playing with Jimmy; be undefeated; and have a cool uniform."

Erik smiled. "Well, what about you? You'd be on Thunder Red with Mac Scruggs. You'd be pretty good too."

"Uuugh! I just want the Marauders to be better. We shouldn't be this bad."

The boys sat together in silence for a few moments.

"We've played three of the top four teams in league," Erik said. "We might do better with the rest of the schedule. If you get your head screwed on straight."

"Yeah, but even the Thunder teams. We should be able to play with them. I'm as good as Jimmy. So are you."

"I don't know."

"And Kenny and Abbey and Will and Matty and Dylan are good too. And Jamie's a great goalie. Jackson and Gabe are good. Leon and Mario do their bit. We should be good. We just need to get organized."

"You left out Parker and Terry."

"Well, Terry really is pretty bad. And I don't know what happened to Park. He used to be solid. Now he wanders around in a daze. One run and he collapses."

"I think we could use a coach with more experience," Erik said tentatively.

To Erik's surprise, Nick did not dismiss the idea out of hand. "Maybe you're right, but who?'"

Erik had no answer to that and said instead, "Hey, I've been meaning to ask you. There's an indoor tournament this weekend in Winchester. We're too late to sign up, but we could go watch. It's a lot of the players from the league. You wanna go?"

"Sure. We could do some scouting. I'll check with my mom and pop, but I don't think it'll be a problem."

AT PRACTICE THAT afternoon, Mr. Steiner announced that he just wanted the team to scrimmage. "I am out of ideas for drills. Let's try to enjoy ourselves today and forget about the last four games."

Erik and Nick chose up teams. Erik chose Will first, then Nick, to everyone's surprise, took Kenny. Erik picked Matty, and Nick surprised everyone again by choosing Abbey.

When all the players were divided, Nick said to his team, "Listen, I'll play 'D' with Mario. Leon, Kenny and Abbey play midfield, and Terry, you go up and score us some goals."

The first time Nick touched the ball, Nick made sure he passed to Kenny. His second pass went to Abbey. And for the rest of the game, Nick stayed on defense and distributed the ball evenly. He found Leon in the open where Leon could take advantage of his dribbling. He threaded neat passes to Kenny, leading to a couple of goals. He also played some nifty combinations with Abbey, which led to a goal from Mario and several chances for Terry to score.

After the practice, there was a round of high fives. "It helps when you pass," Kenny said, grinning. "Then you don't completely suck."

It was on the awkward side for a compliment, but Nick was determined not to take it badly. "Nice finishing. See if you get a couple like that tomorrow."

"Absolutely," said Kenny.

Abbey gave Nick a high five as well, but she didn't smile at him. After practice, he went up to her as she was changing out of her cleats. "You still mad, Abs?"

"Maybe."

"C'mon," Nick said, holding out his hands, raising his eyebrows, and cocking his head.

Abbey turned away. "Okay, we're cool."

"Do I get a smooch?"

"Idiot." Abbey stood up and picked up her bag. But there was no more anger in her voice. As she passed, she punched Nick in the arm.

Nick faked falling, then winked and said in his best Humphrey Bogart imitation, "See y'around, doll."

Abbey walked away hiding a grin.

THAT EVENING, MR. Steiner knocked on Erik's bedroom door after supper.

"Are you busy?"

"No, Dad. No. Just homework. DeMille has us starting on bases."

"Oh, yes. I loved learning to calculate in different bases. Did you know that computers all work in base 2?"

"No."

"Well, let me know if you need any help."

"Okay, Dad. But what I will need help with soon is my Egyptian project. The bibliography is due next week and I can't find any really good books in the school library or at the L." The "L" was what the locals called the town's public library. It was the Lancaster Library and it had been originally founded by someone called Leonard Langbein, and that seemed reason enough. "So I was wondering if you could take me into Milford one day to see if there was anything good in the Hereford Library."

"Sure, I could do that. How about this weekend?"

"Well, Mom was taking me and Nick to Winchester to see some of the indoor tourney on Saturday."

"Don't you ever get enough soccer?"

Erik thought for a moment. "Not really."

"How about Sunday morning? I could take you to Milford first thing, and we could have lunch out when you're done."

"That would be great."

"Actually, I came in to talk to you about the Blue Marauders. How do you think it's going?"

"Today was all right," Erik said. "Nick made up with Abbey. And a little with Kenny, too."

"Yes, that was a good sign. But, honestly, I'm feeling out of my depth. I want to support your soccer, but it's not a sport I know much about. Also I've been pretty busy with work lately. I'm trying to find more money for the company. If I don't come up with something soon, we'll have to lay off staff."

Erik didn't say anything.

"Well, how would you feel if I gave up coaching?"

"I guess I'd understand. But who'd coach us?"

Here Mr. Steiner breathed deeply. "I've had some conversations with the other parents about who might take responsibility."

"Not Gabe's dad," Erik said. "He thinks we're training for the Marines. He knows nothing about soccer."

"I know that, but I did talk to him. Actually, he called me to express concern about the team's lack of intestinal fortitude."

"Really?"

"I'm not sure those were his exact words, but a lot of people have been giving advice. I haven't found the ideal coach yet. I put a call in to Benjamin Rush, the Bedford coach, to see if he knows anyone in the area. I also have a call in to Mr. Garrity."

"It won't be Mr. Garrity, right?"

"I'm sure he would be too busy, but he might be able to help us find someone."

"He's totally slimy."

"I'm not sure how you can say that. You don't know him very well, and you can't judge Mr. Garrity by Kenny."

"I'm not. Kenny is annoying, but he's okay. His dad is much worse. Always talking on his cell phone, watching us, wearing his shades."

"As I said, I'm sure he'll be much too busy to coach."

"Okay, Dad," Erik said, not fully reassured.

"One other thing, Erik."

"Yes?"

"The on-field spats, the fighting. I am thinking it may help to name some captains."

"I guess."

"I am thinking of naming you, Nick, and Kenny as co-captains."

"Kenny? Kenny is the cause of most of the fights."

"To be fair, I think Nick shares some of the blame. But, my thinking is that if they're both captains, they might try harder to work together. Also, we don't want the Marauders to be just a group of kids who have known each other since kindergarten. We want to show that we are open to new kids, kids from other towns."

"There's Matty."

"Yes, but he's not very vocal, is he?" Suddenly, Erik's father's expression softened. "Do you think it's a terrible idea to name Kenny?"

"I guess not, Dad. If you think it's a good idea. Just let me tell Nick first."

CHAPTER 8

Victory

Mr. Steiner named his three co-captains in the huddle before the game on Friday. He gave each one a captain's armband. Nick, prepared by Erik, kept quiet when the announcement was made. He didn't care about being a captain himself. He knew the team would follow his lead anyway. But Kenny? Nick wasn't sure what Mr. Steiner was thinking. Erik had asked him not to fuss though, so he didn't.

Dylan did, but only privately to Erik. "Hey, Erik! What's your dad smoking to make Kenny a captain? This isn't Kenny's team."

"I know. He just thought the non-Lancaster players should have a representative."

"Yeah? Well that seems pretty lame to me."

It did to Erik too, but there wasn't much else to say, and there was a game to play.

It was a cool Friday afternoon in Dover, an attractive colonial city two hours east of Lancaster. Dover housed most of the state's governmental offices and a growing high-tech industry that drew talent from several bigger cities to its south. It also served as a low-tax bedroom community for those cities.

The Dover team, the Deacons, played on municipal fields located at the crest of one of the four hills that surrounded the city. The fields, beautifully groomed and cared for, were enclosed by old pines. Below the leaf line of the trees, one had spectacular views of the Dover hills and surrounding green valleys.

"It's beautiful," Will said.

"Everything is so clean in this country," Mario agreed.

"Clean and boring," Jamie said. "C'mon. Let's warm up."

As the game began, Nick held to his resolution to play modestly and distribute the ball to his teammates, and the Marauders dominated early. Ten minutes in, Nick walked past Erik on a corner and said, in a surprised voice, "These guys can't play with us. We have a ton of time." And they did. The Marauders had time to trap the ball. To look around. To dribble or pass. The Dover Deacons were chasing, but not catching up, and the game was taking place almost entirely in the Dover half. Erik had three shots, one of which really should have been a goal. Kenny nearly scored on a nice cross from Dylan. Will hit the crossbar from just outside the eighteen-yard box. The only thing stopping them was a superb performance by Dover's goalie. He was clearly the star of the team.

The Marauders finally scored three minutes before halftime on a long corner from Erik that found Will sneaking into the far side of the box. Unmarked, Will had time to control the ball with his chest, step forward, and hit a low shot to the near post, catching the goalie flat footed. At halftime, the Marauders raced into the huddle jubilant at their first lead.

As the second half began, the Marauders continued their pressure, even without Matty and Erik in the line-up. However, Dover didn't give up, and when Mr. Steiner rested Kenny and Nick, disaster struck. The Dover goalie noticed the Blue Marauders pushing too far up and, grabbing the ball after a misplaced cross, ran to the edge of his box and punted long to his center forward. The forward, standing at midfield with Terry as the only defender, won the ball, raced to the goal, and scored before any of the other Marauders could react.

Mr. Steiner immediately put Nick and Kenny back in, although they were due for another five minutes on the sideline. He believed in equal playing time, but right now it was more important to win a game.

Nick said to Kenny, "We've got to put the pressure back on them."

Kenny threw back his head. "Pass me the ball, McCoy. I scored four goals against this team last year."

Nick grimaced. "Just one would be nice."

The Marauders had an opportunity to widen the lead a few minutes later, when Nick got the ball forty feet out from the Dover goal. Expecting him to pass, the Deacons gave him space. He pushed up the middle, stepping around first one, then two, defenders. Erik made a clever run, drawing his defender away and leaving Nick with just one man to beat at the top of the box.

Nick considered his options. He could try to beat his man and take the shot himself. Or he could thread a pass to Kenny, who was slashing into the box a step ahead of a wing defender and calling desperately for the ball. Or he could lay the ball off to Abbey, several steps behind Kenny, but wide open because the defense was following Kenny. Nick slowed momentarily to lure his own man closer, then hit a nicely weighted ball across to Abbey. She slammed it on a one-timer into the lower right-hand corner of the goal. It was a perfect play, except that, somehow, the goalie got his hand on the ball and pushed it aside.

Kenny was furious. "I was open!" he screamed.

"Abbey was more open!" Nick yelled back.

To Nick's surprise, Kenny did not yell back. He nodded, grinned, and gave Nick a thumb's up sign. Nick shrugged. Maybe he had misjudged Kenny.

In the end, it didn't matter because the second Marauder goal came moments later, when Kenny played a ball through to Erik. As the goalie came out to him, Erik pushed the ball to Mario, who calmly let it bounce off the side of his foot into the goal.

Mario made up for his modesty in front of the goal with a wild celebration. "Gooooaaaal!" he shouted, as he raced away from the net, holding his hands out like airplane wings. He was still flying when he was caught, first by Dylan, and then by the rest of his teammates, who jumped on his back and buried him under a mass of tangled arms and legs.

The referee blew time five minutes later, with the score still 2–1. The Blue Marauders had their first win. The team swarmed each other like they had won the championship. "The first of many, boys!" was Dylan's cry, quickly adopted by the others.

After shaking hands with the dispirited Dover Deacons, Nick felt a pat on his back and turned to see Kenny grinning at him.

"Great game, man!" Nick said.

"Well, Dover sucks, but yeah."

"We played well, too."

Kenny shrugged and stepped closer to Nick. He pointed over to where Abbey was talking animatedly with Dylan and Will. "Look, I understand why you want her around. She doesn't do any harm back on defense, but next time let's not bet the game on her."

"She was open," Nick said, realizing that Kenny was still sore about not getting the pass earlier in the game. "More open than you."

"Yeah, and she hit a patsy little girl shot straight to the keeper. I'm just saying, hit me on that pass next time. Give us a chance to score." Then he added, with a grin, "Not just you."

Nick was still thinking about how to respond when Kenny motioned for him to turn, and Nick saw that Abbey and Will had come up behind him.

"Nice to see you two talking. See what a little teamwork can do?" said Abbey.

"Yeah, I was just telling Nick what a good game he played. You guys were awesome too. Loved the goal, Will," Kenny said. "And your defense was monumental, Abbey."

"Thanks," Will replied.

"I should've score that one time," Abbey said.

"Hey, you took a good shot," Kenny said, and winked at Nick.

"We're stopping for pizza on the way home," Abbey said, "There's a little place just on the first exit outside of Dover. You two want to come?"

"Sure," Kenny said.

"I'll ask my mom," said Nick. "She's got the twins with her, and we're giving Leon and Parker a ride home."

In the end, everyone stopped for pizza, and the dinner was raucous and fun, except that Nick couldn't put Kenny's comment about Abbey out of his head. Of course, she was just one of many players that Kenny did not consider worthy of his magnificent talents. But watching them at the pizza parlor—somehow Kenny ended up sitting next to Abbey—Nick kept thinking about it.

When Abbey and Nick found themselves together in line to order another slice of pizza, Abbey said, "See, Kenny's not so bad."

Nick thought about telling her about the earlier conversation, but wasn't sure how, or if it would be like snitching. Instead, he just grunted. Abbey laughed. "Oh, yeah, I forgot. You guys have that whole macho boy, head butting, who's got the biggest antlers on the veldt thing going. But it's nice to win a game, right?"

"Nicer than losing," Nick agreed. "Now we just need ten more."

"And vat vould zat fraction reprezent as a percentage of our total games?" Abbey said, imitating Mr. DeMille as a German SS officer.

Nick laughed. "Hey, Erik and me are watching the indoor tourney in Winchester this weekend. You wanna come and hang with us?"

"I'll see you there. I'm playing."

"Really? With who?"

"Kenny asked me. He and his friend Jimmy—you know, the guy from the Thunder Green—have a team."

"You're playing with Kenny and Jimmy?" Nick's voice was filled with disbelief. He ignored the cashier, who was asking him what he wanted to order.

"They wanted me to play," Abbey said.

"But Jimmy's on the Thunder."

"So what! The teams are all mixed up. There's someone from Winchester and from Kilby on it too. Anyway, Kenny's on our team."

"Your order, please!" the cashier said more loudly.

Nick's mind raced. Abbey's arguments were annoyingly foolproof. But obviously she should not be playing with Kenny. Obviously!

"Look, do you want something or not?" the cashier asked.

"NO!" Nick shouted at him and stomped off.

"How about you?" he asked Abbey.

"No!" she said, and stomped off in the other direction.

The cashier shrugged at the next customer as if to say, "Kids. Who can understand them?"

ON THE WAY to the Winchester Indoor Arena the next day, Nick huddled with Erik in the third row of seats in Erik's mother's minivan, recounting his conversations with Kenny and Abbey.

"What a slime!"

"Yeah! Can you believe she's playing with them?"

"I wish we were playing," Erik said. "But . . . I don't understand what she sees in him." Erik and Abbey went way back, too. Everyone talked about Nick and Abbey, but in fact, Erik and Abbey had more in common. In particular, they had seen a lot of each other off the soccer field during the previous summer. They had enrolled in the same summer theatre camp that put on a production of *Oklahoma* in July. They had gone to the movies a couple of times after rehearsal on things that had sometimes seemed almost like dates. But Erik had never told anyone else about it, not even Nick.

"He's rich," Nick said bitterly.

"Yeah, but I don't think that's it. I don't think Abbey would care about that."

"Yeah, well, trying to think up Kenny's attractive points is not what I think of as fun."

THE WINCHESTER INDOOR Arena, originally a group of warehouses, was a vast space that had been converted into a temple of indoor activities. As well as two hockey rinks where the soccer tournament was held, it housed several basketball courts, a golf range, a climbing wall, a video arcade, a laser tag game, and a paintball arena.

When Nick and Erik arrived at the Arena, a little before noon, the place was crawling with kids in different colored soccer shirts. Looking at a schedule, they learned that there were eight teams in the tournament, divided into two groups. Each team had been assigned names of a previous World Cup winner. After the morning matches, Brazil and Germany had topped their groups, with Italy second in Brazil's group and France second in Germany's group. The first semifinal, between France and Brazil, wasn't until one thirty.

"So what you wanna do?"

"Let's head to the snack bar and see if we see anyone we know."

On their way, they ran into Mike, a marginal player for the Thunder Red whom Erik knew from summer camp, and his friend Henry, an English kid who was not on any of the Tri-State teams. Erik asked them how they'd done in the tournament and they laughed.

"We sucked," said Mike. "We lost all our games."

"Do you know if Kenny's team is still in it?"

"Oh, yeah. He's on Brazil. They breezed through, of course. But they got Jimmy and Tommy on the team too."

"Tommy?" Nick asked.

"The short red-headed kid on Thunder Red. You must have seen him at try-outs. He's amazing."

In the end, Nick and Erik joined Mike and Henry for lunch and heard all about the morning action. Nick had brought a sandwich from home, so he waited at their table while Erik and the other boys ordered food.

AFTER LUNCH, MIKE suggested laser tag. Erik and Henry wanted to play, but Nick noticed the price tag, $7.50 per person per game, and his mother had only given him seven dollars for the day.

"I'm out," he said. "I want to hit the video arcade. I'll meet you at 1:30 to watch Brazil."

"C'mon Nick," Mike said.

"Yeah, man," Henry said. "We need you. I bet you're a natural born killer."

Actually, Nick did consider himself a laser tag prodigy. He'd played at a bunch of birthday parties and he had an aggressive style that was very effective. But he shrugged off the protestations and went to look over the video games. He wanted his seven dollars to go as far as possible. He figured he'd want a Gatorade later, which would be $1.75. He could also get a tootsie pop for 25 cents. That left him five dollars for the arcade, which meant he had to choose games he could milk for long runs.

Most of the shooter games were sucker bets. Even if you did well, they never lasted longer than five minutes. But there was a golf game he was good at, and a motor cross game that was one of his favorites. You sat on the motorcycle and controlled it with your body. It was fair and pretty easy to win extra lives. Also, there was a retro game—Mine Sweeper—that Nick could keep going for ages. He played all three and was on his second round of golf when Erik jogged his elbow, resulting in a severe shank.

"Hey!" Nick said.

"It's time for the Brazil game."

"Where are the others?"

"They wanted to play more laser tag."

"Just let me finish this hole."

Nick salvaged a bogey, then the boys hurried over to the hockey rinks. Both teams, Brazil and France, were already on the field, and the game kicked off moments after they had found seats in the stands.

Brazil dominated the game. Nick and Erik were amazed at how differently Kenny played with his Thunder friends. He looked for his teammates, hit quick passes, made cuts, and hardly ever yelled at his teammates.

"What a jerk," Nick said.

Abbey sat on the bench almost the whole game. She got in just the last five minutes in the first half, and another five minutes in the second. Still, she played her usual solid game, always in position, reading the game, and shutting down the attack on her side. When the final whistle blew, Nick and Erik went over to say hello.

"Looks like you chose a winning team," Nick said.

Abbey grimaced. "Yeah, they're good."

Kenny and Jimmy came up. "Good game, Abbey," Jimmy said.

"Solid job, girl," Kenny said offering his hand to slap. "Hey, Mc-Coy, Steiner, what you guys doing here?"

"We just came to do some scouting," Erik said. "You guys looked good out there."

"Well, France sucked," Jimmy said modestly. "Mostly Kilby kids. You should have sent a Blue Marauder team."

"We didn't hear about it 'til too late," Erik said. "But, really, your passing was great. You had 'em running in circles."

"We need more of that on the Marauders," Nick said.

"Gotta have someone to pass to," said Kenny. "But yeah, we should work on it."

Just then, Mr. Garrity strode over. "Kenny, Jimmy, good game! You too, Annie. Listen boys, I videotaped the game. I want to go over it with you before the finals."

"Uhh, Dad," Kenny began, "maybe Jimmy needs to get a drink or something first?"

"Afterward. And go find Thomas. He needs to see this, too."

Kenny flashed a resigned look at Jimmy.

"I'll find Thomas, Mr. Garrity," Jimmy said.

"Great. Kenny, come with me!" Then Mr. Garrity looked at Abbey, Erik, and Nick. "Some of this stuff's pretty esoteric. You wouldn't be interested."

"He's sure right I wouldn't be interested," Nick said when Mr. Garrity had left.

"He's such a pain" Abbey said.

"I can see where Kenny gets it."

"Kenny has to be perfect all the time!" Abbey said. "He can't ever make a mistake."

"Oooh, poor Kenny! His silver spoon tastes bitter. Boo hoo."

"Nick, you are really an idiot. You have it easy with your mom and dad. They let you do what you want."

"As long as it costs under $10."

"Are you jealous of his money?"

"I'm not jealous at all," Nick said. "I think he's a jerk who's spent the whole time since he came on the team acting like he's better than everyone else, so I'm not gonna feel sorry for him. And I really don't get why you're so infatuated."

Abbey opened her mouth to speak, but thought better of it and just walked away.

ITALY WON THE other semifinal, and it looked like they might give Brazil a match in the final. But Kenny, Jimmy, and Thomas were too much even for Italy, and Brazil took the title 3–1.

Abbey played only occasionally, and she disappeared before Nick and Erik could congratulate her. Neither of them had the heart to talk with Kenny again. So, after the match, they sat in the stands and watched the Arena slowly clear out. Finally, Erik looked at his watch and turned to Nick. "We should go outside and see if my mom's back."

As they made to the exit, a barrel-chested man in Adidas sweats shouted at them.

"Hey, you two! Come over here!" It was Mac Scruggs. "You the boys playing with that Blue Marauder team?"

"Yeah," Nick said.

"I offered you a place on Thunder A, didn't I?"

"Yeah."

"Well, I caught your game against Dover, and I was right about you two. You have promise. But that's it. Promise. So now you have a 1–4 record and the worst goal differential in the league. Pitiful. And you're not going to get any better playing with rec-league-team rejects. But listen, everyone makes mistakes. Next season, you can try out for the Thunder again. Just make sure you meet with me first. I'll need to know that you are really committed. Got it?"

"Yes sir," Erik said.

Coach Scruggs glared at the boys for a few more seconds, then left.

Erik turned to Nick. "I guess that's good thing, right?"

"I'd rather slice my jugular open," Nick said.

THE FIRST THING Nick did when he got to school on Monday morning was corner Dylan to ask him about the Egypt projects.

"When are the bibliographies due?"

"The 28th," Dylan said.

"Then we've got a week. Erik had me worried. He told me he was working on it on yesterday and sounded all panicked about getting it done."

"Yeah, man, but remember, De Pill is having conferences with everyone to go over their topics."

"He is?"

"He told us last Tuesday."

"I have no memory of that."

"Maybe you were with Basquiat. It was right after math."

"Oh, great! What are you writing about?"

"Science. Medicine, astronomy, and stuff. I wanted to do architecture, because then you could include lots of cool pictures and drawings. But Jamie took that already. What about you?"

"Uh," Nick said, wondering when his friends discussed their projects. He did not remember hearing any talk about it. "Mummies maybe."

Reaching their classroom, Nick saw that Mr. DeMille had posted a sign-up sheet so the kids could schedule their meetings during recess on one of the next four days. Nick took the last available slot, on Thursday afternoon, ensuring himself at least some time to consider his topic.

LATER IN THE day, Erik passed Abbey in the hallway. She was talking with Tabitha and Yvonne, and she waved him down.

"Good tournament this weekend," Erik said.

"Yeah," she said. "Hey, let your dad know I won't make it to practice today?"

"How come?"

"I just need a break from soccer."

"Okay," Erik said. He wanted to say more, but Abbey had turned back to her friends and no one was paying attention to him. He looked at them for a moment and then wandered away.

"Did you see his look when you said you wouldn't be at practice?" asked Tabitha. "That was Erik's sad puppy face."

"I love that look," Yvonne said.

"Totally devastating," Tabitha agreed.

Abbey frowned. "Yeah, well."

BEFORE PRACTICE THAT afternoon, Erik stopped in at The Village Store to buy a soda. As he was paying for it, Rory Patenaude poked his head out of his office and called out, "Is that Erik Steiner?"

"Yes, Mr. Patenaude."

"Wait a minute, I'll walk you over to the field."

Erik waited while Mr. Patenaude maneuvered his bulk through the narrow aisles of the store.

"I've been meaning to have a talk with you," Rory said.

"Does Georgi want his money back?" Erik asked. He had carried fifteen bucks with him for the last two weeks in case he ran into Georgi, but he didn't have it now.

"Oh, that. No, no. Georgi's calmed down. Pretty good sales at the last home game. But he is upset about the standings. Nick promised the Blue Marauders would make the playoffs."

"Oh," Erik said, startled. "We'll never do that now."

"Yeah, not to worry. What we need to talk about is your father."

"My dad?"

"Rumor is he'd like to stop coaching if he could find someone else."

Erik wasn't sure where the conversation was headed. "Do you want to coach us?"

"God, no! I know less about soccer than your father, that's for sure." Mr. Patenaude stopped in front of Caton's Garage. "But you just won your first game. Do you think he still wants a replacement?"

Erik was flattered to learn how closely Mr. Patenaude followed the team. "I guess so," he said. "If we find the right person."

Mr. Patenaude laughed. "Well, I'm sure that rules a lot of folks out."

Erik did not say anything. It was never a good idea to run down one grown-up in front of another.

"Listen," said Rory. "There's a fellow who lives on Four Corners Road. Been here some time, with his wife. Ten years, maybe. They're potters. They make pots. Name's Jan Tielemans." Rory pronounced the first name "Yan." "Do you know him?"

"No," Erik said.

"He's Dutch. From Holland. And I understand he played some soccer over there. May have done some coaching, too. I want you to talk to him. He can be gruff. But I think he could help you out."

"Okay, thanks Mr. Patenaude. I'll mention it to Dad."

"Good," said Rory, ducking into the garage. "Now you go to practice, and I'll have a word with Dan."

When Erik got to the field, he was surprised to see Nick and Kenny passing together. They were chatting about the weekend's tournament.

"You, Jimmy, and that Thomas kid made a killer midfield," Nick was saying.

"That was the Thunder midfield all last year when we were undefeated. They broke up Jimmy and Thomas on the two Thunder teams this year, and of course, Coach Scruggs got all pissy that my dad didn't get the application in on time."

"What's his problem?"

"He's just super strict. But he's, like, totally connected as a coach. He knows all the college coaches. And guys in the MLS."

"So how's the Thunder Red compared to Thunder Green?"

"They're about the same. Thunder Green have Jimmy, but Thomas is on Thunder Red. I'd rather mark Jimmy than Thomas."

"It'd be sweet to beat 'em."

"Yeah. But we should move Abbey out of defense. She isn't fast enough to stay with those guys. You saw that Sunday."

"I didn't see anything Sunday. She was solid."

"You missed the morning games. She let two goals in."

"Abbey? No way. She never makes mistakes."

"They weren't mistakes. She just wasn't fast enough. She got beat to the ball. She could dominate the girl's league, but this is another level."

"Then why'd you ask her to play in the indoor tourney?"

"Got to lay the groundwork," Kenny snickered. "Her family goes to St. Thomas for spring break. We may be there too."

"Oh, un-huh." Nick shut down his brain and kept passing. The Blue Marauders needed Kenny, and Erik would be mad if they started fighting again.

The rest of practice was pleasant and fairly uneventful. Mr. Steiner ran them through his positional drills again, but after twenty minutes he decided he was as bored with them as the rest of the team. He called the boys in and asked them what they wanted to do for the rest of practice.

"Juggling contest," Leon said.

The suggestion met with a wave of approval, and it gave Mr. Steiner an idea, which he explained to the team. "The next several practices, I'm going to let you take turns as guest coaches. We'll have two guest coaches for each practice. You get together beforehand and plan out what you want to do. Run it by me and, assuming it's not too crazy, you'll lead practice. How does that sound?"

"Wicked!" Dylan said. "Me first. I want to be the first coach."

"Fine. Leon, you work with Dylan for tomorrow. I'll make a sign-up sheet for the rest of the week."

Mr. Steiner felt incredibly relieved. The kids were going to really enjoy this, and he was going to have a break from desperately trying to find new drills.

NICK DID NOT feel like stopping at the library that night, so he told his mother that he would work the next day after practice.

"Will there be enough time after soccer practice?"

"Sure, half an hour should be fine," Nick said, confidently. After all, he thought, how much can there be to say about mummies?

ON TUESDAY, NICK and Abbey were assigned as partners in art. Nick asked her if she'd be at practice.

"I don't think so. There's an organizing meeting for the talent show today, and I want to go to that."

"We have a game on Wednesday."

"Yeah."

"You'll play, right?"

"Do you want to do Matisse, Miro, or Mondrian?" The art project required that everyone choose a print of one of the modernists they had studied and copy it. "I want Mondrian."

"Whatever," Nick said.

"I like this one." Abbey held up one of the Mondrian paintings. "Clean and peaceful."

Nick shrugged. He could take it or leave it. Leave it more than take it. He really would have liked to do a Pollock. But everyone had been assigned a letter of the alphabet and he and Abbey had "M." At least Mondrian would be easy.

"So should we use paint for the white parts, or just leave them blank?" Abbey asked.

"Why don't you want to go to practice?"

"I said, I want to do the talent show."

"Sure, but we really need you tomorrow."

"No, you don't. You need someone a lot better than me. I should've stayed on the Thunder Girls."

"What are you talking about?"

"I sucked on Sunday. I let in those two early goals, and then the coach hardly even played me."

Nick took several seconds to understand that she was still upset about the indoor tournament. "I don't believe it. You never suck."

"You weren't even there. Ask Kenny."

"Who cares what Kenny thinks?"

"I don't, but he's a more objective judge than you."

"Kenny? He just likes to run people down."

"Do you really think we have a chance beat Thunder Red this Saturday?" Abbey asked with sudden sharpness.

"Absolutely. We totally turned it around last game. We can play with anyone."

"You and Erik, maybe. What about Dylan, Gabe, Leon, and the others?"

"Are you kidding? Dylan is incredibly fast. Gabe will totally disrupt any attack. And Leon's an amazing dribbler." But Nick had to stop because Abbey was smirking at him. "What?"

"Don't you see? You just love your friends. Everything Lancaster is totally great to you. It's sweet, but it's not objective. Those guys couldn't even make the Thunder team. The Marauders have no real chance against them. It's like you and Erik and Kenny against all of them. None of the rest of us could even make their team."

"What is it with you? You've been hanging around Kenny, and suddenly none of us are good enough for you?"

"That's not what I'm saying."

"Sure, Lancaster sucks. We're small town; we don't know what we're doing; we can't compete with kids in Milford 'cause we don't fly to St. Thomas for vacation."

"Oh, grow up, Nick!" Abbey said.

That was the last word on the subject. For the rest of the class, they worked in silence, exchanging hostile stares whenever they had to pass paint and brushes to each other.

NICK DETERMINED THAT he was not going to let Abbey's sour mood upset him. At practice he lazed around with the other boys swapping stories while they waited for Dylan and Leon to finish preparing for their drills. Mr. Steiner was late, the sun was shining and the kids, for a change, were in no hurry to start playing soccer.

"Hey, Kenny," Nick said, "did you go to any soccer games when you were in France?"

"No, but I did in Italy."

"When were you in Italy?" Gabe asked.

"Fall term of fourth grade. My babysitter was a total Inter fan, and she took me to games. One time they were playing Fiorentina, and there was this huge fight in the stands. The game was delayed for, like, thirty minutes while the riot police came in."

"Where you near the fights?" Terry asked.

"Sure. There was a guy two rows up from me wearing a Fiorentina shirt. When the Milan dudes starting getting on him, I swear he pulled a knife."

"How big was the knife?" asked Jackson.

"Like this," Kenny said, holding his hands about eight inches apart.

"What happened?" Nick asked.

"Like ten guys jumped him and started kicking the hell out of him. Then the security guys came over and dragged him away."

"Who won the game?" Nick asked.

"Inter, of course. After the riot, the ref didn't call a single foul against Inter the rest of the game."

Dylan and Leon interrupted, giggling. "This will be SO awesome."

"What you got planned?" Nick asked.

"We're going to do a whole Olympics thing," Leon said. "Like a decathlon. Running, dribbling, shooting. Everything."

"Hey, Erik," Dylan said, "where's your dad?"

"I don't know. Maybe we should just get started."

"Let's do it," Nick said, determined to be enthusiastic. "Dylan and Leon, you tell us what you want, and we'll follow along."

But as practice went on, he kept hearing Abbey's voice in his head, every time Dylan missed a trap, or Jackson bounced a ball off his shins, or Gabe misjudged a header. The voice of doubt ate away at his confidence. It said, maybe his teammates weren't that good; maybe they shouldn't be in the Tri-State League; maybe they were in over their heads.

Mr. Steiner showed up about halfway through practice, but he mostly sat on the bench and watched. When the other parents began to arrive to pick their kids up, Mr. Steiner called the team to the sideline. "Remember there's a game tomorrow? Here against Braeburn at five o'clock. Does anyone know if Abbey's coming tomorrow?" When no one answered, Mr. Steiner told Erik to find out. "How about Parker and Matty? Does anyone know where they are?"

"Matty had a doctor's appointment," Erik said. "He'll be here tomorrow."

"And Parker?"

"He wasn't in school," Leon said. "Maybe he's sick. He's sick a lot."

"We won't count on him, then. I'll see the rest of you tomorrow."

As the team broke up, Mr. Steiner found Officer Drybzyck behind him. "Nice game last week, Larry," he said. "We'll see if that turns the season around."

"Thanks, Russ. The boys played well."

"Rumor has it you want out of coaching. Just thought I'd let you know I'm looking at my schedule to see if I can help out more."

Mr. Steiner wondered how the rumor had reached Russ Drybzyck. "Thanks Russ. Things are okay at the moment, though."

"Just wanted to let you know. Have a good day."

Mr. Steiner was still nodding to Russ when Mrs. Garrity approached, dressed in riding gear.

"Coach Steiner," she said. "My husband and I think you are doing a wonderful job with the boys. A good win last Saturday, and Randy was so pleased that you took his advice on giving Kenny the captain's role. It's wonderful what leaders can accomplish when given a chance, isn't it?"

"Wonderful, yes," Mr. Steiner said neutrally.

"By the way, Randy wants to talk to you about your little business. He asks that you call his secretary to set up an appointment."

"Sure, that would be fine. Thank you, Mrs. Garrity. And if you could remind him that I left him a message about finding a new coach." Mr. Steiner trailed off, realizing that Mrs. Garrity had stopped listening. She had taken out her cell phone and was waving to Kenny to hurry up.

Erik, who was standing next to his father, followed the conversations with interest and dismay. He waited until they were in the car driving home and said, "Dad, you aren't going to let Gabe's dad coach, are you?"

"I don't even know how he found out that I was looking for a replacement."

"But you won't let him coach, right?"

"It's not my intent."

"What about the Dutch guy that Rory told me about. Have you called him?"

"To be honest, Erik, I'm not sure how I feel about asking a total stranger to coach the team."

"Well, Rory thought it was a good idea. Shouldn't you at least talk to him?"

"Perhaps. But I think I should talk to the other parents first. They need to be comfortable with him as the coach."

Erik's hopes sagged. That was the kind of reasoning his father used when he wanted to kill an idea.

Mr. Steiner, however, was not thinking about finding a new coach. He was thinking about his conversation with Mrs. Garrity.

Mr. Steiner wondered whether he needed to make it clear to Erik that his decision to name Kenny a captain had not been influenced by Randy Garrity. Even if the *idea* had originally been raised by Garrity, the *decision* had been made by Mr. Steiner alone, and only because he was convinced it would be best for the team. Just as it had been his *decision* to move Nick out of center midfield to free him up to do more attacking.

"When did coaching soccer become such a damned ethical minefield?" Mr. Steiner thought, feeling sorry for himself.

CHAPTER 9

Thunder Storms

Wednesday morning was cold and wet. Showers, and possible thunderstorms, were predicted for the rest of the day. Mr. Steiner got a call from Brad Flynn, the coach of the Braeburn team, suggesting they cancel the game. The two teams were scheduled to play again in a week's time in Braeburn, and Coach Flynn kindly offered to travel to Lancaster for the match.

Mr. Steiner was delighted not to have to coach the game, and even more delighted to have finally met a fellow coach who seemed genuinely helpful.

"Ah, Dad. It's just a little rain," Erik said. "People play soccer in the rain all the time."

"Not in thunderstorms. Why don't you invite your teammates over here after school to watch a movie or something?"

"Better," Erik said, "I have a Tivo of Saturday's U.S.-Mexico Federations Cup game."

EVERYONE ARRIVED AT school shivering. Summer was fading into fall, but the wardrobe of the seventh graders had not yet made the transition. Most of the students arrived in shorts and flip-flops, and they got soaked in the short dash from the parking lot to the front entrance of the school. Inside, the school boilers were running full tilt, and the kids with glasses found them quickly fogged up as water evaporated from their clothes. It was going to be a long day, with no outside recess to provide relief.

Mr. DeMille, of course, was in a good mood. "Today, we can get some real work done. We will do an in-class book report. I have a number of articles on Ancient Greece. Each of you will select one to study and summarize. At the end of the day, you will present a summary of the findings to the class. The goals are to read efficiently, to summarize precisely, and to present in an engaging manner."

The class groaned.

"We can't do all of that in one day!" Dylan said.

"That, Mr. Vaughn, is where you are wrong. I am quite confident that you can do it in the time assigned. Take it as a challenge."

"Do we work together?" a girl called Laurie asked.

"No. You will work as individuals. If you run into problems, I will be here grading. Now, if there are no other questions, I suggest you get started. Please come up here, four at a time, starting with the front row, and select an article."

The rest of the day, the seventh graders read their articles and prepared their presentations. Only an occasional whisper, and the sound of pencils scratching, disturbed the sound of the rain on the large plate glass windows along the southern wall of the classroom. Finally, with just over an hour left in the school day, Mr. DeMille called time and asked everyone to stop writing. Each student made a five-minute presentation and then handed his or her report to Mr. DeMille, who sat in front of the room, smiling broadly.

"Now, that wasn't so bad, was it?" said Mr. DeMille. "Well done, everyone. I will see you all tomorrow."

"I never worked so hard in my life," Dylan said as the crowd of students filed out.

"I'm exhausted," Jamie said.

"I've got a hand cramp," Leon said.

"I've got a brain cramp," Gabe said.

"Tell us something we don't know already, Gabriel," Tabitha said.

Gabe reached out and gave her a charley horse. "Who's going to Erik's?" he asked.

Abbey, Jamie, Leon, and Parker indicated that they were going, but Nick said he would have to join them later.

"I have to stop by the L first. I'm meeting with De Pill tomorrow to discuss my project topic, and there's, like, nothing in the school library."

"You haven't got a topic yet?" Jamie asked.

"Of course, he hasn't," Tabitha said. "Nicky's like that baseball guy in the poem. He won't try to swing until he's got two strikes on him."

"Casey," Abbey said.

Yvonne turned to Nick. "I'm meeting my mom at the L. I can help if you want."

"There's more on Egypt at the high school library," Leon said. "And you can get those books out through the elementary school if you want."

"Ah, Leon," Tabitha said. "Always the matchmaker. Or are you just in Abbey's pay."

"Shut up, Tabby," Nick said. "Yvonne, that'll be great."

"Hey, Tabby," Erik said. "Are you coming over?"

"To watch a soccer game?" Tabitha said.

"Come on, Tabby," Dylan said. "It's not just soccer. It's great company too." He smiled winningly.

"No thanks. I'd rather have my fingernails pulled out."

"Yeah, well, we'll miss you terribly," Gabe said.

"Yes, you will," said Tabitha.

WHILE NICK AND Yvonne headed to the town library, most of the rest of the soccer team headed to Erik's house. Mrs. Steiner made popcorn, and as the kids settled in, Erik asked, "Hey, does anyone know some guy called Jan Tielemans? He lives on Four Corners Road?

"It rings a bell," said Gabe.

"He's a potter or something. Rory Patenaude said he's Dutch, and he used to play soccer. He might be able to coach us."

"Your dad's quitting?" Jamie said.

"I don't know. I think maybe he wants to."

"My dad can help out," said Gabe.

"Yeah," Erik said carefully. "But it's not like he knows more about soccer than my dad. It would be great to find someone who played the game."

"Where'd he play?" Abbey asked. "Was it like, college or semi-pro or something?"

"I don't know."

"Google him!" Leon said.

So while the other kids watched the U.S.-Mexico game, Erik sat at his father's desk and googled Jan Tielemans. There were a lot of people named Tielemans on the web, but when Erik added "pottery" to the search, he finally found something useful. A squib about someone named Jan Tielemans with an exhibition at the Central Valley Craft Community. The last line read: "During his soccer playing days, fans at De Kuip nicknamed him the 'Teapot,' perhaps explaining his interest in these forms."

"Hey, Abbey, come here," Erik said. He showed her what he had found.

"Weird."

"Yeah. It looks like he had a bunch of funky tea pots in the exhibition. Have you ever heard of a team called De Kuip?"

"Google it."

Erik typed in the search and got an image of a stadium. "It says that it's the home stadium of Feyenoord," Erik said. "It looks big."

"Look up Feyenoord."

Erik did and he found the Feyenoord home page. "It's like the premier league in Holland," Erik said. "You think he played for them?"

"How cool would that be?" said Abbey.

After another few minutes, Erik hit gold. A list of players on the 1982 Feyenoord team that won the Dutch league title. Jan Tielemans as player-coach, and there was another name on the roster that Erik recognized, Johann Cruyff.

Another search and they found a clip of Cruyff dribbling through the entire German defense in the 1974 World Cup final.

"Do you think it's the same Jan Tielemans?" asked Abbey.

"Why not?" Erik, said, though he could hardly believe it himself.

"Because what's he doing in Lancaster?"

"We have got to get him to coach us."

"Nick'll go nuts," Abbey said. Erik laughed, imagining Nick's reaction.

BUT NICK'S REACTION was less enthusiastic than Erik expected. Nick arrived at Erik's house just as the U.S.-Mexico game was ending. Jamie asked if he'd found a topic, but Gabe broke in before Nick could answer.

"Yes, Mr. DeMille," Gabe said in a babyish voice, "The subject for my Egypt project is Yvonne's lips. I plan to study them extensively."

Nick laughed, but glanced at Abbey to see her reaction. "I think I'm doing mummies. I hate the darn things, but this was the only book left in the library." Nick threw the book he was holding onto Erik's couch. The title was, *The Meaning of the Mummies: Life and Death in Ancient Egypt*.

"Oh, man," said Jamie. "I looked at that. It's pretty heavy going."

"When I met with DeMille he wanted to know what I was going to say in my paper. Have you thought of that?" Leon asked.

"Not really. What's there to say about the darn things?"

"Well, like, how they figured in religion and what they symbolized," Leon suggested.

"Yeah, I guess that's what I was thinking about."

"You could talk about the difference between mummies for rich people and poor people," Erik said. "I don't think poor people even got mummies."

Leon said. "Because mummies made you immortal, and only the rich got that. It's like cryogenics nowadays. I read a sci-fi book once about how rich people start freezing themselves and generations of servants have to take care of their frozen bodies."

"Why not just unplug the freezer?" Dylan asked. "Whoops! Sorry."

"That's what I'd do," Gabe said. "Oh, and I accidentally transferred your bank account to mine."

"That was all part of the story," said Leon. "There was a lottery every year, and like a thousand of the servants got to be frozen too. So the poor didn't want to rock the boat and screw up their chance of becoming immortal."

"Speaking of immortals," Erik said, "remember I told you about Rory mentioning the guy Jan Tielemans?"

"Yeah," Nick said.

"Guess where he used to play?"

"I don't know. Man United." Nick was joking.

"Close. Feyenoord. First division Dutch team. He was player-coach. And Johann Cruyff was on the team."

"Should that mean something to me?"

"Yeah. He was just captain of the Dutch team, and one of the ten best players in history according to fifa.com."

"Are you serious?"

"We just looked it up. Isn't that great?"

"No, it sucks. No one that good is going to stand around and remind Dylan not to toe the ball."

"I don't toe it."

"Right. But the guy'll never waste time with us."

"We just have to convince him."

"How?"

"I don't know," said Erik. "We have to think about it. C'mon, Nick, it'll be a challenge. Look, everyone ask your parents about him, and we'll compare notes tomorrow. Maybe we can bike over to his house Friday after school. What do you say?"

Nick grinned. Erik was a good planner. That's why he always won at Risk.

MR. DEMILLE GRILLED Nick hard about his topic the next day. Nick recalled Leon's phrase and said he hoped to explore how mummies figured in religion and what they symbolized. Mr. De-Mille blinked for a moment in surprise before saying, "Well, that's reasonable. What are your current theories?"

"Uhh," Nick tried furiously to remember more of his conversation with Leon and Erik. "Well, the mummies made you immortal, but only rich people got to have them. So I'm trying to figure out how they got the poor people to take care of the mummies. Maybe the poor people thought if they did a good job, they could become mummies too."

Mr. DeMille leaned back in his seat and looked at Nick, appraisingly. "What I believe you are suggesting, in an exceptionally garbled form, is that perhaps mummies, and the associated promise of eternal life, played a role in enforcing social and moral codes of behavior. I will be interested to see your bibliography. But it is a promising topic."

Nick grinned like a cat who'd found the cream.

PRACTICE WAS A continuation of the skills competition planned by Leon and Dylan. Nick would have preferred a scrimmage—soccer, not just soccer-related games—but at least Abbey showed up. She seemed to be over her snit.

After practice, the team (with the exception of Kenny, who had been whisked away by his mother as usual) sat around comparing notes on Jan Tielemans. Abbey said her parents won one of his teapots in a raffle.

"My mom said his stuff is really expensive," Leon said.

"My pa says he raises chickens," Will added. "He's been out there delivering fencing and stuff."

Gabe also knew something. "My dad said he made a real stink at town hall when he first moved up. There was some issue about whether he could drill a well. I don't know. But he made a lot of people mad back then."

"He pays on time," Jackson said. "My dad poured cement for him back when he redid his foundations."

Nick said, "My dad wouldn't tell me anything. He just kept saying we should definitely ask him to coach, and then chuckling. I think he thinks we're going to make fools of ourselves."

"So where does that leave us?" Erik asked.

"Nowhere," Gabe said. "We don't know anything about this guy. He could be, like, a convicted child molester. That would explain why he stays away from school activities."

"Yeah, or he could not have children," Abbey said.

"I'm just saying my dad could help coach," Gabe said.

"The man played professional soccer in Holland," Nick said. "Where did your dad play?"

"Ha, ha! He played football at the U, wise ass."

For Erik, Gabe's comment decided the matter. "Okay, Nick and I will head over to his house tomorrow. And hope he doesn't shoot us."

AFTER SCHOOL ON Friday, Nick and Erik biked to see Jan Tielemans. Nick had suggested a phone call first, but Erik had been firm. It was better to talk face to face. It would make a better impression.

"We don't even know if he'll be in," Nick said.

"At least we can scope out his house. Besides, do you have anything better to do?" Erik asked.

Nick had shrugged. Not really. But it was a seven-mile ride. Four Corners Road was on the extreme western edge of Lancaster, down Lancaster Hill, then up Dobb's Notch and along the road that led to Warrick. As the boys reached the top of the notch, they could see the storm clouds moving across the Sokoki Valley.

By the time Nick and Erik reached the single digits on Four Corners—they were looking for number 37—the road had flattened out and turned into dirt. The houses were also more modest in size. Finally, they spied a mailbox with the right number and a poster sitting on a cooler that read, "ORGANIC EGGS — $4.00 a Dozen!"

A small yellow cottage surrounded by red geraniums sat at the end of a short driveway. Across the road from the little house was a large field with a number of old wooden buildings, including a big grey barn with a new tin roof, a sugar shack, a woodshed, and what looked like an outhouse.

Erik and Nick climbed gratefully off their bikes. "We better be quick," Nick said, "if we want to beat the storm home."

Erik nodded, "You ready?"

"Yeah, sure."

The two boys walked up the driveway to the little yellow house and knocked on the door. They waited for a little while and then knocked again more loudly. There was still no answer.

"Let's check out the barn," Erik said. So they went back across the road.

"Mr. Tielemans?" Erik shouted as they approached.

A woman with long grey hair stuck her head out of a side door. "You're looking for Jan?" She pronounced it *Yan* too.

"Yes."

"He's out back collecting eggs. Go around to the right. You'll find him."

Erik and Nick followed the directions and came out around the other side of the barn. The temperature had dropped several degrees, and the sky was getting darker. Behind the barn was a large fenced-in area with a series of chicken coops. Inside, a man was moving from roost to roost collecting eggs. The man faced away from them, so all they could see was his broad back and legs. He wore a blue cable-knit sweater, dirty khaki shorts, and sandals with socks.

Nick called out, "Mr. Tielemans?" There was no answer. "Uhh, Mr. Tielemans?"

"Ya-ah! That's me," the man responded without turning to face them.

"Can we talk with you for a moment?"

The man turned to face them, putting down his basket of eggs. He had a rough, red face, deep-set eyes, and messy, grey hair. "I'm busy. What do you want?"

His "w"s were almost "v"s, and his intonation had a European rhythm. His voice was deep and a little gravelly.

"We wanted to ask you about coaching our soccer team," Erik said. They boys could see immediately that he would turn them down, but Erik hurried on. "We started a team this year, and we have a lot of good players, but we need a coach who knows about soccer. Rory Patenaude said you had a lot of experience."

Mr. Tielemans held up his hand. "Stop, stop. I am too busy, and I'm not interested. Good day." And with that, he picked up his basket and started collecting eggs again.

"Uh, Mr. Tielemans," Nick began, hoping to think of something that could persuade him to talk further.

But Mr. Tielemans waved an angry hand at them without turning around. "Not interested. Go away!"

The boys looked at each other and trudged back to their bicycles. They had biked up to Four Corners on a lark. They had known it was a long shot. It was unreasonable to expect someone they'd never met to drop everything and agree to coach their team. Nick wasn't even sure that a new coach would make any difference. But as they walked back to the road, both boys felt sharply as if all of their hopes had been resting on Mr. Tielemans, and as if his abrupt dismissal was the last straw for their season.

Then the rain began. It was only sprinkling, but the valley below was dark, and they could see that this was the first edge of a big storm. Should they try to call Erik's mother? See how far could they make it before the heavens opened? They could pull over into someone's barn if there was lightning.

Nick wanted to get out of sight of the Tielemans's house and nodded to Erik to start up. But just as they were climbing on to their bikes, the woman who had spoken to them before popped out of the side door of the barn again and called to them, "Boys! What are you doing?"

"We're just going home," Erik said.

"You can't bike in this. Put your bikes in the woodshed and come inside."

The boys did as they were told and went into the old barn through the side door.

It was not the tumbled-down barn they had expected. A new pine stairway led up to a reconstructed loft running most of the length of the barn. The floor was made of wide, polished boards and covered with a collection of small carpets. A series of skylights was cut along the western slant of the roof, with a large circular window at the south end. At one end of the loft there were three easels, several tables filled with paints and brushes, and a large number of canvasses, mostly covered with sheets. At the other end were more tables, two potter's wheels, and a lot of buckets. All along the walls were shelves filled with strange, colorful pottery.

The grey-haired woman stood at a stone sink washing her brushes. She glanced back at the boys and told them she would be finished in a moment. While they waited, Nick and Erik examined the shelves filled with pots.

"There, ready now," the woman said. Her sweatshirt was dotted with paint. "Well, come on. I'm driving you home. Where do you live?"

"I'm down near the Thrupenny River, at the bottom of Lancaster Hill," Nick said.

"I'm on Lancaster Green," Erik said. "But you don't have to drive us, Mrs. Tielemans. If you let me call my mom, I'm sure she'll pick us up."

"Nonsense! It's the easiest thing in the world for me to drive you home. And I'm not Mrs. Tielemans. I'm Mellen. Kate Mellen."

"Sorry, Mrs. Mellen."

"Call me Kate. I mean, I am married to Jan, but I don't go by Tielemans."

"Okay," Erik said.

"Now that we have that out of the way, I'll bring the Ranger around, and you can load your bikes."

It was raining pretty hard when they went out again, and the boys were happy to be riding home in Kate's truck rather than on their bikes.

"So what did you boys want with Jan?" she asked.

"Rory Patenaude told us he played soccer," Erik said. "We were hoping he might coach our team."

Kate Mellen laughed at that. "What did he say?"

"He wasn't interested."

"Well, that doesn't surprise me. I wonder how Rory even knew that Jan played. It's not a secret, but it's not the sort of thing he talks about much."

"Is it true he played for Feyenoord?" Erik asked.

"Now, what would you know about Feyenoord?" Kate replied, surprised.

"They're one of the best teams in the Dutch league. They won the title in 1982 with Johann Cruyff." Erik paused apologetically, "We googled it."

Kate laughed. "Well, Jan's story is his own. He hasn't been involved in football for a long time, and he has his reasons. Still, I always tell him that it's no good for us to get too isolated."

"You think he might change his mind?"

"Oh, I don't know about that. He's a stubborn man. And he's been awfully busy lately. He divides his time between pottery and egg farming, and each profession is a jealous mistress." Kate looked at the boys. "I mean, they both demand a lot of attention."

"It's not a real big farm," Nick said.

"No, it's just hobby farming. But it doesn't work if we lose money on it, and our biggest contract just got cancelled, the Milford Food Coop. They found some company in Texas that can provide cheaper eggs. Can you imagine? Organic, sure, but flown fifteen hundred miles to your door. Anyway, it's left us in a bit of a bind, with an extra thirty dozen eggs a week unsold."

Erik realized that they were coming up on his house. "If you turn here, I'm the third driveway on the left."

"Oh, sure. And here I am prattling on. I just mean to say that you shouldn't be put off by Jan's brusqueness. He's not so scary once you get to know him."

The boys did not see how that helped, since they would never get to know him. They hadn't even been able to confirm that he played for Feyenoord.

"Thanks for the ride," Erik said.

"I'll get off here too," Nick said.

"Okay, boys. It's been nice to meet you. Think about coming out another day. I'll give you a tour of the studio. Most afternoons are good, just call ahead. And you can take some eggs home."

"Thanks Mrs. Mellen," Nick said, "I mean, Kate." But he doubted they'd go. It seemed a long way for little reward.

Then Kate added, "And don't give up on my husband. He just may need a little prompting."

WHEN THE SUN rose on Saturday, the rain was over but there was a nasty chill in the air. Mr. Steiner rolled over in bed and groaned. His wife, who had been up for an hour, came into the room and opened the curtains, "Larry, you really must get up. It's past seven o'clock and you're due in Milford by ten."

"We have to play the Thunder Red today," Mr. Steiner said.

"Yes, and I'm taking Elena apple picking."

"That means I have to face that horrible man on the sidelines."

"Which man?"

"Mac Scruggs."

"Oh, the one who called you up and yelled at you about forming a team and said you'd never eat lunch in town again?"

"That's him."

"Well, he sounded like a perfectly awful person. I'm sure he's terribly unhappy. But he won't bite."

"Ha ha! It's not you who has to shake his hand," Mr. Steiner said. But he got up.

A FEW HOURS later, Mr. Steiner arrived at the Milford Green with a carload of kids, wishing he had another layer of clothing. He was pleased to see that Nick and Charlie McCoy were already there. He intended to keep Charlie close at hand so he didn't have to face Mac Scruggs alone.

Unfortunately, before he reached Charlie, a short man with red face, spiky grey hair, and a slightly hunched back met him as he walked across the field to the visitors' bench.

"Coach Steiner!" the man said, sticking his hand out. Mr. Steiner grabbed it automatically and immediately found his hand crushed in a vice-like grip. "I met some of your boys this weekend. It's a terrible thing you're doing to them."

"Uhh, Mr. Scruggs, I presume," Mr. Steiner said, snatching his hand away.

"A couple of them actually have talent. It's a crime to waste it."

"Well, I think that is for them to decide," Mr. Steiner responded. He would not let himself get bullied.

"Yes, well, we'll see about that. Today I think you're going to learn what a disciplined squad brings to the table. There's a tendency in this league not to want to embarrass amateurs. It's not a feeling I share."

Mr. Steiner paused to compose a stinging response, but Mac Scruggs had turned on his heel and walked away. Mr. Steiner continued on to the visitors' bench fuming. Never had he wanted to win so badly.

He looked at the Thunder Red players, dressed in crisp white uniforms decorated with red flames. They were loose and confident, talking and laughing as they passed the ball around in small groups. Then he looked at his team. Ten minutes to game time and Jamie and Jackson had not arrived yet. Mario and Abbey were still pulling their cleats on. The others stood around taking shots at Nick in goal. The team only had two soccer balls out. "We have more balls than that," Mr. Steiner thought irritably. Where were they? Hadn't Erik brought them from the van?

Mr. Steiner called the players in, just as Jamie came running breathlessly from the parking lot.

"You're late!" Mr. Steiner barked. "And where's Jackson?"

"I think he's coming, Dad," Erik said.

"I ask everyone to come a half hour early to games. Just once I'd like to see you do that! Parker, you start for Jackson. But I want to see you running!"

"Sure thing, Mr. Steiner."

"I want all of you running," Mr. Steiner said, impatient and raising his voice. "This team is so sure of themselves. I want you to wipe the smiles off their faces. Put a body on them and push them around a bit. I want to see you win this game!"

As the boys ran out onto the field, Gabe's father cheered. "Bravo, Larry! You tell 'em!"

Charlie McCoy approached quietly. "Too much caffeine?"

Mr. Steiner sighed. "I let that awful Scruggs person get my goat."

Charlie McCoy laughed. "We'll beat 'em. You'll see. I got a job up in the North Country this afternoon so I have to take off in twenty minutes. But if you need anything until then, I'm your man."

"Thanks, Charlie. I'll let you know." Mr. Steiner liked Charlie McCoy, but this offer to help—for twenty minutes when there was no chance of needing it—was not atypical.

DESPITE MR. STEINER'S pep talk, the game followed the expected script. The Marauders could not keep up with the Thunder Red. Thomas and the other midfielders moved the ball around the field easily and relentlessly. The Marauders chased and chased, but were always a step behind. The first goal came on a through ball hit between Jackson and Gabe. A Thunder Red attacker darted through, collected the ball, and beat everyone else to the goal by ten yards. He had plenty of time to line up a shot and beat Jamie.

By some miracle, the Thunder Red was only up 3–0 at halftime, but it was enough. Mr. Steiner's anger had sapped from him. He watched his team be decimated in all aspects of the game. He saw how the Thunder Red moved the ball fluidly from one opportunity to the next, and try as he might to dismiss Mac Scruggs as an ignorant tyrant, he admired it. He had no idea how to teach his team to do that, or even to describe to them what they should be doing.

When the Marauders trudged in at halftime, he could see defeat in their faces. Their heads hung low, and they avoided each other's glances.

"Listen, boys, Abbey," Mr. Steiner began.

"How the hell can we win if Nick refuses to pass to anyone!" Kenny interrupted. "I'm done! I'm not playing anymore!" He stomped away from the team, but not before Nick yelled out, "I'd pass if anyone on the damn team would ever try to get open!"

"Boys," Mr. Steiner began again.

"The problem is, the middies and the forwards need to get back on defense and cover their damn men!" Gabe interrupted. "We're all alone back here with, like, seven of their speedy midgets."

"No, man!" Dylan said loudly. "Defense has got a push up and challenge for the ball at midfield. We're giving them way too much time. We're never going score if we drop everyone back!"

"Don't look at the defense, look at the midfield!" Terry said just as loudly. If we push up, they send their forwards behind us. But their midfielders have all day to make the pass."

"People have to stay in position," Matty countered. "I'm covering my man, but I can't cover three or four guys."

"Boys, pipe down!" Mr. Steiner said now, much louder. "They are a good team, and they're are running us around. Let's just stay in our positions and mark our men. And let's try to get one back. We'll be okay." Mr. Steiner looked around to see if his message was getting through, but his voice lacked conviction, and he could tell the team did not believe him.

"Hey, is Kenny playing?" Terry asked.

Mr. Steiner looked around. Kenny was not there, but Mr. Garrity was standing on the sidelines watching the proceedings.

"I'll see," Mr. Steiner said. "For now, Nick moves to center midfield, and Terry, you play left."

As the team went out to warm up for the second half, Mr. Steiner put his hand on Erik's shoulder and held him back. "Hey, kiddo," he said gently, "What's up? You've been awfully quiet."

"They're just so much better than us."

"Don't think that, Erik. You're a fine player. Just do your best. If you get beat, it's the coach's fault, okay?" His father squeezed his shoulder, and Erik gave a grudging smile.

Then Mr. Steiner went over to Mr. Garrity.

"Randy, did you see where Kenny went?"

"Voting with his feet, I guess."

"The team needs him."

"It's not going well."

"No, it's not! But that's no excuse for a player to jump ship!" Mr. Steiner walked back to the bench without waiting for a response, and a few minutes later Kenny reappeared, flushed and angry.

"Hey, where am I playing?"

"Oh, you're back."

"Coach Scruggs told me I had to."

Larry Steiner rolled his eyes and turned away. "You're on the bench. You'll get in when I'm ready."

The second half was little better. The Blue Marauders somehow kept the Thunder Red off the scoreboard for the first twenty minutes. But substituting in waves and making full use of his twenty-man squad, Mac Scruggs urged his players on whenever play slowed. "Push the ball. Run! Run! Make them work!" he barked incessantly from the sidelines. One goal fell, and then another. And when the final whistle blew, the score was a humiliating 7–0.

The handshake was a miserable affair. The Thunder Red players seemed to be laughing at the Marauder players when they offered their usual remarks: "Great game," "Tough match," "Well played."

But the misery of the players was nothing to that of Mr. Steiner, who stood at the back of the line, waiting to shake hands with Mac Scruggs, certain that the man would try to twist the knife. He was not disappointed.

Mac Scruggs grabbed Larry's hand and squeezed hard, not letting him pull away. "It's a terrible disservice you've done to these boys. Terrible. Ruining their soccer careers."

Larry Steiner believed in being polite, even when it was hard. He believed in acting like an adult, even when provoked. He wasn't a patsy. He worked and negotiated hard for what was important. He stood firm for his principles in face of tremendous pressure, both in running his company and in his volunteer activities. But Larry Steiner believed that one could stand firm without resorting to name calling and schoolyard taunts.

So as Mac Scruggs squeezed his hand, Larry told himself to remain calm. Don't overreact. Be mature. Smile and move on. Instead, against his own better instincts, Mr. Steiner snatched back his hand and muttered in a strangled voice that was nevertheless loud enough to be heard by both Scruggs and a number of players: "Asshole."

Mr. Steiner saw Mac Scruggs's spiteful smile and immediately regretted his outburst. He'd played right into Scruggs's hands.

"Now, Mr. Steiner. There's no need for that kind of language. What sort of example do you think you're setting? There are rules in this league against swearing, and they apply to the coaches as well as the kids. You just have to be careful you're not kicked out of the league for it."

Larry Steiner turned to stalk off, but caught himself. He turned back to Coach Scruggs. "I apologize," he said. "You're right. What I said was entirely inappropriate."

Then Larry Steiner hurried away, leaving Mac Scruggs with a satisfied grin.

CHAPTER 10

An Eggsellent Plan

On Sunday the sun rose like any other day. A dense morning fog burned off revealing a beautiful fall day. Bright sunshine lit up the leaves that were beginning to take on their fall colors, and the air was crisp without being cold. Up and down the Central Valley, people woke up, looked out their windows, and felt glad to be alive. But these people were not Blue Marauders.

NICK WOKE UP with a sense of dread, knowing that something awful waited for him that day, but not sure exactly what. He racked his brain and tried to remember what was going to be so terrible. Maybe it was just facing everyone after the loss on Saturday. That would be grim. The best thing he could think to do was go back to sleep.

It was 10:30 when his mother came in. "Your sisters and I are going to the grocery. Do you want to come?"

"No, Mom. I'll hang out here."

"Your dad will be back at noon, and he may need some help with the raking."

Nick wondered if raking was the task he had been dreading. Or was it that the Patriot-Steelers game was going to conflict with the

Chelsea-Man U game that afternoon? Erik had invited him over to watch the soccer, which would be great. But Nick also loved sitting at home and watching football with his dad. A difficult choice, but hardly the stuff of dread.

If his dad was going to rake, Nick thought he might be better going off to Erik's. Once Nick's dad started raking, he didn't stop until every single leaf particle was removed from the yard, and sometimes from within a two-yard "security boundary." Last year, Nick and his dad had fought because his dad wanted Nick to rake under the large lilac bush growing in front of the house.

"But Dad, that's not the lawn at all," Nick had said. "It's like raking in the woods."

"You don't pick those leaves up and they'll blow over the lawn within the hour. So stop your whining and get working."

Of course, if Nick went to Erik's he'd have to relive the game against the Thunder with Erik and, worse, if he was around, Erik's dad. Sure the kids were upset after the game, but it had been scary seeing Mr. Steiner lose his temper with Coach Scruggs. Mr. Steiner never got mad.

Nick decided the best course would be to lie low and see whether his dad's raking project was likely to materialize.

ERIK WOKE EARLY and went for a bike ride on a trail behind the high school. He was trying to sort through some troubling emotions. Erik loved playing with his friends, but he hated the Blue Marauders. He wished Nick had never started the team. He wanted to play for the Thunder. He pictured all the goals he'd score with Jimmy or Thomas feeding him the ball.

Then he wondered if he would even start on the Thunder teams. Their forwards were pretty good, and Erik had been pretty useless. In the whole first half of the Blue Marauder season, he could remember only eight or nine good plays and just three measly goals.

And as much as he loved playing with Nick, Nick could also be a pain in the neck, always with a chip on his shoulder about Lancaster, always fighting with Kenny. And Abbey had pretty much ignored him of late. It was like he was wallpaper. Always there, taken for granted.

He couldn't play for his dad all his life. Not if he wanted to play high-level soccer. Sure, Coach Scruggs seemed scary and mean. But Coach Courtland, from the Thunder Green, seemed okay. So did Coach Rush, from the Bedford team. And they were like professional soccer coaches. If Erik played for them, he'd really find out how good he was. No favoritism, no coddling, just soccer.

Of course, if the Marauders got Jan Tielemans to coach, that would be a different story. If they had a coach who could teach them to play properly, they might win a few games, and everything would be okay. Then it would be like Nick said, Lancaster against the world. Nick was right that they had the players. They could play with the Thunder if they could get their act together and work as a team.

But Tielemans had said he wasn't interested, so that was that, right?

On the other hand, his wife had said, "Don't give up on my husband." Something like that. So maybe there was hope, although Erik couldn't see how.

AFTER FINISHING HIS homework and making himself a sandwich, Erik marched into the living room to watch the Premiership "Week-in-Review" pre-game show. He was surprised to see the TV already on and Nick draped over the sofa.

"When did you get here?"

"Five minutes ago. Dad was raking. I had to get out of the house pronto."

"Cool." The two of them sat and watched the television for a while.

"Hey, Nicky," Erik said, "I've been thinking. Why aren't we better?"

Nick sighed, "Oh, man, Erik, I don't know. I don't even want to think about the Marauders. I already said I was sorry I roped you in."

"But seriously, we've got at least five kids who could start on any team in the league. You, me, Kenny, Will, and Jamie. Maybe Matty and Abbey. And Dylan's got some serious talent, if we could just figure out how to use it."

Nick grunted.

"So maybe we should lose to the good teams, but the games should be close. And we should beat the bad teams at least. But we don't. Our record is 1–5, with a cancellation. If you assume that's a loss, we have the worst record in the league. It makes no sense."

"Maybe we're not that good. Me, at least."

Erik did a double take. "You believe that?"

"What can I say? Losing all the time gets to you. But it's definitely not you. I would a million times rather mark Jimmy or Thomas than you. I never know what you're going to do. I figured out what they were up to in, like, ten minutes."

"Thanks. But the same is true for you. You'd beat either of them one-on-one."

Nick smiled, mostly in relief. He really did think that he was the best soccer player he knew. "So why are we losing?"

"I don't know, but I really think it would help to get Mr. Tielemans to coach."

"He said no. We biked out, and he told us to buzz off."

"Maybe we can try again."

"Wow, look at that shot," Nick said as Manchester United rattled the crossbar from forty yards out.

"That's the Russian guy," said Erik. "I wish he played for Chelsea." And the boys settled in for some serious television watching.

Erik was surprised when Nick returned to the subject of Jan Tielemans at halftime. "You remember how his wife went on about how bad the egg business was going?"

"Yeah."

"What if we were to sell eggs for them? We get a bunch of people to buy a dozen eggs every week or whatever?"

Erik looked at Nick with astonishment. "Nick, that's totally it. We'll sell his eggs, and he'll coach us. It'll absolutely work. You're a genius!"

Nick looked back at Erik, surprised in turn by his reaction. The idea did not seem particularly promising to Nick. Then again, if Erik was sure it would work, maybe there was a little genius in it. Nick liked that possibility.

Erik had already picked up the phone. "I'm going to call around. We need a team meeting so we can figure out how we want to do this."

As Nick watched the second half, Erik was busy with his calls. Abbey was out, but he reached their other classmates. Everyone except Will could come over that afternoon at three.

"Will's looking after Angie, and his dad won't be back 'til five," Erik reported. "He sounds down."

"Hey, talk to your mom. If she can pick 'em up, maybe both Will and Angie can come up now and watch soccer with us. I'll play 'Go Fish' or something with her while we watch."

Erik's mom agreed to pick up Will and Angie right away. Meanwhile, Erik kept making calls. Jackson wasn't going to come over, but he would sell to the eighth grade. Mario and Terry would sell in their schools.

"You going to call Kenny?" Nick asked.

"I guess so," Erik said. "I should, right?"

"Nah, screw 'im."

When Will arrived with his sister, Nick did card tricks for Angie while keeping one eye on the soccer. Erik and Will sat in front of the television making lists of potential customers.

The others came over after the game ended. Dylan and Leon arrived first, then Jamie and Gabe. Finally, Parker showed up looking unusually fresh.

"You look like you washed or something," Nick said to him.

"Still do that sometimes. But I like to grunge up when I got a gig."

"Okay, too much information," Will said.

"So what's the big meeting all about?" Parker asked.

"Remember that guy we told you about, the one who used to play in the Dutch League? We asked him to coach and he said no, but Nick's come up with an idea that might convince him."

Parker laughed. "An idea from our Nick?"

"Believe it or not. The guy has an egg business, and some supermarket just canceled its contract with him. So we're going to sell eggs for him."

"You figure he'll be so grateful that he'll have to coach the team?" asked Parker.

"Something like that."

"Well, it sounds pretty crazy to me, but I'm in. How many do we have to sell?" Parker said.

"And how much do we sell 'em for?" asked Dylan.

"Oh, man," Erik said. "We didn't even think of price. How much are eggs?"

Everyone looked at each other. Jamie said, "I think when my mum and dad used to sell eggs they were, maybe, five dollars for a dozen."

"No way," Gabe said. "Eggs are, like, one dollar. They're, like, food for poor people. Ask Leon."

"For God's sake, Gabe," Nick said, "you are the biggest racist in the Central Valley."

"But he's right," Leon said with a straight face, but he put on a fake accent. "We Latinos love eggs. *Huevos rancheros* and all that. And Lord knows how poor we are."

"Does anyone have anything useful to add to this discussion?" Erik asked.

"Oh, I know!" Nick suddenly blurted. "It just came to me. When we biked up there we saw a sign. It said 'eggs for sale.' I'm almost certain it was four dollars a dozen. Do you remember, Erik? We were biking up looking for the house. We saw the mailbox and then the little yellow house. Next to the mailbox was the sign. It was four dollars, wasn't it?"

"That does seem expensive for eggs," Will said.

"Yeah, but I think Nick's right," Erik said. "Probably 'cause they're organic and free-range chickens and all."

The boys made plans to blanket the community with egg sales. Erik explained that the idea was to get weekly, biweekly, or monthly commitments from people. A one-time sale probably wouldn't help Tielemans very much.

"Is there anyone else we should get to help?" Erik asked.

"You've got to call Tabitha," Dylan said. "She knows everyone."

"You should ask Ryan, too," Gabe suggested. Ryan was one of their classmates who did not play soccer. "He's a total nerd, but he loves stuff like this. You know how he always wins the Sally Foster prizes and most box tops and stuff."

"Why not just ask everyone in seventh grade?" Jamie suggested. "They'd all help out."

Erik nodded. "Fine. We should get going right away."

"Wait," Leon said. The others looked around, dreading what he would say. Leon often saw problems no one else did. "What about delivery? It'll be a pain in the neck to deliver 35 dozen eggs a week to different houses. We need a central pick-up place. Somewhere like the Village Store."

"That's it," Erik said, relieved that Leon had solved his own problem. "Rory'll do it, I'm sure. It was his idea we talk to Tielemans in the first place."

"All right, so what's the deadline for making sales?" Leon said. "When are we going to give the results to Mr. Tielemans?"

Again, the problem seemed solvable. After some discussion, the team decided to take Monday and Tuesday off practice so everyone could go out and sell. They'd ask people to commit to buy a dozen eggs a week for at least three months. Then they'd tabulate the results on Tuesday evening and talk to Mr. Tielemans Wednesday afternoon.

"We have a game on Wednesday," Gabe pointed out.

"Not 'til five o'clock, and it's at home," Erik said. "We can go after school and come back."

The boys felt a great sense of accomplishment when the plan was fully laid out, at least until Leon spoke out again. "Do you think any of this will help? I mean, it's a great plan and all, but we have the worst record in the league, and he's just a coach."

There was a long pause. Leon felt suddenly embarrassed and Gabe jumped on him. "Yeah, well, it's pretty rich coming from you, Peon. It's not like you're helping us win games."

Leon blushed, but Nick said, "Hey, back off Gay-Buh. We've all been terrible. Anyway, Leon's got a point. Erik thinks Jan Tielemans is a magic man, but I'm not so sure. Probably we'll just keep losing, but at least this way we're trying to do something."

THAT EVENING, THE boys started selling to their parents and relatives. Four dollars struck many as expensive for a dozen eggs, but the soccer players made their sales pitch. Nick explained to his father that the eggs were organic and free range.

"The eggs are free range?" Charlie McCoy had asked in mock astonishment.

"No, Dad, the chickens, obviously. But they're good. They'll be healthy."

WHEN THE APPEAL of the eggs themselves fell flat, the soccer players changed tactics. "It's for the Marauders. We want to keep the team going, right?"

Not all parents were persuaded by this argument. "But what do the eggs have to do with the Blue Marauders?" Gabe's mother asked.

"Well, there's this guy that we want to coach the team. Only he won't 'cause he's too busy selling eggs. We thought if we helped him sell eggs, he'd sign up as coach."

"But the team has a coach. And you know your dad can help out too. He always tells Larry that he's available, but Larry just wants to do all the coaching himself. Does Mr. Steiner know about this?"

"I don't know. I guess so. The point is, this other guy used to play soccer."

"So did your father."

"Dad played football."

"Yes, but he played club soccer in the spring his senior year. He was very handsome."

"No, Mom, this other guy, Mr. Titleman, I think, was a professional. He played in Holland."

"You want someone from Holland to coach you? How's his English?"

"It's great, Mom. C'mon, we need to sell these eggs. Just buy a dozen a week. Sixteen lousy bucks a month. It's hard to explain, but it would really help out."

"Well, okay."

BY THE TIME the kids showed up on Monday, they had all made their first couple of sales and were ready to blanket the school. Even Tabitha, although she pointed out to Erik that it was sort of a bizarre thing for her to be doing. After all, her parents' farm produced and sold organic eggs to a lot of the local families, as well as several local grocery stores. So this was like helping their competitor. Erik apologized, but Tabitha laughed and said it was fine. "The farm's going real good right now. I'll ask my dad if he needs extra supply for any of his big buyers."

As the students waited for the bell to ring for the beginning of school, seventh graders roamed around buttonholing the elementary school kids in the playground, trying to sell them eggs. Most of the younger kids were terrified, but several agreed to buy eggs, if only to get the big kids to leave them alone. When Abbey pointed out to Erik what was going on, they went around and convinced their classmates to sell to parents only. After that, the seventh graders hung around the parking lot, waiting for any parent foolish enough to get out of his or her car while dropping off children.

NEWS OF THE egg drive quickly reached the morning crowd at The Village Store. There was a lot of misinformation about what the kids were up to until Charlie McCoy showed up to buy a cup of coffee, and put it in simple terms.

"Look, the kids want this guy, Jan Tielemans, who lives up on Four Corners Road, to coach their soccer team. They figure if they help him out, he'll help them out. And you know what? It's a damn good idea. Isn't that what living in a town like Lancaster is all about? Helping each other out?"

The theme was enthusiastically reiterated by Rory at Polly's during lunch time. It was not entirely coincidental that Rory ate lunch there that day, and sat for almost two hours over multiple cups of coffee. By the end of the day, it is not far from the truth to say that the adults in town were as excited by the project as most of the seventh graders.

NICK, UNFORTUNATELY, FAILED to appreciate the excitement. The first thing that happened when he arrived at school was that Dylan came up behind him, slapped him on the back and said, "How'd the bibliography go?"

That was when Nick remembered what he had been dreading all Sunday. His bibliography about Egyptian mummies was due that day. DeMille was going to kill him.

Putting on a brave face, Nick asked, "You get your's done?"

"Of course, man. I found five books and six websites."

Nick sighed. "I forgot. I guess I'll have to do it tonight."

"Whew, man. Would I not want to be you," Dylan said.

"Hey, did you have any books that talked about mummies?"

"Sure. Some of 'em did. Want to see what I have?"

Nick considered. He had five minutes before the bell for class. Maybe he could jot down some stuff. But DeMille said he didn't just want a list of titles—you had to say how you were going to use them. And he'd probably collect the homework right away—he usually did. So it wasn't like Nick could get it done at recess. Nick sighed. "Nah, forget it. I'll just have to face the music."

"That sucks. Could you plan, like, a death in the family or something? Oh, hey, there's the bell," Dylan said.

Nick followed after him with heavy footsteps. It wasn't that he expected any terrible punishment. He had missed assignments before, and it was never that big a deal. He'd have to make up the homework, and maybe he'd miss recess for the next couple of days. Big whoop!

What Nick was really dreading was Mr. DeMille pretending that it *was* the biggest deal in the world and trying to humiliate Nick in front of his classmates. It frustrated Nick that many of his friends seemed to like DeMille. They didn't seem to notice how he treated the kids like him, the kids who weren't stars.

As they walked in, the first thing Mr. DeMille said was, "As you hang up your backpacks, put your folders away, and please have your bibliographies ready."

Following Mr. DeMille's instructions, the seventh graders sat with their bibliographies out on their desks. Erik, Leon, Abbey, and Yvonne had brightly colored covers. Dylan and Gabe had neatly typed cover pages stapled in front. Tabitha and Megan had decorated their work with elaborate hieroglyphics drawn in colored pencil. Some kids just had a sheet of notebook paper, unstapled and slightly wrinkled. Nick had nothing at all. He saw DeMille's eyes flash toward him and then look away.

"Now I will come and collect your bibliographies. This is likely the first time you've prepared one, and it is an advanced piece of work. But you will quickly discover that developing a good bibliography is a vital skill in high school and, for those of you lucky enough to attend, college."

As Mr. DeMille took the homework from each of the students, he stopped at their desks and flipped through their work, nodding his approval or frowning. At Yvonne's desk he flipped open the cover and looked through the four neatly typed pages in silence. Then he held up the report to the class and said, "This, class, is how a bibliography is meant to look. Typed is preferable to printed, although it was not a requirement. The cover page adequately describes the content and keeps the presentation neat. Inside, the entries are well spaced and the descriptions of the work are short and to the point. Well, done, Yvonne!"

He stopped at Tabitha's desk and held up her work. "Very pretty, Ms. Williams, but in the future a plain cover is adequate, and indeed presents a more professional aspect."

At Will's desk, Mr. DeMille gave a satisfied murmur. "More than adequate, Mr. Cooper."

He arrived at Nick's desk next, and Nick shrugged, empty handed. Without comment, Mr. DeMille moved on.

At Laurie's desk, he accepted two sheets of paper, slightly wrinkled and unstapled. "A stapler, next time, Ms. Orleans, and perhaps an iron?" The class tittered. "I also note that you list your resources but do not say how you will use them. Please redo, and get it to me by Wednesday.

At Dylan's desk he reviewed the report and commented, "I see you cite Wikipedia as a source."

"Yes, Mr. DeMille. There was tons of stuff on it."

"Wikipedia, Mr. Vaughn, may have certain useful functions, particularly for getting a broad overview of a subject area. But I caution you against relying on it in a research report. Indeed," Mr. DeMille paused and then raised his voice, "everyone pay attention, please! Internet resources, generally, are not to be relied on. I will review the sources cited, of course, but I urge everyone to remember that a research paper is different from a tweet or a blog entry. And to review the ground rules discussed earlier, at least five sources in your bibliography must be books or journal articles. Anyone who has forgotten that, and has relied solely on internet sites, will have to revise their work."

When Mr. DeMille had collected everyone's work he held up his hands for silence. "There are twenty-one students in the class and I have twenty bibliographies. Whose am I missing?"

Nick rolled his eyes. DeMille knew very well "whose" he was missing. Grudgingly, Nick raised his hand.

"Mr. McCoy," Mr. DeMille said, his voice full of surprise, "and where is your bibliography?"

Nick was silent.

"At home perhaps? You forgot to bring it?"

That was a tempting lie, Nick thought. He'd just have to do it tonight and bring it in tomorrow. But Mr. DeMille was mocking him, and Nick knew it.

"I forgot it was due today."

"When did you think it was due?"

"I don't know. I just forgot it on Sunday. We were . . . busy."

"Busy?"

Nick realized it was useless to talk about the egg project. Unfortunately, Jamie did not. "We started a big project selling eggs, and it kinda took over," Jamie said.

"Well, twenty of you managed to hand in your reports. Was only Nick involved in this 'egg project'?"

"No," Jamie said. "But it was his idea."

"Mr. McCoy, is this correct? Did selling eggs seem substantially more important than doing your school work?"

"No, sir."

"And to what purpose was the project begun?"

Nick was silent again, and so was Jamie. Gabe jumped in. "There's this guy. We want him to coach our soccer team, but he doesn't want to. We thought if we sold eggs for him, he might help us out, see? Hey, do you want to buy a dozen eggs, Mr. D? They're organic."

"No, Mr. Drybzyck, I do not. What I want to understand is why Mr. McCoy determined that this project was more important than his homework. It is for the soccer team, you say?"

Nick stood silent. And this time so did the others. "What team is this?" There was silence. "A local team?"

"It's our team," Will said. "Nick started it. We're playing in the Tri-State League."

"And you considered this team more important than finishing your work, is that right, Mr. McCoy?"

Nick was silent so Mr. DeMille continued. "Perhaps your bibliography was all but finished. You had done most of the work necessary. Just a few finishing touches left?"

Nick was silent.

"Have you even started it?"

Nick thought about the one book on mummies he had gotten out of the L. But it was just one book. "No," he said.

"Ahh. So it is hardly likely that one exciting event on Sunday prevented you from completing it, is it? It seems there were several weeks that you might have worked on it, weren't there Mr. McCoy?"

"Yes." Nick was looking down and whispering. He did not feel shame as much as anger. He was afraid that if he looked at Mr. DeMille, or tried to talk in a normal voice, his anger would get the better of him, and make matters worse.

"So there was something else that seemed more important, I suppose. The soccer team, for example. It takes up much of your time?"

Again, Nick was silent. But Dylan, still failing to follow the plot, was not. "Oh, boy, sure, Mr. D. We play all the time."

"And yet you, Mr. Vaughn, managed to turn your report in." Dylan was silent so Mr. DeMille continued. "Well, we've wasted enough time on this. We'll discuss this further in private. In the meantime, we have word study to get through. Everybody please open your *Word and Language* books to page 135."

At recess, Nick had to stay behind while the other kids went out. Mr. DeMille informed him that he would be speaking to Nick's parents. "It is clear to me," Mr. DeMille said, "that you cannot handle both the academic requirements of seventh grade and your soccer commitments at the same time."

Afterward, Nick joined his classmates at the basketball court.

"Did he harsh on you?" Dylan asked.

Nick shrugged. "He's gonna call my parents. I think he wants to convince them to stop me playing soccer."

"That's crazy," Jamie said.

"Like what? You'd be, like, suspended for a game?" Erik asked.

"Or worse."

"He can't do that," Erik said. "It's not a school thing."

"Yeah, that's why he has to go through my parents. He'll get them to do it."

"That's just mean."

"I've been telling you, man."

"I'm sorry, Nick. He was awful today," Abbey said.

"Thanks, Abs."

"Your dad won't agree, will he?" Jamie asked.

"No way!" said Dylan. "His dad knows what's important."

"Right, steroid boy! His dad will know school is nothing compared to soccer," Tabitha said. "Look, it's a problem."

"Yeah, but leave it, guys. It's my problem, and it'll work itself out."

"You need any help with the report?" Dylan asked. "I can let you copy my sources."

Yvonne said, "If you want, we could meet at the high school library after school and look through the stacks."

"Uhh, guys? I think Nick is meant to do this assignment *himself*," Abbey said.

"I just want to make sure he's finished by Saturday," Yvonne said, mirroring Abbey's frosty tone and stomping off.

"Saturday? I was planning to finish it this afternoon," Nick said.

Leon looked at him dubiously. "It takes a while, Nick. I mean, you have to figure out what's relevant. I went through four books for every one I listed."

"Fortunately," Gabe said, "we are not all Peons. It took me four hours max. And I included everything I looked at."

"Whatever. I'll figure it out. But what's Yvonne's deal with Saturday?"

"We've got a game against Kilby," Erik said. "We need Nick to be focused."

Tabitha laughed. "Perhaps you are *forgetting* something, boys. Saturday is Yvonne's barn party. I think she's more concerned with Nick not being distracted from dancing and romancing."

"Man, give it a rest, Tabitha," Dylan said. "Do you ever think of anything else?"

Tabitha twirled around prettily. "Not when you're around, Mr. Vaughn," she said in the accent of a southern belle. "Come on, Abbey. Let's leave them to their soccer."

Abbey smiled sheepishly at the boys and followed Tabitha across the school yard.

FOR THE REST of the day, Nick felt uneasy about the phone call his parents would be receiving that night. But Mr. DeMille worked even more quickly than Nick anticipated, arranging a conference with his mother for that afternoon. Nick sat for a painful fifteen minutes while Mr. DeMille explained Nick's dereliction of duties to his mother.

At the end of the presentation, which made Nick sound like a cross between Genghis Khan and Attila the Hun, Nick's mother turned to him and asked, "Well, what do you have to say for yourself?"

Nick sort of shrugged, but his mother was not having it. "Don't be cute with me. Why didn't you finish the assignment?"

"I guess I just forgot about it. I was waiting to do it on Sunday. I meant to, but I forgot."

"Of course, that's part of the problem," Mr. DeMille interjected. "This was not an assignment to be 'pulled together' in one day. It takes several days and some planning to complete."

Mrs. McCoy cut him off. "I think I understand that Nick's behavior left something to be desired. The question is, how do we move on from here?"

"Well, I believe it's important to help Nick understand that academics must be the focus of his efforts. Nick is not incapable of hard work. He puts significant effort, for example, into sports and into entertaining his friends. But these are also sources of distraction. I fear he may not be able to focus on both his school work and his soccer season at the same time."

"What are you suggesting?" Mrs. McCoy asked.

Nick could control his fury no longer. "He doesn't think I should be able to play soccer! He's been trying to get me to stop playing all year." Now Nick stood up and turned to Mr. DeMille, yelling at the top of his lungs. "What the hell is your problem? It's the only thing I care about in this whole sucky world! I certainly don't care about your stupid class!" Nick turned and ran out, slamming the door behind him.

His mother went after him, but he ran out of the school, grabbed his bike, and disappeared before she could catch up. Not knowing where he was headed, she returned to finish her talk with Mr. De-Mille. Afterward, she picked up Nick's backpack and drove home to wait for Nick to return.

Nick did not come home that afternoon, and when it began to get dark, Mrs. McCoy put the twins in the car and drove out to look for him. Up the hill, around the town green, past the school, and then down to the Village Store. Back home, she called Erik's house but the phone was busy. She tried Will, Dylan, and Abbey too, but no one had seen him.

Charlie McCoy came home around six that evening and found his wife sitting at the kitchen table with the telephone in front of her.

"What is it, Beth?"

"Oh, Charlie, Nick hasn't come home!" Beth took a breath and then told him the whole story of the visit.

Charlie weighed the information. "He really wanted to keep Nick out of soccer for three weeks? For one late homework? That's crazy."

"Well, I thought so too. I didn't agree to it. I said we'd hold him out this week and that he would have to turn in his assignment and apologize to Mr. DeMille."

"Well, he'd miss a game. I'm not sure he should miss a game. Maybe just a warning this time."

"Charlie! That's not important. The point is, he's not come home."

"He's a smart kid. He won't do anything too dumb."

"Should we call Russ?"

"Not yet. Give him another few hours. I'll call Erik's again. And the pizzeria. Maybe he's there."

Charlie opened a beer and made the calls. Erik's phone was still busy, and Nick was not at Georgi's.

"Don't worry, honey. He's just blowing off steam. I still don't think he should miss the game on Wednesday, though. It's not fair to his teammates."

"Charlie, I am not going to argue with you. It's what Mr. DeMille and I agreed to, and it's how it's going to be!" Beth held the twins on her lap and spoke with intensity. "Now go out and find Nick!"

Charlie knew better than to keep talking. He looked regretfully at his untouched beer, pulled on his jacket, and went to the door. He'd drive by the Steiners' house. Nick was probably there.

CHAPTER 11

Bearing Down

The reason that Beth McCoy had not been able to get through to Erik was that Erik was coordinating the egg drive, and had been on the phone the whole evening. His dad had helped him set up a spread sheet on the computer, and every time someone made a sale they called it in to Erik and he added the information to his master list of subscribers. The goal was forty dozen a week. By six o'clock, as Charlie McCoy was driving up the hill to Erik's house, they had reached twenty-eight dozen, and at that moment Erik got a call from Tabitha. "Hey Steiner, how's business?"

"Beginning to slow down, but we're doing pretty well."

"Well, I just talked with my dad, who talked with one of the stores he sells to. They said they'll take an additional fifteen dozen a week if he can guarantee they're organic. Dad says he'll take those fifteen dozen from your Dutch guy."

"Wow, that's great, Tabby."

"Yeah, well, two conditions."

"Anything."

"Don't say that, Erik. You don't even know what I'm going to ask. And you'll have to see if your Dutch guy agrees."

"Okay."

"First, the price is $2.25 a dozen. That's what Dad charges and he's not taking a fee."

"Oh." Erik had no idea what Jan Tielemans would think of that idea.

"Second, the eggs are branded from the Williams' Farm. Which means they come in our egg cartons."

"That doesn't sound like a big deal."

"Maybe it won't be. But Dad says you better tell him, 'cause some of the farmers here are touchy about that kind of thing."

"I'm more worried about the price."

"For what it's worth, Dad says it's still a pretty good price from a store. You have to expect a discount if someone is buying a lot of eggs."

"That makes sense, I guess. It's great of your dad. Couldn't he have sold the extra eggs himself?"

"Maybe, but I guess he wanted to help out. I told him he shouldn't—that soccer, and especially your team, is the bane of my existence. I think he did it just to spite me."

"Thanks, Tabby. That puts us at forty-three dozen a week. Which is pretty awesome. I don't even know if he has that many."

"He can always buy some more chickens. Maybe Dad can sell him some. Okay, buddy, I gotta go. Mom is on my case about cleaning my room."

"If it looks anything like your locker . . ."

"Hey, we can't all be neat freaks."

NICK, MEANWHILE, WAS beginning to think it was time to go home. He had zoomed out of the school on his bicycle wanting to get as far away as possible. But now his anger had melted away, and he was left feeling resigned and depressed.

He knew he was a dumb kid and would never amount to much. The world and everyone in it—teachers, coaches, guidance counselors, the lot of them—conspired to keep kids like him in line. They'd take one look at him and point him to the door. Sure, his dad had done okay, but he had that mechanical gene that Nick somehow lacked. He wondered if he should join the army after high school. Maybe that was the best place for him. Although he was never as into the whole guns and hunting thing as kids like Gabe. And all the movies made drill sergeants just look like particularly jerky teachers.

The sun was setting, and Nick was still fairly far from home. He knew he'd have to go back eventually and take his medicine. At least the weather was nice for being outside. The low sun shone through the canopy of brightly colored leaves, and the air was crisp without being cold. Nick looked around and realized he was near Parker's house.

Nick had lived in a house on the same road as Parker until he was nine. They had been best friends as little kids, and afterward too. Even at the beginning of last year, they had spent a lot of time listening to music together. It wasn't until the end of the year that they had begun to see less of each other. Nick had started hanging out more with Erik, Dylan, and Will. Nick wasn't sure who Parker's friends were these days. He had sort of dropped out.

Nick smiled at the memories as he reached Parker's long ranch-style house with the weird A-frame on one end. He'd had a lot of good times here. Parker's mother, Mrs. Botelli, worked in a nail salon. His dad did construction and plowed for the town in winter. There weren't any cars in the driveway, but Parker might be home anyway. His parents were pretty calm about letting him stay at home alone.

Nick knocked and rang the bell. A few minutes later, the door opened.

"Nicky! What'ya doing here, man?"

"I was in the area. Needed a change of scenery."

"It's been a while. Come in."

As always, thanks to the influence of Parker's mother, the house was exceptionally neat.

"You wanna listen to some music?"

"Sure. Can I get a drink first?"

"How about a Coke?" said Parker, heading into the kitchen.

"Let me get a drink of water first."

"And some cheese doodles?" Parker grabbed an unopened tub from the counter.

"Perfect," Nick said, filling a glass of water. Parker's house always had good snacks.

Together they walked to Parker's room. Nick said, "So you're not out selling eggs?"

"No, man. Erik called me, and I did ask my mom and Granny. But that's not really my scene. Is that why you're here?"

"Nah. Remember I didn't have my bibliography today?" Parker grimaced eloquently. "So DeMille talked with my mom this afternoon and basically said he wants me to stop playing soccer."

"And you freaked?"

"I tore out of there on my bike while they were still talking, and I've been riding around ever since."

"Does your mom know where you are?"

"I doubt it."

"You want to call her?"

"Not yet."

"Okay, you decide. Let's go 'spin some platters.' That's what they used to say, on old-time radio. I want to show you a drum solo I've been working on."

Parker's room was a sea of chaos in the otherwise spotless house. The only thing that wasn't covered with CDs, dirty clothes, or used snack food containers was the drum next to the bed. Nick picked up the sticks and hit the cymbals a few times.

"Go on, give it a try."

Nick sat in the chair and tried to remember some of the beats Parker had taught him last year. After a few minutes, he put the sticks down. "God, I've forgotten everything."

Parker jumped up and grabbed the drumsticks. "Let me show you what I'm working on." Parker played a long riff. "Recognize it?"

Nick shook his head.

"'Somewhat Damaged' by Nine Inch Nails."

"Oh yeah. I hear it now. Do it again."

Parker played it through a couple more times and then went over to his computer. "You wanna hear the new Limp Bizkit?"

"Sure."

Parker pulled the album up on his computer and the two sat in silence for a while, listening. After several minutes, Parker turned down the volume. "Hey, Nicky, I've been thinking."

"Yeah?"

"You know, soccer isn't really my thing anymore."

"Yeah, I know. But you were good, man."

Parker shrugged. "I'm only playing 'cause you asked. For old time's sake. I would've quit, but you guys have so few players. I didn't want to let you down."

"I'm glad you stayed with it."

The two boys listened in silence for a little while longer. Then Parker opened his desk drawer and pulled out a pack of cigarettes.

"You smoke?" Nick said.

"I started in June."

"Isn't it disgusting?"

"Only at first. I kinda like it now. You wanna try?"

Nick couldn't help looking around to see if anyone was watching them. "Do your parents know?"

"They don't care."

"I think mine would freak."

Parker lit his cigarette and took out another for Nick. "Give it a try."

Nick took the cigarette and sniffed it. He held it between his fingers and faked smoking.

"Everyone starts sometime," Parker said, holding out his lighter. "See what you think. Put it in your mouth and breathe in while I light."

Nick did as Parker instructed. The cigarette flared into life, and Nick got a puff of smoke in his lungs and coughed violently.

Parker laughed. "That's what happened with me the first, like, twenty times. That's why you gotta practice before you go public."

Nick tried another little puff and coughed again. "It feels like my throat is burning."

"It gets better," Parker said, sitting back down on the bed. "DeMille sucks, doesn't he?"

Nick nodded but couldn't speak to answer. He was too involved in trying to figure out what to do with his cigarette. So the two boys sat in silence, listening to Limp Bizkit and smoking, or trying to smoke.

"Hey," Parker said. "Flick your ash in the garbage can. I don't want to burn the house down. Mom really would care about that."

Nick went to the garbage can and flicked his ash off, but he did it too hard and the cigarette went out. Nick smiled apologetically, then crushed the rest of the cigarette in the can. "It feels weird," he said.

"Like you're in a daze, right?"

"Like I'm about to be sick."

"That's how it is. You get used to it." Parker leaned back. "I want to quit the team."

"Don't," Nick said. "We need you. Anyway, what else are you going to do?"

"I don't know. This, I guess."

"C'mon. The team's going to turn around, Park. This new coach will be cool. I mean, he used to be a professional, for God's sake. Besides, if DeMille won't let me play, we'll need you more than ever."

"You'll be playing, man. Don't worry. Your mom and dad know you." Nick didn't say anything. "Look, I bet your mom's already told DeMille where to get off. She's a cool lady."

Nick thought about that for a minute. "I should be getting home."

"Sure you don't want to call your parents? It's getting dark."

"Nah, I've got a light on the bike."

"Okay."

"Will you stay with the team?"

"I'll think about it. Seriously, I will," Parker said.

"Then try to cut out the smoking, man." Nick grimaced and stuck out his tongue. "It's disgusting."

Parker smiled and held up his cigarette. "Peace, man."

"Thanks, Park. You're the best," Nick said, and went home to face his parents.

THE NEXT MORNING, Nick had to take the bus to school. He sat next to Yvonne and explained to her that his mother had been way more furious about him staying out and not telling her where he was than the fact that he had not done his bibliography. For the bibliography, he'd miss soccer for the rest of the week, including the game against Braeburn on Wednesday. But if he handed the assignment in by Friday, and apologized to Mr. DeMille, he'd still be able to play against Kilby on Saturday.

"But for leaving and not telling her where I was going, she took my bike away," Nick said.

"For good?"

"Until I can earn it back by yard work and stuff. So I basically have to pay for it all over again."

"How long do you figure that will take?"

"All fall and winter. If I do a bunch of raking and shoveling."

"So *that's* why you're on the bus."

"Yeah, I'm a bus drone now."

"At least you're not grounded. Then you would have missed my party."

"Saturday, right?"

"Dad's already set up the sound system in the barn. Some of the girls I take swing dance with are going to come and help show you all how to do it. It'll be great."

"Sure." Nick suddenly found Yvonne's hand in his. "Hey, have you talked to Erik? How did the egg sale go?"

Yvonne squeezed Nick's hand and let go. "It was going great yesterday afternoon. I haven't heard since."

At school they learned that Erik had commitments of forty-six dozen a week, including the offer from Tabitha's dad. "Nick, we should bike over this afternoon and tell him about it," Erik said.

"Uhh, no can do," Nick said, and explained his bikeless state.

"You can borrow my sister's," Erik said. "You're the same height."

"I think that may get me in more trouble. I think the point is, I'm not supposed to go biking. It'd be against the spirit. Mom might really get pissed."

"Well, let's see if we can get a ride. Maybe your mom, or mine, can give us a lift."

"Let's talk after school," Nick said uncertainly. "Right now, I have to talk to the Pill."

Yvonne whispered as Nick walked away, "He has to apologize."

Erik yelled out, "Good luck!"

Nick gave a thumbs up without turning around.

AS IT HAPPENED, the apology was fairly painless. Mr. DeMille sat placidly while Nick stumbled through saying he was sorry, then waved an imperious hand to dismiss him. "I'll be waiting for your bibliography on Friday."

There was no soccer practice that afternoon, and Nick wondered if his mother knew that she'd banned him from soccer on a week when there was only one practice planned. Maybe she'd figured missing the game on Wednesday was punishment enough. In any case, Nick didn't feel it was his duty to bring it up.

ERIK COLLARED NICK as school let out. "C'mon over to my house. I'm sure my mom will take us over if I ask. I don't want to go by myself."

Nick thought for a second. "I can't, Erik. I've got to work on this stupid bibliography. Leon and Yvonne are headed to the high school library, and Yvonne said she'd help me find some sources. If I don't finish by Friday, I'll miss the game against Kilby."

"Okay, but I was hoping for some moral support. Tielemans is a pretty scary guy. I mean, what if he doesn't like what we did?"

"Take someone else with you. Dylan maybe? Or Will?"

IN THE END, Erik went with Jamie, and Jamie's father agreed to drive. So while Nick walked to the high school library with Yvonne and Leon, Erik and Jamie climbed into Mr. Farrell's old red Subaru station wagon and went to meet Jan Tielemans.

The trip to the Tielemans's house took a lot less time in a car. Erik was still trying to figure out what he would say when Mr. Farrell pulled up in front of the house. As he did so, Mr. Farrell reached for a crumpled newspaper on the seat next to him and unfolded it with a shake.

"Aren't you coming in, Dad?" Jamie asked.

"No. I believe this is your fight," his father replied. "I'll be here if you need to make a quick getaway."

Erik hesitated climbing out of the car. "What do you mean, Mr. Farrell?"

"Just a joke, Erik. You'll be fine. Go along now."

Erik and Jamie looked at each other nervously as they walked toward the yellow cottage.

Erik knocked softly, and Kate Mellen opened the door. "Well, hello. This *is* a surprise. Who's your friend?"

"Hi, Mrs. Mellen," Erik said. "This is Jamie. He's our goalie."

"Call me Kate, remember?" Mrs. Mellen said. "Nice to meet you, Jamie. I take it you're here to see Jan?"

"If he's in," Erik said.

"He's having his coffee in the kitchen. We've been expecting a visit. Follow me."

Erik and Jamie followed Kate through the mudroom and down along a narrow hall, the walls of which were covered with artwork of all types and sizes. The hall opened onto a surprisingly large kitchen, with glass doors leading out to a sun porch overrun by a profusion of flowers and potted plants.

The kitchen was bright and warm, heated by the light of the sun and by a blue wood stove burning in the corner. Jan Tielemans sat at a gleaming maple table, sipping coffee from an oversized cup.

"Jan, Erik is here," Kate said, ushering the boys in. "He's the boy who came to ask you about coaching football. And his friend Jamie. Who plays goalkeeper. Boys, can I get you anything to drink? Tea? Milk? Water?"

"No thanks," Erik said.

"A glass of water would be great," said Jamie.

"Coming up, one water." Kate bustled around cheerfully.

"So?" Jan Tielemans said. "I think I told you I was not interested in coaching your team, didn't I?" His voice was deeper, gruffer, and more accented than Erik remembered. His *was* sounded like *vas* and his *think* became *dink*.

Erik gathered himself. "Uhhh, yes, you did. But, well, we just wanted you to know how much it would mean to us."

"So you recruit everyone in town to 'help' out?"

"Well, we tried," said Jamie. "We got a lot of people."

"And now I can't go outside without someone offering a favor. Rory will not accept money for a cup of coffee. 'No charge to Coach,' he says. Tim Thomas throws in an extra bag of peat in my order. 'Nothing too good for the Marauders,' he says. At the dump, Frankie comes over and helps sort my garbage, like I cannot do it myself. I come home, and someone has fixed the fence along the chicken coop. They leave a note, 'Good luck with the Marauders.' You have quite a mafia."

Erik and Jamie looked at Mr. Tielemans, astounded. They had heard of none of this.

"Even that policeman is in on it. He stops me because a back tail light in the truck is out. Then he says, 'Normally, I'd give you a citation. But just a warning for the Marauder coach.' And he winks. Bloody idiot. He would never have stopped me normally. For all I know, he broke the tail light."

"Officer Drybzyck did that?" Erik asked, in amazement.

"Yes, yes. I thought Americans weren't corrupt. Suddenly my paper's being delivered. It's never been delivered before. We have not even asked for delivery."

"Wow," said Jamie. "I wonder who that is?"

"One of your cronies," Mr. Tielemans replied angrily.

"I think everyone has been perfectly delightful about it," Kate said. After bringing Jamie's water, she had sat down across from her husband. "I had a haircut the other day and Pamela didn't charge for the highlights. She said she wanted me to look good at the games."

Erik said, "We had no idea."

"Isn't that the point? You come over and tell me I owe you for these favors?"

"Well, uhh, . . . not for those favors. We came to tell you about the eggs."

"What about the eggs?" Mr. Tielemans asked. It sounded like, "Vat about ze eggs?"

"You wife told us that you lost a big contract recently, and that you were worried for your business." Jan looked sharply at his wife. "We thought we could help you find replacement sales. The whole seventh grade helped. We've got commitments for forty-six dozen a week."

"Thirty-one dozen are at four dollars a dozen, just like it says on your sign," Jamie added.

"Commitments from who?" Mr. Tielemans asked.

"People in town. Friends and family and neighbors," Jamie said.

Erik hurried on. "And you know Williams' Farm? They supply some grocery stores with organic eggs, and they said they need another fifteen dozen a week. Mr. Williams said it'd only be for $2.25 a dozen, if that's okay," Erik finished out of breath.

The boys waited in suspense through a brief silence. Kate was smiling broadly, and Jan looked at his wife and the boys suspiciously before barking at her.

"*Wat is hier aan de hand? Wat heb je gedaan?*"

"*Ik heb niets gedaan.*"

"*Dat heb je wel. Ze zeiden, dat je hen verteld hebt over onze zaak.*"

"*Ja, dat wel. Maar alleen om jouw onbeleefdheid uit te leggen. Dit had ik nooit verwacht.*"

"*Het is onverdraagelijk om iedereen met onze zaken te hebben bemoeien.*" Here Jan Tielemans's voice began to rise, and the boys began to be worried.

"*Rustig, Jan,*" said Kate. "*De jongens zijn zeer genereus geweest. Je zult dat moeten toegeven en zien wat zij gedaan hebben.*"

Jan Tielemans mumbled, almost to himself. "$2.25 from a grocery order. That's good business. But the others . . . ." Then he turned to face the boys. "How many separate orders for the thirty-one dozen?"

"About forty," Erik answered.

"How will I distribute? That's many, many deliveries. How will I collect the money? I'll be driving all over town. People will change their minds."

"We worked it out," Erik said. "You deliver to the Village Store, and Rory will collect the money. It's only for six months, but we'll make sure everyone pays. They're our friends."

"Better than a grocery contract," Kate said. "The stores commit to longer, but they cancel without recourse."

Jan leaned back in his chair, threw up his hands, and turned to look out the porch doors. Kate and the boys watched him. Slowly he turned back to them. "Yes. It is a great help, what you offer. I acknowledge it, and I thank you for what you've done." He sighed wearily. "Tell me what you want of me."

Erik said, "We have a soccer team. It just started this year. We play in the Tri-State League, and . . . well, I guess we're not very good. I mean the team's not good. But we have some good players."

"Erik is awesome," Jamie said. "So's Nick."

"Jamie's a great goalie." Erik suddenly felt self-conscious, remembering who Jan Tielemans was. "At least, we're okay for around here. For kids. Except we can't seem to compete with the other teams in the league."

"The teams from the big programs," Jamie put in.

"The ones who have had programs for years," Erik said. "We thought we'd be able to, but . . . . We thought some real coaching would help."

"Who coaches now?" Mr. Tielemans asked.

"My dad. But he mostly just organizes things. We coach ourselves mostly."

"You think because I have some experience, I will coach better than your father?" The boys nodded. Jan shrugged and muttered, "You'd be surprised."

Sensing Mr. Tielemans's continuing resistance, and fighting his disappointment, Erik said, "We were just trying to help. You don't have to coach."

"Yeah, selling the eggs was cool," Jamie said. "Everyone will still buy 'em."

Jan Tielemans stared hard at them. "I believed I was through with football. Soccer, if you prefer. I still believe it. Despite all that you have done." Kate frowned, but Jan Tielemans continued. "I have to think it over. I'll come to see a practice." He held up a hand, "But no promises."

"That's great," Erik said. "We have a game tomorrow at four o'clock. You can come to that if you like, though Nick's not playing. He has to finish a bibliography but . . . ."

"Enough," Jan Tielemans said. "Kate, show the boys out. I have to think."

Kate smiled. "Come on boys." She led them down the hall. "Do you need a ride home?"

"No, my dad drove," Jamie said.

"Then maybe I'll see you tomorrow. Jan's hard to predict, but you did well. And you did some good, too."

MEANWHILE, NICK AND Yvonne had seated themselves in the high school library to get some serious research done while Leon, feeling like an unnecessary third party, had split off to see if there were any new sci-fi books that looked interesting. Having selected one, he settled down in one of his favorite carrels to read.

After about ten minutes, he began to get curious about how Nick's research was going. One of the things that made him curious was that he knew that to get from the main reading room, where Nick and Yvonne were sitting, to the library shelves that held the books on Egyptian history, you had to walk by his carrel. He had yet to see either of them.

Ten minutes later, he felt curious enough to get up and go actually have a look at what they were up to. They did not notice him, but he saw they were talking animatedly, and they had in front of them several *Rolling Stone* magazines.

"Well, it doesn't matter," he thought. "It's Nick who'll suffer if the report is not done." And then another couple of minutes later, he thought, "Actually, we'll all suffer if Nick gets kicked off the Blue Marauders. In fact, it's pretty selfish of Nick to be horsing around."

Leon went to the Egyptian history section and selected seven books. Staggering under the weight, he carried them down out of the stacks into the reading room. Peeking around the books, he could see Yvonne and Nick with their heads together, giggling. He pushed between them and dropped the books on the table.

"Leon," Nick said in surprise, "What's up?"

"Books on ancient Egypt and mummies!" Leon said sternly. "You came to study, so you'd better darn well study. I don't want you missing any more games!" With that Leon turned and walked off.

Nick watched him leave, open mouthed. He looked apologetically at Yvonne. "I guess he's sorta right."

Yvonne was already packing up her things. "I have to go anyway and get some party planning done." She gave Nick one of her special smiles. "I'll see you Saturday, right?"

"Of course," Nick said. He watched her leave and then turned to the stack of books Leon had deposited on the table. "Focus, Nick," he thought to himself.

WEDNESDAY AT SCHOOL, Erik and Jamie told the seventh graders about their meeting with Jan Tielemans. The kids on the soccer team were excited, wondering whether he would show up for their game. Only Nick was quiet, feeling for a change like he was not quite part of the group. He was not playing soccer that afternoon, and his mind was on his bibliography.

Nick had taken five books home from the library the night before, and he'd worked past dinner on them. But none of the books were much help. They all repeated the same stuff about mummies and there wasn't nearly enough for a three- to five-page essay. None of them said whether poor people got mummified. One book had a long description about the actual process of mummification, which Nick figured could take a page of his report, but which, frankly, bored him to tears.

Nick needed to find more sources, but he had no idea where to do so, and he still had to write the whole thing up by Friday, which seemed a daunting task. There were so many stupid little commas and underlinings and things to get right in a bibliography.

Seeing Nick sitting by himself at the picnic table during recess, Erik came up and said, "So what's up, man?"

"Nothing," Nick answered.

"Isn't it totally cool about J.T.?" The kids had settled on J.T. as the acceptable shortening for Mr. Tielemans's name. "When I was sitting there listening to him and suddenly realized that that our plan had gone viral, I was totally blown away. Everyone in town was supporting the Blue Marauders. Can you believe that we just started the team, like, a month ago?"

"Yeah. Pretty weird," Nick said, wondering where Erik got the sources for his bibliography. Hadn't he gone to the Hereford Library?

"You should be proud. This whole thing was your idea. The team. The egg thing. And now the whole town is into it. Jamie and Ryan are going to put up some posters for the next home game to try and get a crowd. That should make Georgi happy, at least."

Nick didn't say anything right away, so Erik continued. "Hey, since you can't play, will you hang out and keep your eyes peeled for J.T.? You can answer any questions he might have about the Marauders. And grill him about Feyenoord while you're at it. I got

Dad to order me a history of the team from Amazon. We're just not sure if it's in Dutch."

Nick looked up at Erik. "I can't go to the game. I mean, I really want to. But I think I have to get my bibliography done. Time's running out so fast. Hey, where else do you think I could find books on mummies?"

Erik laughed and then, to his surprise, saw that his friend was serious and laughed again. "Show me what you have, and I'll see if I can suggest anything. But, Nick, man, you've got to come to the game. Everyone'll expect it."

LATER THAT DAY, Nick was talking to Abbey about his bibliography, and she said something similar. "Come on, Nick! It's only two hours. Stay up late if you need to. It'll make a huge difference to the guys to see you cheering."

"It might make a difference if I was playing!"

"No, that's not it. The Lancaster kids have rooted for you for years—soccer, basketball, baseball. Whatever. Remember when you started doing yo-yo, and everyone took it up? They'll care that you show up to cheer for them for a change."

Nick considered this. He was not used to being in the position of a spectator. Abbey continued, "Half these kids—Parker, Leon, Jamie—are only playing because of you."

"Nah, Jamie's playing because of you."

"Garbage! He was going to play whether I played or not. These guys are just following your lead. Gabe, Dylan."

"Gabe?! No way."

"Yes, way. It's not just because you started the team. If you'd have played Thunder they would have shown up to cheer you there."

Nick again considered this surprising comment. His friends usually did what he suggested, but he never thought much about it. He just figured he had good ideas.

"If you blow off the game because you aren't playing, they'll be pissed. You owe it to them."

"How about you? Will you be crushed if I don't show up?"

"I said 'pissed' not 'crushed,' so don't push your luck."

NICK WAS CONVINCED when Parker came up just after this conversation and asked if Nick was going to be at the game.

"I guess so, Park," Nick said, wondering how his bibliography was going to get done.

"Good! I've been thinking over what you said the other day. I'm going to keep playing. At least for this season. Without you, I guess the team needs all the subs it can get."

AFTER SCHOOL, NICK rushed to the high school library. Leon had given him the website of some professor of Egyptian history at SUNY Buffalo with links to a whole bunch of articles about Egyptian history, and he wanted to look and see if there were any he could use in his bibliography before the game began.

At 4:30, he headed over to Erik's house to hitch a ride to Caton's Field. Mr. Steiner was loading the minivan with gear when he arrived. Erik was in the back seat, listening to tunes on his iPod Touch.

"Nick," Mr. Steiner said, "I understand you can't play."

"Yeah, I'm just a spectator. Can I catch a ride down to the field?"

"Jump in."

Erik nodded to Nick, without taking his ear buds out. He was concentrating, and he didn't want Nick to ruin his focus.

THE BRAEBURN TEAM wore West Ham colors, maroon and light blue, and all the uniforms had the numbers and names of the players on the back. The coach was a tall, younger man, probably just a few years out of college. He came right over to Mr. Steiner to shake hands.

"I'm Brad Flynn. You must be Larry Steiner. I appreciated your letting us cancel our game last week. A lot of coaches in this league would have insisted on playing."

"Not worth getting struck by lightning," said Mr. Steiner.

"No, especially when you're stuck at the bottom of the league tables. This is my second year with the boys' team, and the club's still a bit of a mess. Braeburn only has a hundred and thirty seventh graders this year, citywide! And only sixty-two boys. Not much of a demographic to build a team on."

Larry Steiner smiled. "Lancaster only has twenty children in the seventh grade."

"Well, you must pull around the region. You've got a good crowd here."

Mr. Steiner looked around, surprised. There were fifty people at least, and one of the bleachers was completely full.

"Anyway, it explains why we can't compete," Coach Flynn continued. "Look at Winchester. They have a pool of over five hundred boys."

"I guess we just have to do the best we can," Mr. Steiner said, still marveling at the crowd.

MEANWHILE, ERIK REMINDED everyone that J.T. might be coming to watch the game. Kenny wanted to know who J.T. was.

"We might be getting a new coach," Erik explained. "This guy who lives in Lancaster who used to play in the Dutch first division. He coached Johann Cruyff."

"Yah, right!"

"It's true. His nickname was 'The Teapot.'"

"The 'Teapot'? Is he a fairy?"

"He won the Dutch championship," Erik said.

"I'll believe it when I see it. C'mon! What would a guy like that be doing in Lancaster? If he existed, Coach Scruggs would be on it, and he'd be coaching the Thunder."

"Okay, believe what you want. Just play well!" Erik said and stomped off.

"Wow, temper, temper from Mr. Icy." Kenny turned to Abbey. "I guess he's sad because Nicky Nick isn't playing?"

Abbey rolled her eyes. "He's mad because he thinks you're being a jerk, Kenny. And for your information, it happens to be true."

Kenny was still wearing a "What did I do wrong?" look when Mr. Steiner called the team together. Nick joined them, feeling out of place.

"Okay boys. Oh, and girls, Abbey. We don't have Nick today, so Terry will start at left midfield. I don't know much about this team, but we should play our game. Stay in position and remember to mark a man. We've got a good crowd today. Let's make the town proud. Hands in."

"1 . . . 2 . . . 3 . . . TEAM!"

Standing outside the circle of players, Nick yelled along with his teammates. His blood was pumping with pre-match adrenalin, with no way to relieve it. Frustrated he could not play, he went to the far side of the field, where he could, at least, run along the sideline, yell instructions, and help the referee make calls.

The Blue Marauders came out with energy and took the ball at Braeburn right away. But the game soon turned ugly, with a lot of unconsidered kicking and rushing by both teams. No one was more surprised than the Marauders when they found themselves up 1–0 at halftime. The only play in the first half that they could really look back on with pride was a save by Jamie, who dove at the feet of the Braeburn center forward on a breakaway. He had taken the ball in the stomach and a cleat in the face, but he had saved the goal and preserved the halftime lead.

Unfortunately, the collision also opened a cut on Jamie's forehead that had to be bandaged. He came off, and Terry took his place in goal.

"Game's not over yet," Mr. Steiner told his team. "Take a drink, take a breath. We have a long second half to play, and we have to keep concentrating. Play defense and get the ball up to our forwards. One goal won't be enough."

As the huddle broke up, Erik asked Nick, "Have you seen J.T.?"

"Not yet. I've been watching the game."

"Man, I'll be bummed if he doesn't come. I was sure he would."

"I'll look next half. Just focus on the game. You need another goal."

Early in the second half, Erik got that goal after stealing a lazy pass across the penalty area from one of the Braeburn defenders. Then Dylan added a third ten minutes later, knocking in a loose ball after the keeper bobbled a shot from Mario. As it turned out, they needed every goal. Down to just one sub, the Blue Marauders began to tire, and the momentum shifted. The midfielders stopped running back on defense, the defenders were caught out of position, and Braeburn peppered the goal with shots. Thankfully, many of them were wide and high. But finally, two of them got through, and Braeburn was pushing hard for an equalizer when the final whistle blew.

The Marauders looked at each other in relief. It hadn't been a beautiful game, but it was a win. A win in front of the home crowd. A win without Nick. A win, Erik hoped, with their new coach watching.

After shaking hands with the Braeburn team, Erik scanned the spectators, but he could not see J.T. He rushed over to where Rory Patenaude, dressed in shorts despite the 50-degree temperature, was talking with Georgi, and asked if they had seen him.

"No. But I wasn't looking for him," Rory said.

"I watched game," Georgi said. "Very sloppy. Two of those goals you did not deserve. I expect better with my name on the shirt. But, okay crowd. I get some business, I think."

Erik slipped on his sweat pants and gathered up his sports bag. Then he helped his father take the corner flags down and store them in one of Mr. Caton's out-buildings. He kept expecting to see J.T.

"How is Jamie?" Erik asked his father as they got in the car.

"Oh, he'll be fine," his father answered. "Just a little blood. No sign of a concussion according to Mrs. Vaughn."

"I guess J.T. never did show up," Erik said. Then, thinking about what Georgi had said, he added, "Maybe it's better this way. No professional soccer player would want to coach us."

He wished he could talk it over with Nick, if only so Nick could disagree. But Nick had already caught a lift back to the library.

CHAPTER 12

A New Fan

As Erik left for school Thursday morning, his father told him that he wouldn't be able to coach that day. "I have a phone call with the Board of Directors, and it can't be put off. Sorry about that. Remember, it's Gabe and Terry's turn to lead practice."

Erik was out of the house before he remembered to ask his father about J.T. He considered turning back, but decided there was no point. His father would have mentioned it if he'd heard anything. Besides, Erik had started to question whether they needed J.T. Reviewing the remaining schedule, he thought that the Marauders could still turn things around on their own.

With Nick back, they'd definitely beat Kilby. They already had beaten Dover away, so there was no reason they couldn't do it again at home. Then they'd be 4–5 heading into games with Winchester, Bedford, and the Thunder teams. If they could steal a couple of victories it would not be such a bad season: 6 wins, 7 losses. Count the cancelled Braeburn game as a win, and they'd be .500. They wouldn't make the playoffs, but not half bad for a small town in its first season.

It was Nick's kind of thinking, and Erik wanted to run it by him before school. But Nick hadn't arrived by the time the bell rang for the kids to line up. Indeed, he didn't show up until after morning meeting, at the beginning of social studies. He looked pale and disheveled.

"Aah, Mr. McCoy," Mr. DeMille said, "nice of you to join us. I think you had best stay in for recess and get caught up."

Nick slumped in his chair without a protest, prompting whispers and giggles that Mr. DeMille silenced. "Enough! We are here to study the Peloponnesian War, not Mr. McCoy's poor sense of time."

As a result, Erik did not get a word in with Nick until lunch time, and then only after Nick finished updating everyone on the status of his bibliography. He had stayed awake until midnight working on it, and he still needed to look at some books in the Hereford library that afternoon.

Erik waited while his classmates satisfied their curiosity with growing impatience. Finally, he could stand it no longer and cut into the conversation.

"Can we talk soccer now, Nick?"

"God, yes! I never want to think about Egypt again."

"And that's just the bibliography," Dylan said. "Imagine how you'll feel after you actually write the paper."

"You mean we have to write a paper too?" Abbey said, feigning shock.

"All right, give me a break. What's up with the team?"

"Blue Marauder talk!" Tabitha said. "I'd rather get a cavity filled." She moved away and Abbey went with her, leaving just Erik, Nick, Will, and Dylan.

Erik reported that J.T. hadn't been seen at the game, which probably meant he wasn't going to coach.

"It's pretty lousy after all we did for him," Dylan said.

"We said there was no obligation," Will pointed out.

Nick agreed with Dylan. "It's still lousy. He could have at least come to the game."

"The thing is," Erik said, "I've been thinking. Maybe Nick was right. Maybe we don't need him. We should win the next two games easy. We'll be one under .500."

Nick smiled. "Sweep the rest, and maybe we squeeze into the playoffs?"

"It's theoretically possible," Erik said.

There was a moment of silence while the boys considered how unlikely that was.

"There's still a downside to not having a coach," Will said. "Gabe and Terry are running practice today."

Gabe heard his name as he was returning his lunch tray and stopped at their table. "That's right! And we have some awesome stuff planned."

"Let me guess," Nick said, "blocking and tackling drills?"

"Wouldn't you like to know! You'll see at practice," Gabe guffawed, walking away with his tray.

"I won't be at practice," Nick called out, but Gabe ignored him. Nick shrugged, "Maybe the library won't be so bad."

AS THE OTHER kids gathered to put their cleats and shin guards on, Gabe described the first drill. "It's a penalty contest, with Jamie in goal. But there are two guys going for the ball instead of one. Offense *and* defense. "

"The defender has to start a step further back," Terry put in.

"Then when we blow the whistle, they both go for the ball."

"And there's a huge collision?" Erik asked.

"Not if the shooter is quick enough; then it's a normal penalty. Otherwise, boom!"

"What else you got?" Dylan asked.

"Listen to this. Two guys stand at the corners and cross balls in at the same time. The rest of the guys are in the box. The defenders want to clear both balls, the attackers want to score 'em."

"So lots of head banging," Will said.

"Just like a real game. That's what so good about it."

"Except for the two balls," Erik pointed out.

"But we have to get good and tired out first," Terry said. "We'll start with a bunch of shuttle runs that we used to do in football drill that are absolute killer!"

"So hurry up," Gabe said. "Get your butts in gear."

"I'm ready," Dylan yelled, springing up, and sprinting out to join Gabe and Terry.

The others looked at each other and slowed down. Abbey decided that the laces on her shoes weren't tied tightly enough, and she'd have to start again. Erik caught her eye, and she put her head down to hide a grin. For the next few minutes, the team was so absorbed in adjusting their shin guards and shoe laces that no one noticed the arrival of the newcomer until he was directly among them. A man dressed in green Wellington boots, brown tweed trousers, and a hand-knitted grey wool cap, and with a florid, cracked face and an oversized nose.

"J.T.!" Erik jumped up. "I mean, Mr. Tielemans! What are you doing here? I mean, I didn't, we didn't expect you. We didn't see you at the game yesterday, and we thought . . . ." Erik realized he was babbling, and he shut up.

"J.T.'ll do. Finish getting ready."

J.T. walked over to Dylan, Gabe, and Terry in the center of the field. He motioned for Kenny to join them, and, within seconds, he had organized them into a 3 v. 1. J.T. watched without comment while the rest of the team raced to get ready and form their own 3 v.1 drills. When Jackson and Mario arrived late, J.T. looked at them severely and added them to existing groups, creating two groups of 4 v. 1.

Each time the defender touched the ball, or knocked it out of the prescribed area, the defender became an attacker, and the attacker who lost the ball became the defender. With J.T. watching, and the kids eager to impress, the games stayed crisp and fast. When someone made a mistake, they shifted quickly to defense without trying to assign blame elsewhere.

It was less than ten minutes when J.T. signaled the players to stop, but the team felt as if practice must be half over. They gathered around J.T. at midfield, holding their shorts and breathing hard.

"Let's get a couple of things out of the way." J.T. spoke in a deep, accented voice and sounded unhappy. "First, you have done a generous thing in helping me with the eggs, and I want to acknowledge that. My wife and I are grateful.

"I do not like the idea of your buying my services with your generosity. But I understand there is a need and desire for some expertise that I may or may not be able to offer. I have spoken with Mr. Steiner, and he will file papers with the league to name me your coach. You may consider my presence here as, let us say, a token of respect for the town in which we live, which you have helped me appreciate."

The kids remained silent, captivated by the words.

"Second," J.T. held up two fingers. "I did not expect ever to coach again. I certainly did not expect to coach children. I don't have children. I have never liked children very much. So, while we are together, I would ask you to try not to behave like children.

"Third. I did watch your game yesterday." J.T. sighed. "Well, I can say that not everything is terrible. But there is much to learn. And much to unlearn.

"Let me ask a question. What is the purpose of a soccer coach?"

"Winning games!" shouted Gabe.

"It was a rhetorical question. The purpose is to make each of you the best soccer player you can be. At times this may require a reduction of your current effectiveness in order to ensure that a tactic or skill is correctly instilled."

The team concentrated, trying to figure out what he meant as J.T. continued.

"I have talked somewhat today. I hope that is unique. You do not learn soccer by talking, you learn by playing. At these practices we will normally pick a skill and go right into our drills and exercises. Today, the topic is the square pass, the foundation of all of soccer. Every one of you needs work. It must be done with the inside of the foot directly below the ankle. One must be on one's toes, dancing, to receive and pass the ball. You will see, passing and movement are inseparable. And each pass must be hit with authority. Now, before I give the drill, are there any questions?"

There were.

"Did you really play for Feyenoord?" "Did you play with Cruyff?" "Why'd you give it up?" "Did you play in the World Cup?" "What was your position?" "What are Feyenoord's colors?" "How much did you get paid?" "Did you have, like, a sneaker contract for cleats?" "Did you do advertisements?" "Were you on television?" "Did they have cheerleaders?" "Were there fights in the stands?" "Were you ever in a fight?" These and other questions exploded from the team.

Mr. Tielemans held up his hands and raised his voice just a little, "Enough! Of course, I should have expected. You have questions about me. However, we are not here for a history of Jan Tielemans, and I am not inclined to give one. Let it suffice to say that, yes, I did play for the Feyenoord F.C. for eight years. I was manager for two years. That is the past. I now manage the Blue Marauders, and I will focus on that team."

Cutting off further discussion, Mr. Tielemans explained the passing drill. He used no more than two or three sentences, but what he wanted was immediately clear. The players sorted themselves into groups and were soon moving through the drill. Even those who had no real clear idea of what Feyenoord was, or why it should matter, felt that it did. The coach of Feyenoord was now their coach, their "manager," and they had to live up to it. He had asked them not to behave like children, and it seemed important not to.

The first drill was relatively simple. Two square boxes were set up with a rectangular gap in the middle between them. Two players started on the perimeter of each of the two outer boxes, on different sides, and one more player started in the middle rectangle. Players had to make a pass and then move, to an open side of a square box, or into the middle rectangle, if it was open. J.T. walked among the team saying little. He watched Mario for a minute and said, "More oomph." He put his hand on Dylan's shoulder to stop him running, knelt down and turned Dylan's leg out and thumped the foot right below the ankle bone, "Here! Here!" He watched while Dylan hit two passes properly, then looked into Dylan's eyes and said, "Every time!" He twice reminded Gabe to stay on his toes.

A defender, who roamed the entire area, was added, and then a second, so that there was a defender in each square. They wanted to control the ball, or kick it clear of the coned-in area. The attackers realized they had to hit firm, straight passes to get by the defender, and also that they had to communicate with each other, so the ball did not roll away outside the perimeters of the cones. The logistics of the drills would have taken ages to set up with Mr. Steiner or Mr. Drybzyck coaching. There would have been ten minutes of instructions before the kids even touched the ball. Somehow, with J.T. that did not happen. The kids moved seamlessly from drill to drill, and J.T. let them figure out the strategies themselves.

J.T. continued to say little as the Marauders struggled, although he stopped play once when Kenny threw up his hands in disgust because Terry had failed to anticipate a pass. "No blame. Make him look good. Communicate. Look at his eyes. Talk. Point. Nod. Use everything." Before Kenny could object—it was Terry's fault, he should have made the cut—J.T. had moved on.

Kenny was uncertain how to feel about the arrival of J.T. On the one hand, he knew what it meant to play for Feyenoord, and he was nearly as star-struck as Erik. On the other hand, he was miffed to have been wrong about J.T.'s existence, and to have it so obviously proven. Earlier Erik had flashed him a "See, I told you so!" look, and Kenny had rolled his eyes to show how unimpressed he was. Trying to maintain his skepticism, Kenny estimated it was pretty likely that J.T. would turn out to be some freak, pathological liar. But meanwhile, he would make it super clear where his passes were going, so J.T. would realize that Terry was to blame for any mistakes.

After the team had rotated through positions, J.T. modified the drill again, removing the cones, and creating a free-floating 5 v. 2. Then he changed the drill to two touch and to one touch.

There were plenty of missed passes, and the Marauders demonstrated poor execution and stupid tactics, but the kids played hard and figured out what they needed. They understood that the drills were, in fact, mini competitive games. Defenders stayed on defense until they won a ball, and the person who made the mistake took the defender's place. The passers wanted to make the defenders suffer, and to avoid becoming defenders themselves.

J.T. called the players in for a water break, gave them a minute to rest and drink, and then split them into squads for mini games. They played 4 v. 4 or 3 v. 3 and rotated opponents. Before they started, J.T. said only, "Remember what we worked on. Crisp passes. Communicate." And they were off, playing and running again.

To Erik, it was a revelation. Every cut, every pass they made in the mini-games, was one that they had just done in their drills. He wondered if the others realized it, too. He looked around and saw Abbey's face glowing red and happy. He saw Dylan running, as always, but with furious concentration. He saw Gabe making a cut for a ball down the wing. He saw Kenny waving his arms to communicate some sort of movement to Matty. He saw Mario hit a one-time pass to Parker. He saw Jackson bending over, holding his shorts and panting. He realized something good was happening, and he wished Nick was there to share it.

After practice, the team collapsed on the sidelines, sweaty and exhausted. J.T. said, "According to Mr. Steiner, there is no practice tomorrow, but there is a game on Saturday morning at 11:00 in Kilby. I will meet you there no later than 10:45. Practice is over." Then, as the players gathered their gear, he disappeared.

"That was the hardest I've ever worked," Dylan said, gulping air as he lay outstretched on the cool grass with his shirt off.

"You said it," seconded Gabe, pouring the remainder of his water over his head.

"All we did was play soccer," Leon said.

"We never stopped." Mario's voice sounded unintentionally like a whine.

"But it was fun," Abbey said, still glowing red.

Kenny, who for once was sitting with the rest of the team, said, "I still find the whole thing pretty mysterious. How come he won't tell us anything about his playing days? It's like he worked for the CIA."

"Maybe he did," Will said, "like the Dutch secret service. Maybe soccer was his cover."

"He doesn't look much like a professional soccer player, if you ask me," Kenny said. "I mean, he's short and dumpy."

"Maradona was short," Will said.

"And dumpy," Mario said.

"But that nose!" Kenny said. "Man, it needs its own zip code."

"Now I understand why you're so good at soccer," Abbey said. "Your cute button nose." She reached over and tweaked it.

Erik listened to the chatter happily. He couldn't wait to call Nick and tell him everything.

BUT WHEN HE called Nick that night, Nick started talking about his bibliography before Erik could even get a word in.

"I thought it was going to be a disaster, Steiner. My mom dropped me off at the Hereford library, and I couldn't find any of the books I was looking for. I mean, plenty of books about how mummies were made and all the standard garbage, but nothing that talked about the stuff you and Leon mentioned. You know, like who got mummies and how much they cost and who took care of them. Then I talked to this super cool librarian, and she helped me look through the card catalogue, and guess what?"

"What?" Erik asked, unenthusiastically. He wanted Nick to hand in the darned bibliography and get back to concentrating on the important things in life, like soccer.

"The books I needed weren't in the history section at all! One was in sociology and another was in the religion section, which I never would have found. It was on a whole different floor." Nick paused, expecting congratulations.

"That's great, Nick," Erik offered.

"So, now I'm ready to go. I even have a cool picture of a freshly opened mummy for the cover. All black and disgusting."

"Nick, J.T. showed up today."

"What?"

"Jan Tielemans. He was at practice. He's going to be our coach."

"Wow! Did you see him play? Was he amazing?"

"Nah, he didn't play. He was in, like, rain boots. But practice was totally amazing."

"How?"

"It's sort of hard to describe. We just did a lot of passing drills and like, 3 v. 1s, but everyone agreed it was the best practice we ever had."

"Huh?" Nick said. It didn't sound so magical to him.

"Nicky, you had to be there. Gabe and Terry had all these bump and kill drills planned, then J.T. showed up, and the whole practice was, like, totally different."

Nick still didn't get it. "What's the big deal about passing drills?"

"I don't know. But even Dylan was passing properly by the end of it. It just evolved from one thing to another, but it was pure soccer." Erik hesitated. He could tell Nick didn't understand. "You'll see on Saturday."

NICK HANDED IN his bibliography first thing on Friday morning. Mr. DeMille opened it up and flipped through the pages. Nick waited confidently. He knew The Pill wanted to find fault, but if any of his work could ever withstand teacher scrutiny, this was it. Finally, DeMille put the bibliography on his desk without comment, and Nick turned to his classmates and gave a silent victory scream. The class was almost as relieved as Nick.

At recess, Nick heard more about J.T.'s coaching and began to wonder what he was missing. It wasn't just Erik who was infatuated. Even Gabe and Parker had nice things to say about him.

"He didn't say anything about playing?" Nick asked.

"He said, 'I am not inclined to discuss my personal history,'" Jamie quoted, making J.T. sound like Arnold Schwarzenegger.

"So we don't even know what position he played?"

"No, he just coached," Will said.

"Anyone can lead passing drills."

"Maybe, but it felt different," Leon said.

"C'mon."

"It did. You'll see."

LUNCH CONVERSATIONS REVOLVED around Yvonne's party. Yvonne had caused some excitement by e-mailing the class Thursday evening about it. She said the party would begin with a swing dance lesson, and she asked everyone to dress up. She wanted the boys to wear coats and ties, and the girls to wear gowns.

"My God," Tabitha said, "I'm not even sure what a 'gown' is. I have a night gown. Will that do?"

"Sure, Tabby," Dylan said. "White flannel. You'll look great."

"Well, what are you going to wear?"

"Uhh, clothes."

"For which we are all thankful, funny guy. Do you even own a tie?"

"I wore one to my uncle's wedding last year. I look awesome in it."

"That's some tie," Tabitha snapped. "It must cover your face!"

AFTER SCHOOL, TABITHA and Abbey headed to the L to play video games on the library computers. As they walked, Abbey said, "Can I tell you something?"

"What's up, girl?"

"No one else knows—well, Yvonne knows—but I asked Kenny to Yvonne's party."

"Kenny?"

"You know, the boy from Milford on the soccer team? Tall, curly blond hair, blue eyes. Good player."

"Okay, I get the picture. And I see why Yvonne didn't mind you bringing him," Tabitha said. "But isn't he the kid that Nick and Dylan say is so stuck up."

"Yeah, that's why I wanted to tell you. I'm not sure how the boys'll take it."

"Ahh, don't worry, we'll keep 'em polite. But I didn't know you were hanging out with him. The stories I hear make him sound awful."

"Well, he is stuck up. But he's also cute."

"Sure, that makes up for a lot. Are you guys, like, going out?"

"Nah. No. Not yet."

"Wanna say it one more time?"

Abbey smiled. "No. I mean, we've been to a movie together, but it was nothing really. He invited me to a concert next month. And I guess I invited him to Yvonne's party."

"That sounds like going out to me. But if he's so stuck up, what do you like about him?"

"I don't know. He's done amazing things. He's traveled all over the world; he goes scuba diving in Mauritius; he's lived in France. It's cool talking to him."

"I guess that means he's rich," Tabitha said, uncertainly.

"His dad's super rich. But he doesn't like his dad because he puts so much pressure on him. Like, every week he gives him a book, and Kenny has to answer a bunch of questions about it in front of the whole family."

"Every week?"

"Yeah, and his dad videotapes his soccer games and makes him go over all of his mistakes. Kenny pretends it's all okay, but he says it's really horrible. If he ever gets less than an A in any of his classes, his dad hires a tutor, and he has to do extra work."

"So what do you do when you get together? You just listen to his stories?"

"Yeah, mostly. Another thing that's cool is he has his whole life planned out. He wants to go to Harvard and then Harvard Business School, and then work as a banker for like five years before starting an adventure travel company."

"That's weird."

"Yeah, but I've never met anyone who thinks about this kind of stuff. Half the kids in town aren't even sure they'll finish high school. It's amazing to talk to him. It makes you think about getting out of here. You know?"

Tabitha wanted to support Abbey, but she wasn't sure what to say. Her own family had farmed in Lancaster for generations. Abbey seemed to be suggesting that life in Lancaster was somehow less worthy than jet setting around the world. Tabitha knew that Abbey's parents had pretty fancy educations; her dad had a master's degree, and her mother went to medical school. Tabitha's own parents had gone to the local community college. It had never mattered before, but at this moment, Tabitha felt a gulf opening between them. She didn't understand what Abbey saw in Kenny.

"It sure sounds different," Tabitha said.

"Yeah, Kenny's totally different."

Tabitha nodded. They had been standing outside the library for the last few minutes. "Well, don't worry. We'll keep the boys in line at the party. Let's go kill some aliens."

ON SATURDAY THE team met at the school to carpool for the two-hour drive to Kilby. Charlie McCoy, Larry Steiner, and Hector Juarez were driving. Kenny and Mario were meeting them in Kilby, and Officer Drybzyck, who had received an unexpected call that morning, was planning to follow them later.

The cars followed each other north along the highway. Rolling farmland turned into suburbs and then into the outskirts of a significant town, populated by strip malls and factories. Kilby was not a big town, but it had been an industrial center for a long time, starting life in the 1800s as a mill town, becoming a hub for auto parts manufacture as the mill lost steam, and now a center for retail activity as the auto parts business moved overseas. Through its nimble reinvention of itself over the years, Kilby had avoided the worst blight suffered by towns like Winchester.

The soccer fields were in a park that had been built to accompany the town's first "destination mall," constructed out of several abandoned mill buildings. The park itself was also a destination, with six fields, a water park in the summer, a bike path, a skateboard park, and three playgrounds, each designed for a different age group.

Looking for their field, the Marauders spotted the Kilby uniforms first, white shirts with garish orange and royal blue swishes.

The Kilby team looked as impressive as they had on the day of the first game: twenty-two kids being guided though a complicated weave drill by a trio of coaches in matching Adidas sweat suits.

On the Marauder side of the field, Kenny and Mario were already there waiting for the others. Kenny was passing with his father, who was in a suit and loafers, while Mario juggled a ball by himself.

"Why can't Kenny pass with Mario?" Nick asked out loud.

"Not good enough for him," Dylan murmured.

Abbey said nothing.

Then Erik pointed to a red-faced man sitting on the visitor's bench eating a sandwich. He wore a shabby raincoat, brown tweed pants, and a soft trilby hat. It took everyone a second to realize that this was Jan Tielemans, their new coach. He looked up and squinted at them as they approached.

"Ach, ten minutes late. Come. Chop, chop. Boots on."

"I'm Larry Steiner," Mr. Steiner said, sticking out his hand. "We've talked on the phone, but I'm not sure we've met before."

J.T. put down his sandwich, wiped his hands on his pants, stood up, and shook Mr. Steiner's hand.

"I'm Hector Juarez, Leon's dad," said Mr. Juarez. "We met once several years back when you led a sculpture class at the high school. No reason you should remember me."

"Yes, I remember. History, I believe, is your subject."

"That's right," Mr. Juarez said, beaming.

"And I'm Charlie McCoy, Nick's dad. We really appreciate what you're doing."

"Nick? He was not at practice on Thursday?" J.T. made the statement into a question.

"A discipline issue. He needed a reminder to get his homework done." Charlie McCoy called to his son. "Nick, come here and meet Mr. Tielemans."

"Aah," J.T. said, "you are one of the boys who came to my home. You helped organized the egg sales?"

"Me and Erik," Nick said.

J.T. looked him over long enough that Nick began to feel uncomfortable. "Well, I owe you my thanks. Don't miss practice again."

Nick waited a moment, but J.T. did not say anything else, so Nick said, "Yes sir," and went to finish tying his cleats.

The other parents looked at J.T. expectantly until he said, "Excuse me now," sat down, and returned to his sandwich.

In a few minutes the kids were ready, and they rushed out and began taking shots on Jamie. J.T. hurried onto the field. "No, no. No shots. 3 against 1 to warm up. We want passing, not shooting."

The kids organized themselves into two groups, and J.T. went back to the bench. They had been passing for only a few minutes when the referee yelled over, "Five minutes, coach!" Without getting up, J.T. waved a hand to call his players in. They came quickly and stood around him, waiting for his directions. Before he spoke, however, J.T. cast a dark look at the parents hanging around the bench.

Mr. Steiner caught on first, and tapped Charlie McCoy on the shoulder. "Maybe we should go over to the other sideline. Let Mr. Tielemans coach his team in peace."

J.T. waited until the parents were halfway across the field, then he cleared his throat. "Listen well. Remember the passing. I don't care if you win or lose. I want to see some pretty football. When someone has the ball, he should have a teammate to pass to on every side."

The referee blew the whistle for the game to begin, and J.T. frowned momentarily. "We need eleven players." Selecting at random, he pointed at Nick, Kenny, and Matty. "You three start on the bench."

There was a brief, stunned pause in the team, and Erik finally said, "Uhh, coach? They usually start."

J.T. looked at Erik and snorted. "Everyone plays equal time, right? This is what your father explained."

"Yes."

"So it does not matter who starts and who finishes. Come, let's play!"

"What positions should we play coach?" Mario asked.

"Ach, placement. Positions do not mean so much. On attack you must be ready to help at the four compass points, wherever the ball is. On defense, you must mark a man and move with him. Why do you need a place? We'll play without positions. I want to see you move."

The referee blew his whistle for a second time.

"Go, go!"

The Blue Marauders ran on to the field, feeling confused. Gabe headed up to attack, thinking perhaps this was his chance to play forward. Erik, Terry, Mario, Leon, and Dylan all joined him there. Parker stood vaguely in midfield while Abbey positioned herself to cover both her usual right wing back position and the right half.

"We can't all play forward," Dylan said.

The referee, standing with the Kilby forwards at the center spot, looked bemused. He could hardly believe that a team had not worked out positional play so late in the season. "You boys ready?" he asked. "Game's about to begin."

"Spread out," Erik said.

"You spread out," said Gabe. "We don't have positions."

Erik decided not to fight. "Leon and Jackson come back with me. We'll play defense. Dylan, play center mid."

The referee waited for the boys to move back and then called to each goalie. Jamie and the Kilby goalie raised their hands to indicate that they were ready, and the ref blew the whistle.

On the far sideline, Charlie McCoy leaned over to Mr. Steiner. "What are they doing?"

"I have no idea," Larry Steiner said.

Mr. Garrity, who had been talking on his cell phone, now noticed Kenny was not on the field. "What's going on? Why isn't Kenny in?"

"Don't know," Nick's father replied. "Nick's not starting either. Might have to do with his missing practice on Thursday."

"My God, Larry, where did you dig up this Tielemans guy? And why didn't you tell me about the coaching change?"

"It was really the kids' idea, Randy, and it was fairly last minute. But I think it's for the best. Tielemans played professionally in Holland, so he'll be better able to develop their soccer skills."

"Jesus Christ! What a way to run a team! It's clear he has no sense of talent evaluation, sitting Kenny on the bench. And what kind of moron doesn't know how to position his players?"

Mr. Steiner nodded. It was all somewhat mysterious. He wondered if he would have to start coaching again, when the experiment with Mr. Tielemans flamed out. Maybe there was a reason the man had not wanted anything to do with the team.

The game itself was looking ugly. The Marauder players were bunching up, running into each other and having arguments about who was on whose territory. Meanwhile, Kilby was taking advantage of wide open spaces, moving the ball around and finding unguarded spots all over the field.

Kilby's record was bad, but the team was not terrible. They played disciplined, high-pace soccer. The problem was that all their best players were defensive, and they had trouble scoring. They relied on a very mechanical attack, pushing the ball down the wing and hitting crosses into the box. Unfortunately, their forwards were not particularly good in the air, and their midfielders did not have the ability to dribble by their men and make their own shots. As a result, Kilby hardly ever scored, and lost a lot of games 0–1. Coach Beaufort, himself a defender in his earlier days, seemed happy with these hard-fought defeats. Certainly he had done little to change the way the team approached their games over the season.

But with the Marauders unsure of who was playing where, and even the kids playing defense sneaking up frequently to attack, Kilby had plenty of time to operate, and they were emboldened to try some direct attacks. Their midfielders and attackers dribbled right into the Marauder penalty box, getting several shots on goal. The only thing they didn't do was score. Erik, Will, and Abbey managed to close up holes just in time to keep the shots off balance. And Jamie made several excellent saves.

J.T. watched the game impassively. He did not shout instructions or yell out who should be guarding whom or who should play where. The only thing that seemed to get his attention was when one of the Marauders made a long pass.

When Will cleared a ball, J.T. turned to the bench and said, "He had a square pass. Parker was right there." When Abbey knocked a deep ball behind the Kilby defense, J.T. said, "Nicely weighted, but not necessary. She had an open teammate to her left. Build slowly. Make the other team chase."

After what seemed an eternity to the three players on the bench, J.T. substituted Nick, Kenny, and Matty into the game. Erik, Will, and Terry came out. The immediate effect was to cause more confusion. After some hesitation, Matty chose to play forward, while Kenny and Nick started vaguely in the back.

But Nick had not played soccer for a week, and he had no intention of limiting his role. For the rest of the half, whenever the Marauders held the ball, Nick either had it at his feet or was a few feet away, calling for a pass. Sometimes, Nick received the ball on one wing, hit a cross to a player on the other wing and, seemingly within seconds, was making himself available on the far side of the field for a return pass.

Kenny yelled at Nick several times to quit hogging the ball and stay in position, but to no effect. So Kenny started chasing the ball too. Any Marauder with possession would suddenly find himself flanked by Nick and Kenny, both yelling for a pass.

On defense, the disruption gave Kilby several breakaways. Abbey managed to clear most of the balls, but at last, Kilby scored.

J.T. remained impassive, merely turning to his bench and saying mildly, "No positions does not mean no marking."

But on the opposite sideline, the parents' discussion was less calm. "I can't watch this garbage anymore," Mr. Garrity declared. "The man doesn't know what he's doing. And where's that Nick kid playing? He runs around like a chicken with his head cut off."

"He's playing his heart out," Mr. McCoy countered, angrily. "I didn't see Kenny back on defense."

What went unnoticed by any of the fathers was that, despite the goal and the defensive lapses, the swarming Marauders were putting severe pressure on the Kilby midfielders. Except for the breakaways, Kilby was having a hard time holding onto the ball, and the Marauders were dominating the midfield. Although no goal had fallen, the Marauders had had several chances to score.

Nonetheless, when the halftime whistle blew, the team, like their fans, was more focused on their confusion than on what was going right. They walked in, angry at each other and beginning to be angry at J.T.'s lack of direction.

Kenny led the complaints, saying as he came into the huddle, "We need positions, man! No one is getting back on defense." He turned to Nick, "Where the hell are you playing?"

"I'm getting back!" Nick snapped. "More than you are!"

"We should be killing these guys!" Dylan said.

"We need someone who can finish up front," Leon said.

Gabe felt he was being criticized and lashed out. "How many goals have you scored, Peon?"

"None," Terry said. "But he has to be put on attack, because he's useless at defense!"

"Hey, man," Jackson said, "I don't know about y'all, but I sort of wouldn't mind to hear what the coach has to say."

Everyone looked at J.T., who was listening in silence to the arguments, his face a dark cloud. A quiet descended as the kids waited tensely for an explosion. J.T. seemed too furious to speak, and the silence continued unbearably. Finally it was broken with a hiss rather than a bang.

"Listen to me you snot-nosed, *bloedsinnige Baelge*," J.T. whispered. "None of you have a god-damn idea what you are talking about. Your pathetic couple of years fiddling around with a ball is nothing. Nil. A nullity. To sit here and spout nonsense . . . ."

J.T.'s voice faded away when the parents walked over to listen in on the halftime conference. "GET OUT OF HERE!" he yelled at them, shocking both the parents and the kids.

Even Mr. Garrity stopped short. The fathers looked at each other, then turned around and walked the other direction. As they were walking away, Mr. Steiner said to Mr. Garrity, "Perhaps this is a good time to discuss the software we've been developing."

"Sure," Mr. Garrity replied, leading Larry away from the field. "I've got some potentially good news. Some of my people looked at the business plan you sent me, and they think we should arrange some technical follow up."

J.T. turned back to his team and spoke in a voice that seemed less angry but no less intense. "I do not give the merest hint of a fig whether we win this game or not. What I want to see is beautiful soccer. Short, crisp passing to people around you. I want to see controlled ball movement. Understand?" The team looked uncertain. "I like the way you are moving. I *like* the way you are swarming with the ball. And *that* is the only thing that matters."

There was a silence as the kids tried to envision the play he wanted.

"What about defense?" Erik asked, uncertain if J.T. would explode again.

"If they don't touch it, you don't have to play defense." The whistle blew for the start of the second half. J.T. pointed to Jackson, Gabe, and Parker. "You three are out. Now go!"

Once again, the team was faced with the question of who would play where. The players met at midfield and Dylan, Terry, Will, and Abbey volunteered to start on defense. Nick, Kenny, and Matty would play in the middle. Leon, Erik, and Mario would start up front. Erik wondered why J.T. couldn't have made that sort of arrangement for them. Why leave it up to the kids?

Just before the second-half kickoff, Officer Drybzyck popped up unexpectedly behind Mr. McCoy and Mr. Juarez. He was rumpled, red in the face, and short of breath. "Have I missed anything?"

Charlie McCoy considered how much to tell. "Kilby is up one goal to none," he said.

"I thought Kilby was terrible. How's Tielemans working out?"

"A work in progress," Charlie replied. "The team looks a little disorganized."

"Well, it just goes to show," Officer Drybzyck said. "All that soccer skill only gets you so far. The kids need discipline."

The second half started with an early disappointment, as Jackson bungled a simple clearance. Instead of soaring away, the ball rolled directly to Kilby's unmarked center forward, who had no trouble one-timing it into the goal.

There was a moment of stunned silence among the Marauders, shocked to be suddenly down by two goals. Nick snapped them out of it, running into the goal to collect the ball and telling Jackson, "Don't worry. We'll get it back." He looked around at his teammates. "Just keep passing!"

At kickoff, Mario touched the ball to Erik. Erik beat a defender and knocked it to Nick. Nick passed it back. Erik changed direction on receiving it, hit it to Dylan on the wing, and then ran over and asked for the ball back. The pass back was a little soft and Erik had to stretch and twist his body to beat the Kilby defender to it, but he did so. He quickly passed the ball back to Matty, who one-timed it square to Kenny. Kenny waved for everyone to run up the field but then surprised both teams by hitting the ball square to Abbey. Abbey beat a defender and dribbled up the middle of the field before turning, suddenly, and hitting the ball wide to Leon on the wing.

Dribbling down the wing, Leon was surrounded by two Kilby defenders and had little room to move. But one thing Leon could do well was hold onto the ball. He pulled the ball back from the first defender, pushed it past the second, and managed to knock the ball over to Nick, who had run over to help.

At that point Mr. Juarez started calling out *"Olé"* after every successful pass. Soon Charlie McCoy and Russ Drybzyck got the hang of it and joined in, along with Gabe, Jackson, and Parker on the Marauder bench.

Nick hit it back to Will. *Olé.* Who hit it back to Abbey. *Olé.* To Nick. *Olé.* To Erik. *Olé.* To Kenny. *Olé.* To Dylan. *Olé.* To Nick. *Olé.* To Leon. *Olé.* To Abbey. *Olé.*

It was fun watching the Kilby players run after the ball with seemingly no chance to catch it. Or maybe the Kilby players were simply content to let the Marauders play keep-away because they had the lead. Either way, the defensive pressure on the Marauders became less intense as the passing continued. So when Matty received the ball (*olé*) on the left side of the midfield with Kenny and Nick in support, none of the Kilby players moved in to tackle him. And they were caught flat footed when, instead of hitting the easy square pass, Matty slotted the ball forward to Erik (*olé*) cutting into the eighteen-yard box. And Kilby was only just recovering when Erik, instead of trying to slam the ball past the keeper, rolled it square to Leon (*olé*) running in from the other wing unmarked. He received the ball three yards away from the goal line and was able to walk it into the net untouched.

The Marauders jumped up in the air as one and rushed in to smother Leon, hugging him as if he had just won them a championship. Which may have been over the top, considering that it was just one goal, against the worst team in the league, and they were still trailing 2–1.

Certainly Kilby seemed unimpressed. Coach Beaufort quickly subbed five of his starters back in with the grim instruction to "Shut' em down!" Kilby ran harder and began trying to gang tackle any Marauder who had possession. They even got off two shots on goal. But as time wore on, the Marauders increasingly dominated play. They held the ball in Kilby's half and peppered the Kilby goalie with shots.

The equalizer came more from luck than anything else. A pass from Abbey squirted through the legs of a Kilby defender, and Kenny won the race to the ball. After a couple of touches, he sent a weak shot looping through the air. The goalie should have saved it, but he was too far off his line. The ball sailed gently over his head, and a few minutes later the ref whistled the game to a close: a 2–2 tie.

For all their wonderful play in the second half, the Marauders had only managed to eke out a tie against the last-place team in the league. And even that tie relied on a lucky goal, made possible by mistakes by both a Kilby defender and the goalkeeper. No one could say that the Marauders deserved a win, and many would say they should thank their lucky stars not to have lost.

And yet, it was not the result of the game that mattered. What mattered was the first goal. It wasn't just that it was a thing of beauty, which it was. Erik, Nick, Kenny, and Abbey, at least, had scored beautiful goals before. But this goal was not the result of any particular skill by any particular player. In fact, no one's contribution was that extraordinary. Rather, it was an act of teamwork. They had worked together, smoothly and relentlessly decimating the Kilby defense. It had been thrilling and empowering. And they were eager to do it again.

Something else about the goal mattered too, although likely no one noticed. The team had arrived at the field with five fans, each a father of one of the players. They left with six fans.

J.T. had been more than reluctant to coach the Blue Marauders. Not only because, when he moved to America, he had assumed he was done with soccer for good, but also because the idea of watching hours of soccer played by preadolescent Americans made him decidedly nauseous. Similar to the way a composer might feel if he were told that he had to listen to a six-hour medley of his compositions played by children who have just taken up the violin.

He had agreed to coach only out of a sense of obligation to the players who, in their misguided, muddleheaded way, had opened their hearts to him and his wife. He was fairly sure that no one in Lancaster really understood who he was, or what it meant that he had played for and managed a team in the Dutch premier league. If they had known, they would have understood how absurd it was for him to travel to places like "Kilby" and "Winchester" to watch a bunch of thirteen year olds chase a ball around small, lumpy fields.

"But, if that's what they think they want," he had said to his wife, "what can I do? I doubt the children will learn much, but at least no one should get hurt." He winced as he said this, thinking about his own pain at watching terrible soccer. "And maybe there will be one child who can learn from what I say."

But watching the game against Kilby, something shifted. J.T. first noticed something unusual when Nick went in. The boy reminded him of his old rival Neeskins, who could never leave the ball alone. When Erik and Nick started exchanging passes, he began to think that it was possible to underestimate preadolescent Americans. As the sequence that led to Leon's goal unfolded, he had thought, "They have potential." And when Leon dribbled the ball into the back of the net and the team burst into cheers, he had to restrain himself from jumping off the bench and pumping his fists in the air.

He did not mention any of this to the Marauders when they gathered together after the game. "Some nice moments," he said, "But the last goal was dreadful. We should have lost. We'll have a lot of work to do at practice next week."

And by the time his team was shaking hands with Kilby, J.T. was several fields away, a distant figure, heading to the parking lot to find his car.

CHAPTER 13

Party Time

The team itself did not have much time to think about the game. They had to eat lunch, get home, shower, change, and make it to Yvonne's by seven o'clock. Several of them still had to figure out where they could get a tie and jacket.

Yvonne seemed to know, by some sort of sixth sense, when Nick arrived and was there to greet him as he popped his head through the barn door.

"Nick!" she said, grabbing his hands and pulling him through the door, "I'm so glad you could make it." She examined him closely. He wore a blue blazer, black denim pants, a blue oxford shirt, and a blue tie. "You look great," she said.

Nick, who had been looking around the barn, now turned his attention to Yvonne. She wore a clingy silver dress and a pearl choker necklace. Her hair was up off her head, held in place by a couple of barrettes. What Nick noticed most, however, was her skin, her lips, and her eyes. He skin gave off a healthy, golden glow under the dim barn lights. Her lips shone moistly. And her eyelids sparkled with some sort of glittery eye shadow. "So do you," he said, meaning it.

"Come on, come meet some of my friends from gymnastics."

Yvonne pulled Nick over to a punch bowl, where three girls Nick didn't know were drinking from plastic cups. "Hey, guys," Yvonne said, "this is Nick. Nick, this is Jennifer, Sylvia, and Adelaide."

Jennifer was a short girl with strong legs and a blond bob. Sylvia was tall and thin with dark skin and hair. Adelaide was a mix of the two, tall, blond, and super skinny. The girls giggled as Yvonne introduced Nick, and Jennifer said, "So this is Nick?"

Nick smiled broadly. "You guys must be the future Olympians that Yvonne always goes on about?"

Adelaide pursed her lips, "No, likely not. The real stars train year-round in Texas."

"I think he was joking, Addy," Sylvia said, then turned to Nick. "Addy takes everything literally."

"Oh, well, she'll have to meet my friend Jamie. He takes everything literally too."

"Is he here?" Addy asked, looking around.

"Addy . . . ," Sylvia began.

But Addy gave a little high-pitched giggle, "See, you can't tell when I'm joking either."

"So, do you *all* know how to swing dance?" Nick said.

"Well, Jennifer and I take lessons with Yvonne," Sylvia said.

"Then I guess you're our teachers tonight," Nick said. "What is swing dancing, anyway? Is it like the stuff you see on TV?"

"No, that's ballroom. Swing is much more fun." Sylvia grabbed Jennifer's hand. "Here, we'll demonstrate."

Yvonne watched with a pleased smile. Nick had charmed her friends, as she knew he would.

By 7:30, just about everyone had arrived. The girls were mostly hanging out around the tables, complimenting each other on their dresses and hair. The boys mostly gathered on the other side of the barn, admiring their own outfits. Dylan and Gabe were studying Parker, who had arrived in a red silk jacket, black and grey striped stovepipe pants, and pointy patent leather shoes.

"Man, where did you dig that stuff up?" Dylan asked, both horrified and envious.

"Craig's List, man. You can get anything. This whole outfit was five bucks."

"I think you overpaid," Gabe said.

"I think it looks sharp," Jamie said, before being cut off by Yvonne's voice blaring over the speaker system, "Testing, Testing, one, two, three!"

Confirming the speakers worked, and seeing that she had her guests' attention, she continued. "Dad says the pizza just arrived, so first we'll eat. After that we'll do a short swing dance lesson, and then my mom and I will assign partners and get everyone out on the dance floor together. Thanks for coming!"

She gave a little wave, received a cheer, and turned the music back on.

JAMIE WAS ON his second slice of pizza when Abbey finally came walking through the door, wobbling slightly in a pair of her sister's high heels. She was dressed in a sleeveless black dress with a small silver chain around her neck. Abbey's hair, usually tied in a tight ponytail, was loose around her neck and shoulders. Jamie blinked twice before finally yelling a greeting. "Hey, Abbey, the pizza's getting cold, I saved a slice for you."

Abbey waved, and then Jamie, and everyone else at the party, noticed Kenny, a step behind Abbey, following her into the barn.

Kenny entered with the confidence of a peacock, resplendent in a black tuxedo setting off his thick golden curls and bright blue eyes. Jamie and the other boys were momentarily hushed, wondering why Kenny was there. All doubt was removed when he stepped forward, took Abbey's arm, and smirked. Abbey looked over at Jamie and smiled awkwardly.

Abbey was nervous, not just because she had arrived with Kenny, but also because of her wardrobe. She was never girly-girl and she had never tried to be glamorous before. She felt like she was exposing some part of herself that had always been kept secret, and she was unsure how it would be received.

The kids in the room waited for Jamie to speak again, but he was too awestruck by Abbey's look, or too stricken by Kenny's appearance, to get another word out. Finally, Nick walked over to the new arrivals saying, "C'mon kids. You gotta get something to eat before the dancing begins. Yvonne's got a full program for us tonight." He reached out his right hand to shake with Kenny while hugging Abbey with his left. "We almost started without you."

With Nick's greeting, the uncomfortable silence in the barn exploded back into a hubbub of voices and conversations. Abbey looked at Nick gratefully. "You look great, McCoy."

"You're not bad yourself, Stephens." He turned to Kenny. "But what's with you? You look like an undertaker."

By now, Tabitha had joined the group. "C'mon, Nick. Don't be so country. All the well-dressed seventh graders are wearing tuxes."

"Seriously, did you rent it?" Nick asked.

"Of course not," Kenny said, "everyone needs a tux."

"Yeah, right. Come on, let me introduce you around."

Kenny looked at Abbey, but she waved him on with a smile. She wanted to debrief with Tabitha anyway. So Nick took Kenny around and introduced him to the non-soccer-playing Lancaster kids. Nick also introduced Kenny to Yvonne, who seemed very pleased to meet him. "Abbey's told me so much about you," she said. Nick raised an eyebrow at that, but didn't comment.

It turned out that Kenny already knew Yvonne's gymnastics friends. They went to school together.

"So what brings you out this way, Kenny?" Sylvia asked. "Surely this is not your usual haunt?"

"I came with Abbey. You know I'm playing on the Lancaster team this season? The 'Blue Marauders' they call themselves."

"Oh, right. I heard about you not being on the Thunder. You must miss playing with Jimmy and the boys."

"It's only temporary. Coach Scruggs wanted to make a point. But I'll be back next year."

"Meanwhile," Nick said, slightly annoyed, "he gets to play with me and Erik this year, so at least he's learning something. Today he even managed to score his first goal."

Kenny said to the girls, "Actually, the team's a mess. Sometimes I feel like I'm playing by myself out there."

"Sometimes it's like he really is playing with himself out there."

Kenny glared at Nick for a moment, before Yvonne came up and put a hand on Nick's forearm, "Can I borrow you for a second?"

Nick and Kenny kept their eyes locked a couple of seconds longer before Nick took a deep breath and turned to Yvonne. "Sure, what's up?"

Yvonne led him away and said, "I want you to help out with the swing demonstration. Jenny and Sylvia are going to dance together, and you can dance with me."

"But I don't know how to swing dance."

"Well, that'll be what's so good. Everyone will see how easy you pick it up. And it really is easy. Anyone can do it. I just need to walk you through a few steps beforehand. You had enough to eat?"

"Yeah, I'm fine."

"Good. We'll practice in the back where no one will see us." Yvonne led Nick away from the party, down to an empty horse stall in a far corner of the barn. She turned to face him and took a deep breath.

"Hold me like this" she said, and she began to lead him through the basic dance moves.

NOT ALL OF the Marauder boys were taking Nick's relaxed approach to Kenny's arrival. Erik, Dylan, and Leon were huddled in a corner commiserating with Jamie. While Jamie never expected to go out with Abbey himself, Abbey's interest in Kenny somehow seemed like a new sort of betrayal.

"I wouldn't normally care," Jamie said. "It's just that Kenny's so . . . ordinary."

"His dad's super rich," Dylan said. "That's not ordinary."

"What bugs me," Erik said, "is not that she's going out with him, but that he's lying to her."

"What do you mean?" Leon asked.

"Well, he's always telling her how great she played, but he'll turn around to me and Nick and laugh at the whole idea of girls playing soccer. He thinks the only reason we have her on the team is that she's a babe."

"Wow, would that sure piss her off," Leon said.

"He thinks he's better than all of us," Dylan said. "He won't even pass the ball to Leon or Mario."

"Yeah, but the point is he's lying to Abbey," Erik said.

"Well, why not tell her?" Leon asked.

"We can't do that," Erik said. "First, Kenny would just deny it. And, anyway, it would be kinda creepy. Like snitching."

"Well, what if we could get him to tell her?" Leon said thoughtfully, treating the situation like a puzzle to be solved.

"That's crazy!" Dylan said. "Why would he do that?" Dylan imitated Kenny's overly precise pronunciation: "'Before you kiss me, Abbey, I just want you to know the truth. You are one sucky soccer player. No offense.'"

Leon was not put off. "Well, what if he didn't know she was listening?"

The others looked at him skeptically, and the idea would almost certainly have died there if Parker had not joined the group. "Funny you should mention that," Parker said. "I was just exploring the loft in the barn, and there are some places up there that you can hear the conversations below you clear as a bell. I was over in the corner, and I guess Nick and Yvonne were practicing some dance moves down in the far stall. I heard every word they said."

"Yeah?!" Dylan said. "So spill the beans? What were they up to? All lovey dovey?"

"The point is," Parker said, "if Abbey was up there, and you were talking to Kenny below, she'd hear everything you said."

Everyone looked at Erik expectantly, waiting for a decision. It was just an idea, but if he okayed it, it would become a plan. Before he could say anything, however, they were interrupted by an announcement from Yvonne. "Okay, everybody, time for a dance lesson. If you can gather around, Jennifer, Sylvia, Nick, and I will show you some basic swing dancing moves. Then we can put the music on and let everyone go at it. Gather round, please everyone!"

Erik turned to his friends, still waiting for his decision. "I'll talk to Nick," he said, "Then we'll see. For now, act normal."

AFTER EVERYONE HAD watched Yvonne's dance tutorial, laughing at Nick's clumsiness, Yvonne's mother divided all the kids into pairs by drawing names from a hat, first a boy and then a girl, resulting in many groans and laughs. Erik was matched with Jennifer; Leon was matched with Laurie, which was funny because Leon was short and Laurie was so tall; and Gabe was matched with Kathy, which met with some wolf whistles because the two of them had been hanging out in semi-secret for almost a year.

Not all the matches were random. Some of the names were written out as pairs, so that "Yvonne and Nick" were together, as were "Abbey and Kenny," and "Dylan and Tabitha." Yvonne's mother didn't try to hide the fact that some of the pairs were set in advance, but she pretended not to know how it happened, and made a big show of being surprised. It was the same joke over and over, but the kids found it funny each time.

When Parker's name was called, he was nowhere to be found. Yvonne's father was called to step in and take Parker's place, and several of the girls agreed that Melanie had gotten lucky.

After everyone had a chance to walk through the steps, Yvonne's mother turned on the music and the couples danced the first two songs. Then Yvonne had everyone switch partners for the next song. After one more switch, Yvonne's father declared everyone an expert swing dancer and said people could choose their own partners now.

At once, the dance floor was empty except for Nick and Yvonne, Abbey and Kenny, and Michael, a non-soccer player who really knew how to swing dance, with Jennifer. Finally, Nick begged off, saying he needed some punch, and the others followed. The dance floor was deserted.

When Yvonne went off to compare notes with Sylvia, Jennifer, and Adelaide, and Kenny went off with Abbey, Erik finally found himself alone with Nick. Looking around to make sure they could not be overheard, he quickly explained Leon's plan to Nick. At the end he asked, "So, what do you think? Should we go for it?"

Nick scratched his head. "It's pretty underhanded."

"Yeah, but Kenny's treatment of Abbey is pretty underhanded too."

Nick looked around to see if he could see Abbey. "Where are they?" he asked.

"I think they went outside," Erik said. It was hot and loud in the barn, and kids were going outside occasionally for a blast of fresh air or some quiet. In some cases, a couple of kids went out together to talk. Parker, Nick knew, had gone out for a cigarette. But a boy and a girl going out together for a little privacy . . . that meant something different altogether.

"Okay, let's go for it," Nick said, suddenly furious. "What do we need to do?"

"You and I can take Kenny aside, saying we want to talk strategy for the next couple of games. And I'll signal for the others to get Abbey up to the loft. Then at least she'll know what she's dealing with."

Just then the music in the sound system stopped, and Yvonne was at the mike again. "Okay, kids, that's it for the swing dance program. It's getting late, and it's time to start getting down." She put in a new mix and the first few notes of the Beatles' "I Want to Hold Your Hand" began to stream through the speakers. "Where's Nicky?"

"Yo!" Nick cried out.

"Let's show them how it's done," Yvonne yelled.

The music, and the sight of Nick and Yvonne rocking out, infected the other kids, and pretty soon everyone was dancing. Some were in loose pairs, while the rest danced in a big circle, singing in unison along with the choruses of the best-known songs.

The group of dancers gradually diminished as the kids exhausted themselves and went to the sideline for a drink, or outside for some air. Finally, Nick and Yvonne, too, decided it was time for a break and went to get a glass of cider. They beamed at each other, sweaty and red faced.

"That was fun," Yvonne said.

"Yeah. I'm totally worn out."

"Did you see Dylan?" Yvonne asked. "He and Tabitha were awesome together."

"I think Erik and Sylvia were hitting it off," Nick said.

"I noticed that too. I better go talk to her. Don't move. I want to dance again as soon as I catch my breath." Suddenly, Yvonne reached up and gave Nick a quick peck on the cheek. Before he could react, she had moved away.

NICK WAS STILL a little stunned when Erik and Dylan came up behind him and pointed out Kenny, leaning against a beam watching the dance floor, sipping a ginger ale. Abbey was on the other side of the barn talking with Eleanor and Karen. Nick nodded, and he and Erik moved toward Kenny, while Dylan peeled off to find Jamie.

Erik and Nick walked over to Kenny. "Kenny boy!" Nick said. "How you enjoying the dance?"

"Good man, good," Kenny said.

"We've got to talk some soccer."

"What's up?"

"Not out here," Erik said. "Let's go in the back."

"Well, uh, I was sort of waiting for Abbey."

"She'll be fine," Nick said, "look, she's over with Karen and Eleanor. Once those guys get talking, man, they never stop. She won't even notice you're gone."

"Okay," Kenny said. "I guess."

Once in the horse stall, Nick and Erik looked at each other, and Kenny began to feel a little nervous. Finally Erik spoke up. "We just wanted to know if you are really playing Thunder next year?"

"Of course, man," Kenny said, relaxing.

"But with J.T. coaching, we could be really good."

Kenny shook his head. "Even the best coach needs players."

"We got players," Nick said. "Gabe was great today, pushing up against Kilby. We could play him as a target in the attack and move Jackson to sweep."

"That's a terrible idea!" Kenny said, laughing. "Gabe hasn't got the control to play anything but defense. And Jackson is lost half the time. His reaction time basically sucks!"

DYLAN AND JAMIE were having a harder time with Abbey. "Hey guys!" Jamie said, as he and Dylan joined Abbey, Karen, and Eleanor. "What's up?"

"We were just admiring Abbey's hair," Karen said. "What do you think, Jamie? Aren't you the connoisseur of all things Abbey?"

Abbey frowned at Karen, but Jamie smiled. "I think it looks great. But I also think it looks great in a ponytail. I mean, anything's cool."

"Come on, Jamie, take a stand," Dylan said. "Don't be so wishy-washy. I think she should get a buzz and dye it pink. Now that would be a look."

Eleanor and Karen giggled. "I'll do it if you do it," Abbey said. "But I promise it would look better on me."

"Hey, Abbey," Jamie said, "have you been up to the loft? It's pretty awesome."

"Nah," Abbey said. "I think I want to dance more. You wanna dance?"

"Uhh," Jamie stammered. Yeah, he wanted to dance with Abbey, but it would not help getting her up to the loft. "What about Kenny?"

"Oh, come on. I'm not dancing every dance with him. Let's go!"

"No," Dylan said. "Me and Jamie promised to help Leon find his contact lens, remember?"

"Uhh, sure. I forgot."

"He lost it up in the loft. That's why we were headed up there."

"Right, won't you guys help?"

"I will," said Karen.

"Me too," said Eleanor.

Abbey gave an exasperated sigh. "Fine. Go on then!"

"Aren't you coming?" Jamie asked.

"I think four of you are enough. In fact, you're much more likely to crush it than find it."

As Abbey spoke the opening notes of "Purple Rain" came through the speakers, and Yvonne ran over looking for Nick.

"Has anyone seen him? This is our song."

Abbey looked down and made a face at this, but no one noticed.

"I think he went outside with Erik," Dylan said.

As Yvonne moved away, Leon joined the group.

"I thought you were in the loft," Abbey said. "Didn't you lose your contact lens?"

Leon looked confused. "No, I don't think so."

"So why is everyone going to the loft then?" Abbey stared hard at Leon. "Where's Nick?"

"Maybe he's in the loft?" Leon said, now quite unsure of himself.

Abbey turned to Dylan, who met her gaze, and then to Jamie, who shrugged guiltily. "Okay, I get it. Nick put you guys up to something. Well then, I *will* go up to the loft and tell him exactly what I think of it!"

With Dylan, Leon, Karen, and Eleanor trailing behind, Abbey marched up to the loft. Dylan gave a thumb's up signal to Parker, waiting at the punch bowl, so that he could let Nick and Erik know that Abbey was on her way up. Dylan felt good. They were like the team from *Mission Impossible.*

As she climbed the stairs, Kenny was still in the horse stall, sharing his poisonous opinions about the rest of the team. Gabe had no touch. Jackson was mentally slow. Matty played with his head down and never knew what was going on around him. When the ball went in to Leon, it never came back out. Mario was scared of contact. Jamie was too small to play goalie—anyone could beat him with a shot to the top corner of the net. Terry was incapable of hitting a pass. And Parker, please, was just a waste of space. The only Marauder (other than Nick and Erik) who escaped Kenny's wrath was Will, of whom he said, "He's pretty tough. He'd be a decent wing back on the Thunder."

Kenny was just starting in on Dylan when Abbey, having walked the whole length of the loft to make sure Nick was not hiding anywhere, turned on Dylan and Leon.

"Okay, what the deal? Where's Nick?"

But instead of answering, Dylan put his finger to his lips. "Shhh! What's that?" As clear as a bell, they heard the voices of Kenny, Erik, and Nick.

"At least Dylan's fast," Erik said.

"Which might help if he could trap or pass," said Kenny.

"He really scares the defense," Nick said.

"Yeah, right. They're frightened he'll run into the post." There were a couple of snorts of laughter.

Dylan, listening upstairs, flinched. He knew this was all part of the plan to get Kenny talking, but he didn't like them talking about *him*. And Nick and Erik didn't have to laugh at Kenny's lame jokes, did they?

"What about moving Abbey to midfield then?" Erik said.

"You can't deny she's a great player, can you?" Nick said.

There was a brief silence, and Kenny paused as he opened his mouth to answer the question. Something was wrong. Maybe it was the way Nick asked the question. Maybe it was the way Erik's attention suddenly focused on him. Or maybe it was just weird that they wanted him to talk about Abbey's soccer when they already knew what he'd say. Kenny looked around the room, but there was no one else there.

"Yeah, Abbey's great," he said blandly. "I'll miss playing with her."

"Even though she's a girl?" Erik asked.

Now Kenny knew something was up. "What difference does that make?"

"Come on," Nick said. "You told me girls can't play at this level. The only reason to have her on the team is 'cause she's cute?"

Erik jumped in. "That's what you think, right?"

Kenny almost laughed. It was clear to him now. They wanted him to say something bad about Abbey. They were angry that Abbey was more interested in him than in them. "Look," he said, innocently, trying to figure out where the recording device was. "I know you guys always talk her down, but Abbey's a real player. That's why I wanted her on my indoor team."

Kenny enjoyed the frustrated expressions on Nick and Erik's faces. In a way, he thought, it was a shame. For a while he'd thought that Nick and Erik really wanted to be friends, but instead they were just trying to set him up. They were jealous, of course. "Hah," he thought. "They'll have to do better than this to get one over on me!"

"Is she better than Gabe?" Nick asked with little sense of hope.

"Sure," Kenny said with a big smile. "Her control is better, her understanding of the game is better, and she's cuter."

"Could she play with the Thunder?" Nick asked.

"Yeah, she'd be great," Kenny said, smiling some more.

"Forget it, Nick." Erik said. "He's not going to answer."

"I'm not going to answer how you want, you mean," Kenny said. "You two think you're so clever, don't you? Well, you're not. You're stupid, dumb hicks from a stupid, dumb hick town!"

But Kenny's last words were drowned out by Abbey now bursting into the stall and screaming in Nick's face, "I CAN'T BELIEVE YOU ARE PULLING THIS GARBAGE!"

The ironic thing was that Abbey didn't even care what Kenny really thought about her soccer. She knew him well enough that she could have guessed what he would say about girls' soccer in general, and about her in particular. She knew Kenny didn't really rate anyone on the team except himself. But it didn't matter. They never talked about soccer or their teammates when they were together, so she didn't worry about it.

In any case, Abbey knew she also had some opinions about her friends that were none too flattering. Nick needed to grow up; Dylan could be a loudmouth; Erik should stand up to Nick sometimes; Jamie could be a bit of killjoy, and Tabitha could stand to lose a few pounds. As long as they went unsaid, well, people could muddle along.

Now, however, thanks to Nick and Erik, Abbey couldn't pretend anymore. Sure, Kenny never actually said anything disparaging, but his fake praise with everyone listening and knowing he didn't really mean it, was almost no different than just coming right out and saying Abbey didn't belong on the team. It was out there.

Any anger at Kenny, however, was buried deep beneath the rage she felt toward Nick and Erik. She didn't expect anything different from Dylan, really. Leon and Jamie were likely just pawns (and she hated that they'd involved Jamie). But Nick and Erik had no excuse.

"Hey Abbey," said Nick, with a desperate hope he could still smooth things over.

"I HOPE YOU CRAWL IN A HOLE AND DIE."

"Abbey . . . ," Erik began.

Abbey ignored him and turned to Kenny to explain the situation. "They arranged for me to be upstairs so I could hear you bad-mouth me." She turned back to Erik and Nick. "BECAUSE THEY ARE MORONS WHO THINK THE WHOLE WORLD REVOLVES AROUND THEM."

"But I didn't say anything bad," Kenny said. "I defended you."

Abbey's eyes filled with tears she would not let fall. "Yeah, you just trashed everyone else on the team. Don't pretend you're any better than they are! Or not by much." Then, yelling again, "WHY ARE BOYS SO AWFUL?"

Yvonne and Tabitha came into the stall. "Nick!" Yvonne said. "I've been looking for you all over." She paused and studied the scene more closely. Abbey was red faced and furious while Nick, Erik, and Kenny looked pale, guilty, and unhappy. "What is going on here anyway?"

"Nothing," said Nick.

"I can explain," Erik began.

"They were trying to get me to say nasty things about Abbey," Kenny broke in. "But I didn't do it, and I think I deserve some credit for it. Not just being yelled at for no reason." Then, with a toss of his head, he pushed his way past Yvonne and out of the stall.

Yvonne looked around again. She was not sure what had happened, but she was sure about one thing. She turned on Nick fiercely. "It's all about Abbey!" she said. "It always is! Whatever the rest of the girls in the class do, however hard we try, however nice we make things, all you stupid boys care about is Abbey. I organize a party. I make everything cool and fun, and all you boys do is get in a big fight about Abbey and ruin my party!" Now she started to cry. "Well count me out, Nick. I'm sick of it!"

Yvonne ran out crying and Tabitha turned to Nick and Erik. "You really blew it tonight, boys. Come on Abbey, let's get out of here."

Nick and Erik looked at each other in silence for a moment. Nick sank down against the wall of the horse stall, covering his eyes with his hands. Erik walked quietly away, wondering how long it would be before his dad came to pick him up.

CHAPTER 14

Total Football

The participants in Saturday's farce still had lumps in their stomachs when Monday rolled around. They were not ready to see each other. Yvonne and Jamie considered staying home, but lacked the energy to convince their parents they were sick.

Nick tried to put a good face on things. Maybe it hadn't been as bad as he remembered. Sometimes things just blew over. When he arrived at school, he realized this was not one of those times.

His classmates were spread out across the playground in isolated little groups. He waved at Yvonne, but she pretended she did not see him. He went over to Will and Erik, who were standing together on the basketball court, talking in low voices.

"Hey!" Nick said.

"Hey," Erik repeated tonelessly.

"What's going on?"

Erik didn't respond.

"It's supposed to start raining later today and rain all week," said Will.

"We can practice in the rain. It'll be fun."

"If anyone comes," Erik said.

"What do you mean?"

"You may not have noticed, but Abbey got pretty pissed off Saturday night. So did Kenny. Who knows if they'll play anymore? Man, I'm not even sure I want to play."

Nick was stunned. "Because of Saturday? Come on, it wasn't that bad."

"Look, Nick, I'm sorry. I don't want to talk about it." Erik walked away.

Nick looked at Will. "He's blaming me for this? The whole thing with Abbey and Kenny was *his* idea. He talked me into it."

Will looked sort of skeptical, but he did not question Nick's version. "A lot of people are upset. The girls are choosing up sides. Supporting Abbey or Yvonne. And you should see Jamie. He's a mess."

The bell rang, signaling the kids to line up for school. The other kids jostled and shouted with their usual enthusiasm, but the line of seventh graders was oddly silent. Even the boys not involved in the incident, like Gabe and Will, seemed to have caught the mood.

Mr. DeMille did not object to the students' subdued tone. He took advantage of the lack of interruptions to cover several days of science lectures in a morning, droning on and on while the rain started falling outside.

Nick tried to ask Abbey if she'd be at practice, but she turned away whenever he caught her eye.

At lunch, Nick sat next to Dylan. "You'll be at practice, right?"

"Yeah, sure. Nothing else to do," Dylan said, morosely.

"What is *wrong* with everyone?"

"Give it a rest, Nick."

Nick's last remnant of optimism died. He knew Dylan was upset because Tabitha wasn't talking to him. But if Dylan couldn't laugh it off, nobody could.

Nick started thinking about Saturday's events. But try as he might, he couldn't see where he was to blame. The whole plan had been Erik's idea. Nick had tried to be nice to Kenny, even if Kenny had just thrown it back in his face. What was Abbey doing bringing Kenny to the party anyway? And why was Yvonne so upset? Nick had danced with her practically all night.

A COLD, LIGHT rain was falling and Nick, Jamie, and Parker caught a lift to soccer with Leon and his mom. The ride down was pretty quiet.

"Sucky day for practice," Parker said.

Leon grunted in agreement. Jamie was not even talking enough to grunt.

Nick tried to sound enthusiastic. "I hope everyone shows. Erik wasn't sure who'd come."

"I see his point," Leon said.

But it turned out that everyone did come to practice, even Abbey and Kenny. No one was talking to, or even looking at, each other, but they were there. The team changed into their cleats in silence. When they were ready, Nick and Will went off to pass back and forth.

"At least everyone's here," Nick thought to himself, "things will get back to normal once we start playing." But he was wrong about that.

When J.T. arrived a little later, wearing tall green mud boots and a brown corduroy jacket, he quickly set up groups of 4 v. 1. Nick was with Abbey, Dylan, Will, and Mario. He smiled at Abbey as they came together, but she ignored him, staring straight ahead. He wanted to make a joke, but thought better of it. So the group played in silence, punctuated occasionally by "I'm open!" or "To your right!" Sometimes, J.T. stopped play to make a small point of technique. Otherwise the players concentrated on the ball and ignored each other.

After ten minutes, J.T. signaled for a switch to 5 v. 2. Now Jackson and Jamie joined Nick's group, and the game started quickly again. Playing defense, Nick lunged to block a pass from Abbey.

He missed the ball, which went safely over to Will, but their knees clattered. "Sorry," he said. But Abbey, silent, stared straight ahead.

After another ten minutes, J.T. called the panting kids together. "Good working! We have a lot to accomplish this week. There were some moments of real football—soccer—on Saturday. But too much wasted effort and pointless kicking. The goal is to increase the percentage of touches that make sense and are directed to the ultimate goal." He pointed suddenly at Terry, "You! What is the ultimate goal?"

"Winning!" Terry shouted back, confidently.

"How do you do that?"

"Score more goals than the other team."

"And how do you do that? You!" He pointed at Nick.

"Take more shots?"

"That might help. How do you get more shots? You, Erik!"

"Passing?"

"Passing is part of it. *Possession* is the answer. Nine-tenths of the law and nine-tenths of soccer. As long as you hold the ball, you can score and the other team cannot. And the best way to maintain possession is to give the ball to an open man. No one can take a ball away from someone who is not marked." J.T. turned to Jamie. "How do you find an open man?"

"Uhh, I guess you see him."

"With the eyes sure. But also with the brain. That is what we do with 5 v. 2. If you know where the defenders are, you can deduce who is open without looking. . . . Okay, I talk too much. That is what we practice this week. Thinking and seeing!"

"Can't we have positions?" Gabe asked. "Against Kilby, no one knew where they were playing."

"It is not positions. It is shape. Positions are just a way to make the idea of shape simple. But they get in the way. Positions become static and people stop moving." J.T. paused and looked at the kids.

"Okay, I am talking again and you do not understand. For now, remember, when we practice 4 against 4, there are always four defenders as well as four attackers. The shape of defense must be a counterpoint to the shape of the attack." Again he saw blank faces. He clapped his hands. "Come, you will see."

Under J.T.'s direction, the players divided themselves into three teams of four and set up mini fields with a full-sized goal on each end. Erik, Dylan, Terry, and Leon, with Matty as a sub, began playing against Abbey, Nick, Jamie, and Parker, with Jackson as a sub, while the extra team played 3 v. 1 on the sidelines.

J.T. paused the play only occasionally to make a point. He stopped Terry once to show him when a back pass was available. He stopped Parker to tell him what run he should make. He stopped the game to demonstrate how Abbey's positioning had allowed her to intercept the ball. Mostly the teams just played.

The players were still not talking to each other except to exchange information needed for the games. They focused on winning the games. Abbey made several good passes to Nick, and he acknowledged them with a nod, but without warmth. J.T. switched the groups, so Kenny, Gabe, Mario, and Will came in for Erik's team. And play went on. Kenny tackled Nick hard, then helped him up without looking at him. It was cool and impersonal. Everyone just played soccer.

After another switch, J.T. set up a new variation of the game with four separate small goals on an extra-wide field. "Now, you have two goals to attack and defend. This benefits attackers who can switch the ball from one side to the other efficiently." J.T. looked at Gabe. "It benefits defenders who know how to maintain their shape."

Again the teams rotated against each other. When they grew tired, J.T. told them to let the ball do the moving. He taught Gabe how to position himself when the ball carrier moved toward the man he was marking; he stopped Kenny, who made a one-touch pass that should have been controlled first; and he corrected Mario, who tried to turn with a ball into a crowd when a simple pass backward would have sufficed.

Somehow, J.T. managed to fit two more versions of 4 v. 4 into the practice. One was a game with goals at each compass point, with one team permitted to score in the goals on the north-south axis, the other in the goals on the east-west axis; and another was played without goals, where scoring required dribbling over the end line. Explaining the latter, J.T. said, "Winning on such a field requires excellent position play from the defense. And good ball movement from the attackers. Let's see how you handle it."

Twenty minutes later, J.T. called the players to the bench. Several parents were already waiting to pick up their kids, but the stories about J.T. had spread, and they kept their distance. J.T. looked at Erik. "When is the next game?"

"Saturday at home against Dover. It starts at ten."

"Thank you. So we have three more days of practice before the game. It will be wet all week. But if you work like today, you will stay warm. And it is good practice to trap and pass with a wet ball. We will keep working on our seeing and thinking in small groups. And we will see how much you have learned on Saturday."

Once practice was over, J.T. did not wait around, heading at once to his pick-up truck in the parking lot. On this day, for once, with nothing to say to each other, the players were ready to leave almost as soon as their coach.

Nick felt like he had a ton to say. Erik was right: J.T.'s practice was amazing. He couldn't believe how tired he was. All they had done was play some games. It seemed like anyone could have led practice, but Nick had never been at a practice that flowed so quickly, or required so much thinking and running. He had the sort of woozy feeling like after a math test. Not pleasant exactly, but intense. And he'd actually seen improvement. In his own playing, but also in Leon's and Jackson's and Terry's and Mario's. All of them were making passes at the end of practice that they would not have made at the beginning.

Nick almost said something to Erik before he remembered they were sort of fighting. Abbey, Kenny, and Dylan had already left, but Nick understood why everyone had come to practice. It wasn't for the camaraderie; it was for the soccer. Nothing about showing up meant that they were friends. It was strictly business.

"Well," Nick thought, "that's cool, if that's how everyone wants it. I can do it too."

SO THE WEEK progressed with the kids moving from school, to practice, to home, barely talking to each other.

At school, Mr. DeMille seemed intent to test the limits of their endurance, racing through lessons and assigning ever more burdensome homework assignments. On Tuesday afternoon, he announced an important math test to take place Friday morning, ending the unit on fractions and testing everything they had learned to date. It was a big deal to Nick and Will. They had to get passing grades to avoid remedial math for the rest of the year.

On Wednesday afternoon, Mr. DeMille returned the Egypt bibliographies and reminded everyone that the paper was due in thirteen days and he hoped everyone had started by now.

Meanwhile, J.T. kept the team in constant motion at practice, running them through one 4 v. 4 situation after another. They did 4 v. 4 with big goals, with small goals, with wide fields, with narrow fields, with one touch, with two touch, with designated scorers, and with restrictions on how you could score or pass. Each new game brought out a different technique or tactic that J.T. wanted the team to think about. Nick wanted to laugh with Erik at the endless variations of the same game. But somehow the right moment never came up.

At the end of practice on Thursday, J.T. spoke to the team before dismissal. "I have watched you this week. You work hard, but you don't talk to each other. Sometimes this can be effective. At Feyenoord, they once said we were a team that needed fourteen different tunnels to take the field, but we won a lot of games. We will see how it works for you on Saturday."

ON FRIDAY MORNING, Nick was certain that the math test had gone very badly. He sat next to Leon at lunch.

"What do you think you missed?" Leon asked him.

"Everything. I had no idea how to do the last three problems."

"That's okay. Those were really hard. I bet everyone missed them."

"You always say that, then you get everything right."

"Not this time, seriously. We never even covered that stuff. I think DeMille was just trying to see what we could do on our own. I think I only got one of them. If you did okay on the others, I bet you'll pass."

"Really?"

"Scout's honor."

"Hey, Leon, can I ask you a question?"

"Sure."

"Are you still mad about last week?"

"Mad? At who? I just feel stupid about it. You know, the whole plan was sort of my idea. I didn't really think we'd do it. It was just sort of theoretical. I mean, if Abbey wants to go out with Kenny, what do I care?"

"I wish everyone would just move on."

"I know what you mean. But Abbey and Yvonne are still mad. Mostly at you, I think, but they're also mad at each other. And the rest of the girls have taken sides. Half think Yvonne was out of line with Abbey, and the other think she was right on. So they can't let go."

"Girls are crazy. I didn't even do anything."

"We all did something," Leon said. "I'm sure Erik feels guilty. Especially since he's Mr. Perfect, and suddenly he looks really stupid. I think Dylan's still upset at the things you and Erik said about him."

"We didn't say anything about Dylan!"

"Sure you did. You were talking to Kenny about him when we got up to the loft. You were laughing at him."

"Man, we were just doing that to get Kenny going."

Leon shrugged. "I know that. I think Dylan does too. But that doesn't mean you weren't laughing at him. I'm just glad I didn't hear what you said about me."

"C'mon, you guys are great. I can't take the ball off you. And I sure don't want to be a defender trying to beat Dylan to the ball."

"It's like the math test isn't it?"

"Why?"

"Well, you say you can't get the ball off me, but in an actual game you always do."

Nick grinned. "I guess so. But I can't win any games by myself. So the rest of you had better play well on Saturday."

Leon smiled, and Nick felt a little better. Almost everyone was still fighting, but at least he had one friend he could talk with.

BY SATURDAY THE rain had moved on. The ground at Caton's Field remained damp and squishy, but the air was warmer, and the water drops on the grass glistened in the sun. Erik and his father arrived early to set up. J.T. was already there when they arrived, sitting on a bench eating a sandwich and shuffling through papers. Once again he was dressed in his raincoat and tweed trilby hat, that always looked too small for his head. It seemed to be his official soccer match outfit.

"Hey coach!" Erik greeted him.

"Good morning, Erik," J.T. replied. "Good morning, Larry. A glorious day for football, is it not?"

"Sure is, coach."

J.T. continued to eat his sandwich and look through his papers, while Larry and Erik moved the goals into place, arranged the corner flags, and positioned benches for the spectators. When they were done, Mr. Steiner and Erik approached him again.

"What are you working on there, Jan?" Larry Steiner asked.

"I am considering positions for the children."

"I thought you didn't believe in positions," Erik said.

"Perhaps I overstated my case. Positions as a starting point, just not as an end point. They are an indication of *primary* responsibility, but they must not become constraints." Erik nodded. J.T. didn't much look like a soccer player, but Erik had developed a profound faith in everything he said. "You, for example. You play striker so you push too far forward and do not get sufficiently involved in the build-up of the play. It wastes your abilities. I am moving you back to midfield to give you more touches."

Erik was caught off guard. "I've always played striker."

"So you will try something new. I want to see you scoring less and feeding the ball to your teammates more. Also, you need to develop your marking and tackling to bring them up to par with your other skills."

"Who'll play center forward?"

"I think Leon. He holds the ball well. If we put him in center, he can be a nice target and he can feed the ball back to his midfielders and out to the wings."

"But I can do that."

"Yes, yes. You can do many things. That is the point." J.T. looked down at his sandwich, and Erik realized that the discussion was over.

KENNY AND HIS father showed up next. Mr. Garrity, wearing a suit and dark glasses, went right up to J.T., who had just popped the last bite of sandwich into his mouth.

"Coach Tielemans. I don't think we were properly introduced last week. I'm Randy Garrity, Kenny's father." He removed his sunglasses.

J.T. grunted, his mouth still full.

"I've heard some good things about your practice sessions, even if that first game was a bit of a disaster. A tie against Kilby is nothing to write home about."

"Mr. Garrity . . . ," J.T. began.

"Funny place for us to be," Randy gestured around him. "Two years ago, Kenny was All-State U-11 on an undefeated Thunder team, and now here we are. An old hay field behind a broken-down gas station in the middle of nowhere." Randy looked J.T. in the face and smiled. "But I guess you know a little something about being a big fish in a small pond."

"Not really."

"Don't be modest, Coach. I have one or two portfolio companies in Holland, so I've been over there a fair amount. I know you're better than this. That's why I can trust you to take care of Kenny. This is temporary for both of you. In fact, I've been talking to some of my friends, and we've already identified several kids in the Tri-State region with superior skills and no team associations. A Scottish boy, a couple of kids from Ghana, and a Russian goalkeeper—six foot two and still only twelve years old."

"I don't understand, Mr. Garrity."

"I thought of bringing them in earlier in the season, but there didn't seem any point when Steiner was coaching. It's a little late now, but we could try to get you the goalie for the last few games, and the others can come in next year. We both know that you don't have enough to compete with the big teams. The Thunders and the Bedfords. After Kenny, it's a whole lot of dross."

"I don't think you know what we have here."

"Sure, the Erik kid's okay, and his buddy Nick. The short kid's not bad. But they're country kids. They haven't had the training, and they don't have the discipline. What I'm saying is that next season, we can start a real team. My people are looking into fields now. With a coach like you, and the right kids, we could really make something happen."

"Something is happening right here," J.T. said.

"Of course we'll bring over a couple of the better kids with us. Can't have too many subs. But if things work out, I see no reason we couldn't win the Tri-State, maybe the nationals. I think you may be the right person to lead a team like that." Mr. Garrity put his sunglasses back on. "Do we understand each other?"

"Yes, I believe we do."

Mr. Garrity flashed a smile. "Nice talking to you, Coach. Got a flight to Dallas so I can't stay for the game. A car's picking Kenny up. Good luck!" Mr. Garrity walked away whistling.

J.T. HAD MORE than one surprise for the team when he handed out positions. On defense, he had moved Abbey to sweeper, Dylan to right wing back, Jackson to left, and Gabe to stopper.

"I'm a forward," Dylan protested.

"No, you are not. Right now you are a more natural wing defender. Your speed will be an asset at securing the right side. Remember, positions are starting points. If you make an overlapping run on attack, the others will cover for you."

Put that way, Dylan was happier, but Gabe remained uncertain. "Why not put Abbey at stopper, and I can stay at sweeper?"

"Because she reads the game better. Sweepers do not need to be fast; they must position themselves correctly and guide the defense. Abbey is best at that. Your job is to disrupt the attack further up field. But, of course, I expect you will find yourselves switching positions often."

In midfield, Will was in the center with Erik on the right and

Nick on the left. Kenny assumed he must be playing center forward.

"I don't usually play striker," he said.

"No, you will be on one wing, with Matty on the other. I want Leon to play center forward."

"Leon?" Kenny said. It made no sense to him. He would be wasted on the wing.

"Leon will hold the ball in the middle, and distribute it. We need a center forward who will wait for his help. The wingers must find space behind the defense and worry the defenders. Movement is vital. Move, move, move!"

"But . . . ," Kenny began to protest.

J.T. silenced him a ferocious look and then spoke with a strange intensity. "For two years, the main papers in Rotterdam called me a dummkopf for playing Wim Juppes as a central defender. I ignored them, we won a title, and Wim went on to a career on the national team that he would never have had as a midfielder." The team held its breath and J.T. continued in almost a whisper. "One thing a manager decides—has absolute authority on—is where his people play. I might be wrong, but I will not be challenged on this. Does everyone understand?"

The referee blew his whistle, and the starting unit of the Dover Deacons, already on the field, ran and jumped nervously as they waited for the Marauders to come out of their huddle.

J.T. was suddenly calm again. "As it happens, I expect you to win today. But that is not important. Remember, when you have the ball, there is a teammate to your left, to your right, and behind you. It is 4 v. 4. Let your opponents chase the ball while you retain possession. We will show these people how to play beautiful soccer."

AS J.T. GESTURED at the spectators, Erik looked around the field and marveled. There was a real crowd, at least a hundred people. Many of them were from the families of the Blue Marauders, some were Dover parents, but the rest were other Lancaster townspeople. These were the people who had bought eggs or otherwise helped persuade J.T. to coach the team. Perhaps they wanted to see how their investment was turning out.

Nick looked around too, but he mostly noticed one resident who was not at the game. Yvonne. This was the first home game she'd missed. Then he glanced over at Abbey and Kenny. They had their heads down, not looking at anyone. Nick also noticed Dylan. Usually he'd be trading fist bumps, pumping the team up. Instead, he was quiet, staring straight ahead. Nick tried to catch Erik's eye, but couldn't.

"Well," Nick thought, "it worked in practice. No need to start getting friendly now. "

THE REFEREE BLEW his whistle again, and J.T. pushed his players onto the field, "Go, go!"

As the team broke the huddle, Dylan said to Erik, "Hey, we never gave a cheer."

"I guess J.T. doesn't figure it's important," Erik replied.

As it turned out, at least on that day, it wasn't. The Deacons took the kickoff, but when they lost the ball they lost it for good. The Marauders moved the ball around as they had in practice, and the Deacons chased and chased and chased. With Nick all over the field, no Marauder was ever without an easy pass. And once Nick got the ball, he kept it moving. A back pass to Abbey, a through ball to Kenny or Leon, or else a change of field to Erik on the other side.

Whenever Erik had the ball, the Deacon defense panicked. It became apparent that no single one of their players could take the ball away from him, and when they tried to gang-tackle him, Erik had no trouble picking out unguarded teammates running into space.

Erik's passes went through to Leon, who, as J.T. predicted, held the ball well enough to allow his teammates get open around him; to Kenny, who dashed to the goal and hit several hard strikes necessitating great saves from Dover's athletic goalkeeper; to Matty, who dribbled to his wing and hit efficient crosses; and to Nick, as well, who moved seamlessly from midfield to attack. Nick didn't try to force things, even when he received the ball near the goal. If the shot wasn't there, he would send it wide to Kenny or Matty or hit it back to Will or Erik. The Marauders didn't score, but they didn't lose possession either.

In their previous game, the Deacons had had success on attack when they booted the ball up to their skillful wingers. But, on this day, the tactic failed. Dylan's speed allowed him to shut down his side. Even when he was beaten, he would recover so quickly that he had to be beaten all over again. And, more important, Abbey was always in the right place. There were no wild bounces that she did not anticipate, and no attacker made a move past Jackson or Gabe that she was not there to cover for. With her directing traffic and anticipating play, there were no holes in the defense for the Dover Deacons to find.

Miraculously, no goal had fallen by the time J.T. made his first substitutions. He took out Erik, Nick, and Will, put in Terry, Parker, and Mario at forward, and moved Kenny's line back to midfield. The changes reduced the attacking pressure exerted by the Marauders, but the Deacons still found no holes in the Marauder defense.

The first goal fell while Erik, Nick, and Will were on the bench. Abbey hit a ball to Jackson, who booted it to Parker on the wing. Parker collected it awkwardly and dribbled down the wing until two Deacon defenders converged on him. With a bit of luck, Parker managed to knock a pass through their legs toward Mario standing at the eighteen-yard line.

Most forwards who receive the ball near the goal with just one man to beat will assume the challenge of scoring themselves. But Mario was not greedy for glory, and he had three characteristics that the Deacon defenders were not aware of. First, he was a minimalist; he liked the soft touch, the half turn, the feint. Second, he was deceptive. In fact, he was deceptively deceptive; he was much more deceptive than people expected. And third, he was unselfish, sometimes to a detrimental degree.

But there was no detriment in that moment. As the Dover defender raced to challenge him, Mario noticed Matty running in from his left half position, and he let the ball roll though his legs untouched. With the defenders drawn to Mario, Matty had the ball all to himself twelve yards from the net. He hit the shot in stride, and the ball cannoned off his foot into the upper left hand corner, nicking the side bar and caroming in before the goalie even moved.

The crowd cheered and Matty and Mario were ecstatic, but the rest of the team kept their cool, exchanging only the formalities. They were still pretending not to be enjoying themselves. On the bench, Erik began to wonder if this professional approach wasn't what was missing all along. Perhaps the team's success was the result of not letting their personalities get in their way of their soccer.

Whatever the reason, the Blue Marauders continued to play well—even without Nick, Will, and Erik—and a second goal fell just before halftime, off a weak shot from Leon that deflected off a defender and through the goalkeeper's hands. This second goal shattered the spirit of the Dover Deacons, and when the halftime whistle blew, they walked silently back to their bench. On the Marauder side, the players' attitudes also remained muted.

"That was maybe fifteen minutes of good soccer," J.T. said, "And the rest, a lot of kicking. I don't even count the second goal, which was only an accident. Kenny, Leon, and Matty come off. Erik, Nick, and Will, you will start in midfield for the second half. I want to see more passing, even when you are near their goal. Don't panic when you find a shot and remember the 4 v. 4. No more lucky goals like the last one."

Erik, Nick, and Will were feeling a little out of sorts, as they took the field, that the scoring in the first half had come entirely without them. But they took care of that in the second half, each adding a goal. The first of their goals, dribbled calmly into the net by Erik, even met with J.T.'s approval. The second, off a rocket shot by Will from the left corner of the eighteen-yard box, was a thing of indifference to J.T. "Anyone can hit a shot," he said. The third and final goal was the result of just three touches: a goal kick by Abbey, a knock-on header from Will, and Nick's nicely weighted chip over the goalkeeper rushing out to clear the ball. "It counts," J.T. said after the game, "But it is not the way we want to play. Too many vertical lines."

After the fifth goal, the Marauders passed the ball effortlessly around the field as they waited for the final whistle. After they shook hands with the Deacon players, the Blue Marauders congratulated each other. When Nick came up to Erik, he could see Erik's eyes shining. Nick grinned and put his hand out. Erik slapped it gently and said, "That, McCoy, is how to play soccer." Dylan, too, seemed over his funk. He had taken off his shirt, as usual, and was offering bear hugs all around.

J.T. spoke briefly after they had exchanged handshakes. "We have a game on Monday against Bedford. Make sure you arrange your ride so you can leave the minute school is over. You had some good moments today, but everything must go faster. BOOM, BOOM, BOOM." J.T. clapped his hands together quickly. "We will work on it at the next game, and in practice."

It was a less-than-enthusiastic summing up, but it did not dampen the excitement of Nick and the other Lancaster boys, as they ate a post-game lunch at Georgi's and relived the highlights of the match.

CHAPTER 15

Making Up is Hard to Do

Sunday, Nick woke up happy. His mother made pancakes and Nick and his sisters sat around eating and playing Sorry. Afterward, they watched cartoons until almost noon, when Nick's mother came in and clicked off the television.

"You've watched enough! Besides, the girls have to get ready for a play date. Don't you have any homework to do?"

Nick thought about it. He supposed he should start on his Egypt report at some point. But not on such a beautiful, gorgeous Sunday. "Not really. Anyway, I was planning on heading over to Erik's."

Nick called Erik and tried to invite himself over, but Erik's sister was hosting a Girl Scout event, and Erik was trying to get out of the house.

"How about Dylan?" asked Nick.

Dylan lived alone with his mother in a small house in western Lancaster, near the Warrick town line. With his father mostly out of the picture, and no siblings, Dylan and his mother relied on each other as friends and companions. They cooked and gardened and played games together. When his mother was working, and Dylan couldn't arrange visits to friend's houses, he filled his time with hobbies. He built model airplanes, collected coins, or did woodworking projects in his basement.

When Nick and Erik arrived, a little after one o'clock, Dylan and his mother were playing Gin Rummy. Apologizing to Dylan's mother for dragging her son away, the boys went out to the backyard to throw a baseball around. Nick asked Dylan if he'd spoken to Tabitha recently.

"Yeah, we talked after the game last night. She gave me heck, of course, but I could tell she was kinda on our side."

"What do you mean, our side?" Erik asked.

"About Kenny, of course. She has no idea what Abbey sees in him."

"She's not alone," Nick said.

"You know I talked to him," Erik said. "Kenny."

"You did?"

"I ran into him at the movies last night. We got talking about the game. He loved Mario's dummy on the first goal. Anyway, I told him we were sorry about what happened at the dance. I mean, what we did was really totally uncool."

Erik waited a beat to see if Nick or Dylan would disagree, but they didn't.

"So what did he say?" Dylan asked.

"Oh, he was a jerk, of course. He said it was okay, that he was used to people being jealous of him."

"Man!" Dylan said.

"Then I asked him if he really believed it when he talks about how bad the team is. You know what he said? He said he actually liked playing with us. Because there's less pressure. Because no one expects us to win."

"Hah!" Nick said. "I expect us to win. Playing like we are, we'll win the rest of our games."

Erik looked at him skeptically. "We have to play the four best teams in the league. Thunder Green is undefeated, and Winchester has lost only one game. It's a pretty tall order to win them all."

"Pretty much impossible," Dylan agreed. "I'd be happy just to throw a scare in 'em."

Nick knew that the Marauders could do more than scare the big teams. When they played soccer the way J.T. wanted them to, they were really, really good. But it was no use insisting. Instead he said, "If Kenny enjoys playing for the Marauders, he sure has a funny way of showing it."

"That's what he said. Maybe he was just being polite."

Dylan and Nick shook their heads at that. Kenny wasn't famous for his politeness.

"Anyway," Erik continued, "he asked for a ride to the game tomorrow. His mom and dad are out of town, and we have to drive through Milford to get to Bedford. So I said no problem."

"Has anyone talked to Abbey?" Nick asked. "Do you think she's cool now?"

"I talked to Jamie," Dylan said. "He stopped by her house, but she wasn't around. I think she's still pretty upset."

"Man, Jamie is the one I feel worst about," Nick said. "Let's call him and see if he wants to come over."

"I gotta work on my Egypt report," Dylan replied. "My mom's taking me over to the library later. I promised I'd do a couple of hours on it today."

"But it's not due for ages."

"Are you kidding, Nicky?" Erik said. "It's due in eight days. Three to five pages—typed. Just the bibliography took a week."

Erik had a point, but he was always uptight about deadlines, and Nick shrugged it off. "At least let's play something, then, before we have to work."

So the boys played Pickle, which turned into a game of 1000, which turned into a keep-away, which turned into kill the carrier, until Dylan's mother said it was just about time to go and offered Nick and Erik a ride home.

Back home, Nick thought about starting his report, but decided to see if his dad needed some help with the raking first.

ON MONDAY, THE schoolyard was mostly back to normal. Only Abbey and Yvonne remained distant and standoffish.

Fortunately, Mr. DeMille was in a lecturing mood. In math class that morning, he gave a long talk on adding and subtracting in different bases, leaving Nick free to watch the two girls. Abbey sat slumped in her chair near the door, her long legs splayed in front of her. She didn't take notes, but she was paying attention. Yvonne, in the front row, sat with a straight back and took careful notes. One nice thing about DeMille's lectures, Nick realized, was that he spent a lot of time at the backboard, with his back to the class. And that made it easy to pass notes.

Nick thought carefully about who should receive the first note. He'd known Abbey longer, but he figured Yvonne would be madder if he wrote Abbey first. So he picked Yvonne. The note said simply: "Hey, are we cool?"

Nick watched as Yvonne opened the note and looked around furtively. She caught Nick's eye, almost smiled, but then shook her head firmly. "No," she mouthed to him.

Nick sent another note. "Aww, come on! I'm sorry we ruined your party. Let's go to the movies Saturday." As it was being passed, Nick also sent a note to Abbey, "Yo! Can't say I'd vote for Kenny for Mayor but SORRY!"

There was no reaction from either girl to these notes because Mr. DeMille had turned to face the class in order to emphasize a point. As soon as he turned his back to the board, Nick sent two more notes. To Yvonne: "We can ask Jennifer and Erik if you want." And to Abbey: "We were stupid. Think we can shut out Bedford today? They scored seven last time."

By this time, the class had become more involved in passing the notes than in listening to Mr. DeMille's lecture on Base 2. DeMille sensed the restlessness and whirled around from the board just as the last notes were received.

"What is going on?" he fumed. The class looked at him innocently. He eyed his students but could not uncover their secrets. "Whatever it is, stop! I am laying out the fundamentals of the whole next unit. If you miss it you will be behind from the start. And some of you," he looked directly at Nick, "cannot afford to get behind!"

As Mr. DeMille went back to the board, both Abbey and Yvonne turned to Nick and mouthed the word "Stop!" Abbey even drew a finger across her throat in dramatic fashion. But Nick just smiled and prepared two new notes.

This time Yvonne took the note but Abbey refused it. Leon was insistent, and when she wouldn't accept it, he lobbed it gently onto her desk. As he did so, Mr. DeMille twirled around in the middle of writing an equation, saw the note flying through the air, and yelled out in triumph, "Hah!"

Startled, Yvonne jumped, unwisely drawing Mr. DeMille's attention to her tightly closed fist.

"Ms. Stephens and Ms. Martin! Passing notes are we?"

"No, sir. I am just receiving them," Abbey said sullenly.

"And what is that you hold, Ms. Martin? May I see?"

Reluctantly, Yvonne opened her fist and revealed the note.

"I must say I am disappointed that two such normally fine students feel it necessary to disrupt the class like this. Let's see what's so important that it can't wait until the end of class. Read us your note, Ms. Stephens. You'll be next, Ms. Martin."

"I'd rather not," Abbey said.

"Stand up and read, Ms. Stephens." Mr. DeMille waited, with every sign of enjoying her discomfort. "Or we'll be here all day."

Abbey stood up slowly and opened the last note. Scanning it

before reading, she blushed. "I really don't think I should read it, Mr. DeMille."

"Perhaps you should have considered that before. Please read."

Abbey took a deep breath and read the note without expression. "'Don't you think Mr. D. has the cutest legs?'"

There was silence. Mr. DeMille's face was unreadable. The room was filled with the tension of suppressed mirth.

"And your note, Ms. Martin?" Mr. DeMille said, tightly.

Yvonne looked at it. "It's similar," she said.

"Read it!" Mr. DeMille said.

"It says, 'Mr. D. has totally dreamy eyes.' I didn't write it," Yvonne added quickly.

"Nor did I," said Abbey almost as quickly.

Mr. DeMille coughed, and a giggle ran through class. "Passing notes is inappropriate, whatever the content. The two of you can stay in at recess this morning and clean the classroom. Now, sit down, and let's return to the subject of bases." The class erupted in laughter.

Nick raised his hand. "Yes, Mr. McCoy. Do you have something to add?"

"I passed a note too. Should I stay in for recess?"

"Yes," Mr. DeMille snapped. "Would anyone else like to stay in, or can we get back to our subject?"

No one else volunteered, and Mr. DeMille returned to his exposition of adding in Base 2.

After class, the other kids filed out for morning recess until only Nick, Yvonne, and Abbey were left. Mr. DeMille looked at them sternly for just a few seconds and then said, "Well, I have some copying to get done, and I need a cup of coffee. I expect to see this place neat as a pin when I return."

As soon as he left, Abbey and Yvonne turned on Nick. "What the hell are you doing?"

"Hey, I was just trying to find a way to talk to two of my favorite people on the planet."

"You got us in trouble!" Yvonne said.

"Staying in for recess is hardly trouble."

"Yes it is. I've never had to do it before."

"Me neither," said Abbey.

"You guys have never stayed in for recess? What about when you miss a homework assignment?"

"I always do my homework," Yvonne said.

"So do I," said Abbey.

"You've never lost it or forgot it at home or something?"

Abbey and Yvonne looked at each other. "Never happens," Yvonne said for both of them.

"Wow," Nick said, simply. "Hey, we better start cleaning up before De Pill comes back and throws a fit."

"What do we have to do?" Abbey asked.

"Erase the board. Wipe off the tables. Run the carpet sweeper around the rug. That kind of thing."

"Aren't you even going to apologize?" said Yvonne.

"Okay, okay. So I'm sorry. But at least you guys are talking to me." Nick began to put chairs up on the tables, "So, Yvonne, what do you say? You want to get a group together for the movies in Milford on Saturday?"

Yvonne had begun to erase the board. "Maybe. I'll ask my mom. I could see if Jen and Sylvia want to come."

"What about you and Kenny, Abs?"

"What about *us*?" Abbey was wetting a sponge at the sink, preparing to wipe down the tables.

"Come to the movies with us. It'll be cool. Maybe we'll run into some of the Thunder Green crowd, still stinging from the hurt we put on them that morning."

"You know that's the Saturday before our Egypt report is due?"

"Oh, darn," Yvonne said. "We'll have to do it some other time."

"We can't work all Saturday," Nick protested.

"No, because there's a soccer game in the morning," Abbey replied.

"So we study in the afternoon and go to the movies at night. We can get Mexican at Taco Joe's before the show."

"When do you work, Nick?" Yvonne asked.

"Oh, now and then. It all gets done. Did you see the look on De Pill's face when you read your note? It was priceless!"

Yvonne grimaced. "His eyes are definitely *not* dreamy. They're like fish eyes. And his glasses make them bug out of his face."

"I had to talk about his *legs*," said Abbey. "As if I go around staring at his butt the whole time. That is sooo gross."

"Do you think he thought we meant it?" Yvonne asked.

"What a horrible idea! And it's all Nicky's fault."

Without warning, Abbey launched a wet sponge at Nick, hitting him right in the chest. He put his arms up to protest and was hit full in the face by Yvonne's chalky board eraser. He tripped over a desk, fell on the floor, and lay on the carpet, laughing.

"Come on," Abbey said, picking up the trash can filled with wet paper towels. "Let's do some damage." They moved to stand over Nick. Abbey showered him with wads of wet paper towels while Yvonne pelted him with bits of chalk. The girls took turns while Nick rolled around on the floor, half trying to shield himself, and half daring them to hit him.

No one heard Mr. DeMille enter into the classroom until he roared, "WHAT IS GOING ON HERE?"

Yvonne quickly put on her most innocent voice. "I'm sorry, Mr. DeMille. We were cleaning up, and this boy started attacking us. We asked him to stop, but he wouldn't."

Abbey took the straight-man role. "It's true, sir. Yvonne was wiping the board when Nick just started throwing stuff. We were trying to clean up." She held up her waste-paper basket to show that she was trying to clean up. She put the wet wad of paper that she was holding in her other hand into the basket. "See."

"I have no doubt about who caused the trouble," Mr. DeMille said. "Go on outside, girls. I'll deal with this."

On the way out the door, Yvonne and Abbey took the chance, with Mr. DeMille's back turned, to exchange a silent high five. Then Yvonne looked back at Nick and stuck her tongue out. Abbey grinned at him.

It wasn't until lunch that Abbey and Yvonne found out what fate they had left Nick to. "He said I had to stay after school for two hours. To help the janitorial crew."

It took a second for Yvonne to see the impact of this, but Abbey saw it right away. "But we have a game today!"

"Yeah, I told him. I asked if I could stay for two hours tomorrow, but you know DeMille, that just made him happier. He says it will help me learn a lesson.'"

Abbey put her hand on his. "I'm so sorry, Nicky. I had no idea."

Yvonne said, "We were just playing. We never thought you'd miss a game."

"I know. I don't mind what you did. I just wish DeMille didn't hate me so much."

The news spread quickly. "We'll never beat Bedford without you," Leon said.

Erik shook his head. "We were just getting on the right track. This'll completely muck up any chance for the playoffs."

"We still have a chance at the playoffs?" Gabe asked. "Didn't we have the worst record in the league?"

This launched a long discussion of team standings. Erik explained that, if the Marauders won the rest of their games, they could overtake Bedford and the Thunder Red, assuming those teams lost both their games against the league leaders, Thunder Green and Winchester.

"We just have to win all the rest of our games? That's a big *if*," Will commented.

"Well, we won't make it if we don't beat Bedford," Erik said.

THE REST OF the day was excruciating.

"Could you call your parents?" Dylan asked at lunch. "Your dad is cool. He'll talk to DeMille."

Nick shrugged. "He's on a job. Only my mom's around."

"What about J.T.?" But even as he asked, Dylan knew that J.T. wouldn't get involved, and so did everyone else.

"You could sneak out," Gabe said.

"Hoo boy. You really want to get me in trouble. DeMille would try to ban me for the season. And my mom would likely go along with it."

"There are ways," Gabe said, mysteriously. But he would not explain further, and his teammates assumed he was just talking big.

As the end of the day approached, Nick and Erik huddled together talking tactics as the other kids got their stuff ready to go. "You can win without me," Nick said. "You did before. Make sure Will covers their center middie. And if J.T. plays you at halfback, push up and do some give-and-gos with Kenny."

When the final bell rang, Nick watched disconsolately as his friends and teammates marched out of the classroom.

Mr. DeMille, who had been grading papers at his desk, stood up. "No need to be glum, Mr. McCoy. I am sure you will have a lovely time helping Brian and Jeannette clean the toilets." He looked at his watch. "It is 3:10 now. I will take you over to the cleaning staff, and they will show you what you need to do. At 5:10, they will bring you back to me, and we will inspect your work. Assuming that it is satisfactory, you will be free to go. And we will hope that you have learned something about the difficulty of keeping the school in working order." Mr. DeMille grinned. "Is that satisfactory to you?"

Nick nodded, his face flushed and furious.

"Perhaps you can use this time to your advantage," Mr. DeMille said. "As you clean, you can think through what you plan to say in your Egypt report. It is due in one week, so I assume you must have plenty of ideas by now."

Nick looked down. He would not respond to De Pill's provocations. Together they walked down the long school corridor toward the custodial station. Their footsteps rang out in the empty hallway, the sharp clicks of Mr. DeMille's loafers contrasting with the squeaks of Nick's battered sneakers. As they passed the main entrance to the school, they heard a third set of footsteps coming up behind them, loud pops of hard boots marching in a determined fashion. They turned around to see Officer Drybzyck, in full uniform, bearing down on them.

"Is this the miscreant?" Officer Drybzyck asked curtly. He towered over both the short Mr. DeMille and the thirteen-year-old Nick.

"Yes, yes," Mr. DeMille replied, "I have assigned him to detention today. He attacked some girls and made a mess of the classroom in the process."

"It's good someone's taking a firm hand with the boy, Mr. DeMille."

"My thoughts exactly, Officer."

"Okay, I'll take him now. Come on, McCoy. Follow me."

"What are you doing?" Mr. DeMille asked.

"Taking him down to the station."

"I'm not sure that's necessary. This is a school matter."

"Assault is a serious matter, Mr. DeMille. And bullying is a public safety issue. Come along, McCoy." He grabbed Nick's arm and began to lead him away.

"Officer, you can't just come here and take boys out of school!" Mr. DeMille squeaked, hurrying to catch up with them.

Officer Drybzyck stopped suddenly and turned around, causing Mr. DeMille to bump into his chest. "Listen, Mr. DeMille. As I said, I appreciate your taking a hard line with the boys. But public safety is my concern, and I won't be interfered with. I have a zero-tolerance policy when it comes to bullying."

"But I've already talked to his mother. She's going to pick him up here," said Mr. DeMille. "You can't just take the boy away."

"Are you going to stop me?" Officer Drybzyck looked both calm and threatening.

Mr. DeMille was flustered. "At least let me talk to the principal. Maybe I can follow you down to the station and bring him back when you are done."

"Fine, go talk. But we don't need you at the station. I'll contact the boy's parents."

Mr. DeMille hesitated, not wanting to leave Nick alone. Finally, he said, "Wait here. I'll be back." And he turned and hurried toward the principal's office.

"All I did was throw some paper and chalk," Nick said nervously. "We weren't really fighting. We were having fun. Normal kid stuff."

"Go get your bag, and hurry," Officer Drybzyck replied. "We're leaving now."

After Nick returned with his things, Officer Drybzyck donned his sunglasses and pointed him to the school's main entrance. "Lead the way!"

"Aren't we meant to wait for Mr. DeMille?"

"He thinks so! But I happen to know Principal Snowe is gone for the day. Come on!"

They marched quickly into the parking lot and over to Officer Drybzyck's patrol car. Office Drybzyck locked Nick in the back and then went around to the driver's seat. Just as he was climbing in, Mr. DeMille came running out of the school doors.

"Officer Drybzyck, wait!" He hurried over to the patrol car's driver-side window. "Principal Snowe is out. But I really think . . . ."

He got no further. Officer Drybzyck started the car and gunned the engine, drowning out any chance of further protest. Then he drove away.

After turning out of the school driveway, Officer Drybzyck lowered the bullet-proof glass window separating the front and back seats and said to Nick, "You change while I drive."

"What do you mean, change?" Nick asked.

"For the game, of course! When Gabe told me what happened, I sent him and Terry along with Mr. Steiner." Officer Drybzyck looked at his watch. "We should just about be able to make it." He turned the siren on and flashed Nick a grin. "Maybe we'll beat them there."

NICK AND OFFICER Drybzyck did not, in fact, beat the other Marauders to the Bedford fields, mostly because Officer Drybzyck took a wrong turn in Bedford and was out the other side of the town before he realized it. He had to double back to find the road to Pelham Commons, and it was another three miles along a dirt road before they reached the fields.

The road ran along a ridge overlooking the Siennahunk River, and from the parking lot for the Pelham Commons, you had a stupendous view of the fields, the river, and the rolling farmland below. Nick did not stop to admire it. They had arrived just five minutes before game time, and Nick sprinted down the steep wooden stairs leading toward the fields.

Because he was late, Nick had missed the sight of J.T. being greeted by Bedford's Coach Rush fifteen minutes earlier. The Marauders had been warming up with 4 v. 1 drills, and J.T. was alone on the visitors' bench, finishing his sandwich, when a tall, slim man in a coat and tie had come over and extended his hand. "It's not Coach Steiner, is it?"

J.T. had wiped his fingers on his pants and stood up. "No, Tielemans. Jan Tielemans." They shook hands.

"Aah, right. I remember Steiner was a taller, paler chap. I'm Benjamin Rush, the Bedford coach. So you're in charge of this lot now?"

"I am the manager."

"Good. Well, it looks like you got here okay. We'll start in five minutes, if that is agreeable. It begins to get dark early these days."

"Yes, fine."

"I see you've had some improvement lately. Mostly wins against the minnows but, still, congratulations on the progress. I hope we'll have a good game today."

"I think we will."

"I won't push my boys too hard."

"Play as hard as you wish."

"By the way, I mentioned to your predecessor that I run a camp for new coaches." Coach Rush had produced a card and handed it to J.T. "The next session's in April. There's a lot of good pointers on building a team. Feel free to give me a call if you'd like to sign up."

AS NICK RAN into the huddle, J.T. paused and stared at him. "So you are here. They told me you weren't coming."

"I'm here," Nick said.

J.T. frowned. "This is something to discuss later. For now, same positions and the same starting team as last time." The referee blew his whistle twice to indicate it was time to begin the game. "Referees always want to rush people," J.T. said, not rushing. "These boys are not bad. They play disciplined soccer. Be aware that the midfielders do not usually carry the ball a long way on the dribble. They like to keep the ball on the ground and switch the field quickly. They look for space on the wings where the defense has over-shifted. What does that tell us?"

No one answered.

"It tells us the importance of maintaining shape. This does *not* mean standing in one place like a scarecrow! It means movement in unison. You must communicate with your teammates and cover for each other."

The referee blew his whistle again. "Look, think, pass. Now go!"

As before, the Marauders made their way onto the field without the customary cheer. This time, no one complained about their positions. As they jogged out, Gabe punched Nick in the arm, "My dad sprung you, hey?"

On Nick's other side, Erik said, "Hey, Nick. You know what it means? What J.T. just said?" Nick shrugged, and Erik lowered his voice. "He couldn't have seen our first game against Bedford. He'd never even heard of us back then. He had to have watched one of their games."

"So?"

"Don't you get it? It means he's scouting for us. He must have gone to Bedford's game against Braeburn last Friday."

Nick was tempted to ask how Erik knew Bedford's schedule, but he figured it was a stupid question. This was Erik. He'd probably memorized all the schedules before the season began. Then the game started, and all further thoughts were driven from Nick's head.

On attack, Bedford moved the ball fluidly along the ground from the defenders to the three quick midfielders, and then back and forth across the field, much as J.T. said they would. But Nick, Will, and Erik were quick enough to challenge each pass, and with Abbey's sharp eyes and even sharper instructions to her defense, the Blue Marauders did not provide the openings that the Bedford midfielders were used to seeing.

Meanwhile, the Marauders were able to exert their own pressure on attack. Erik soon realized that his defender couldn't take the ball away from him, and as the other defenders ran to double him, they left big spaces to work in. Nothing was easier to hit the ball safely over to Will, or to find Matty or Leon breaking forward, ever deeper into Bedford territory.

The first goal came in the seventeenth minute, when Erik executed a give-and-go with Leon in the penalty area and hammered a shot home about ten yards out. A second fell only moments later, after Nick intercepted a weak pass and ran through the middle of the defense. When he was finally challenged, he touched the ball over to Erik on his left, causing the anxious Bedford players to surge en masse over to Erik's side of the field. Instead of dribbling, Erik one timed a chip back over to Kenny coming in from the right wing. Kenny collected the ball in stride and slotted it effortlessly past the goalie.

Even when Erik, Nick, and Will went out, and Kenny, Leon, and Matty moved to midfield, the defense remained organized enough to keep Bedford out of the goal, although the danger of the Marauder attack faded. And the score remained 2–0.

At halftime, J.T. praised the team's defensive shape and asked for more patience in building up the attack. "We know we can stop them," he said. "We have nothing to fear. So now we must take our time. Move the ball around and look for the right opportunities. Bedford will try to run at you in the second half to take advantage of their numbers. Play your triangles and let them run."

Erik looked around as J.T. talked and was amazed to see the change that had taken place. Everyone was focused on what J.T. said. Even Gabe and Kenny. Erik could hardly believe this was the same Marauder team that had been embarrassed by Bedford less than a month ago. Now the Bedford players were chasing them, and the Marauders dominated even when he and Nick and Will were on the bench.

For the beginning of the second half, J.T. left Mario, Parker, and Terry at forward and put Erik, Will, and Nick back in at midfield.

J.T. explained that Gabe, Jackson, and Dylan would start the second half playing defense in front of Abbey, but they'd be replaced by Leon, Kenny, and Matty after twenty minutes. Abbey would remain in at sweeper and Jamie at goalkeeper.

"Abbey played all of last game," Gabe protested, but without heat.

"I don't mind coming out," Abbey said.

"No," J.T. said. "I leave you in. It is calming for me. Sweeper is like goalkeeper. It is useful to have consistency. Now, go!"

The second half unfolded as J.T. predicted. Bedford cycled players in and out, running aggressively at the Marauders. In the early going, the Marauders struggled with the speed of the defenders, and the Red Demons stole some passes and created several opportunities for themselves. Jamie was tested several times, and had to make one great save to tip a shot over the crossbar and keep Bedford scoreless.

"We need to pass and move," Erik yelled as Bedford prepared for a corner. "Possession."

The corner floated in and Gabe headed it straight up in the air. In the melee that followed, Nick came out with the ball and dribbled it quickly up the field. The Bedford midfielders, who had flooded the penalty box for the corner, were racing back to catch up with him. The Bedford defenders, who had pushed past midfield, dropped back quickly too, worried about a pass over their heads. But once Nick crossed into the Bedford half, he slowed and let the Bedford midfield and defense, sprinting back as hard as they could, run past him. He turned and passed back to Erik, who found himself alone in the midfield. He held the ball motionless under his foot and looked around. Finally the Bedford attackers, who had been walking back from the Marauder penalty box, started to jog toward him. Erik waited until they had almost reached midfield before knocking the ball firmly back to Dylan, standing in the left wing-back position.

Having run up for the corner, and run back on defense, the Bedford players were hesitant to run back to the Marauder goal. So they approached slowly while Dylan and Abbey knocked the ball back and forth. When they began to threaten, Abbey knocked the ball over to Jackson, who hit it up to Will. Will gave one of his grins and imitated Erik, holding the ball under his feet. Everyone on the field was getting a nice rest, except possibly Nick, who ran back and forth to make sure that everyone who touched the ball had a pass to him if they got in trouble.

The Blue Marauders had regained control and now found they were able to hold the ball even as they moved deep into Bedford's half. But the crowd this created in the Bedford penalty box made it difficult to score.

It was Nick who found the solution. He locked eyes with Erik as he dribbled left to right across the top of the penalty box, drawing several defenders with him. When Erik cut hard behind him, Nick somehow slipped his right foot under the ball, turning a half circle away from his markers, and flicked it up and across the penalty box, so that it floated over the Red Demons massed around him, and arced down just inside the six-yard box, and just over Erik's right shoulder as he emerged from the crowd. Erik chested the ball to his left foot and smashed a volley back across the mouth of the goal into the far side of the net for 3–0.

When the Red Demons scored off a lazy mistake just before the final whistle, it did nothing to diminish the Marauders' satisfaction with the result.

J.T. seemed less happy. As the team huddled after the game, he spoke only of the last-minute lapse. "You have to play the whole game. I have seen many losses in the last five minutes. Tiredness is not an excuse. Be tired later, but first win the game. Go shake hands. Nick, I will talk with you afterward."

As the team shook hands, Benjamin Rush came over to J.T. "Well,

well," he said, and looked J.T. over in an appraising sort of way.

"Your boys play well," J.T. said. "But your midfielders should not be afraid to push the ball forward. Too much passing. It's predictable."

"What did you say your name was?"

"Jan Tielemans."

"Dutch?"

"American now."

Coach Rush nodded. "You certainly have coached your boys up a bit."

"Aach, no. I just remove some of the constraints on them."

"Yes, I can see that too," Coach Rush said, then moved away without shaking hands as the Marauders returned to collect their belongings.

J.T. looked around to make sure he was not forgetting anything. He had a bag with several catalogs from Bedford galleries he had visited earlier in the day. He took the old sandwich wrapper out of his pocket and put it in the bag. Then he watched the kids take off their cleats and pull on their sweats. After a few minutes, Nick approached. "You wanted to see me?"

"Why were you delayed?"

Nick hesitated before deciding the truth was simplest. "Mr. DeMille gave me detention at school, but Gabe's dad took me out of it."

"With the teacher's permission?"

"Well . . . it's complicated. Officer Drybzyck sort of gave the impression that he was taking me to the police station, but he took me here instead." J.T. did not say anything.

"But I didn't do anything bad," Nick added. "It was the girls. Mr. DeMille just misunderstood. You can ask Abbey."

"That is not my business. But I suggest you speak to your teacher and serve your detention tomorrow. I will not expect you at practice."

CHAPTER 16

Thunder Green II

Nick tried to put the whole DeMille detention matter out of his mind. The Blue Marauders had just crushed Bedford and, if they won the rest of their games, had a decent shot at making the playoffs. They could not catch the Thunder Green team or Winchester, but if the Marauders won out, and Winchester beat the Thunder Red, they might be in.

Of course, as Leon pointed out, they still had to beat the three best teams in the league. Thunder Green had lost only once and Winchester's only two losses were to the Thunder Green. The Thunder Red had four losses, but were the only team to have beaten the Thunder Green, and had beaten the Marauders 7–0 last time out. So winning out still seemed like a long shot.

These calculations kept Nick's mind away from nasty questions about what De Pill might have learned about him playing soccer yesterday, and the even more difficult question of whether he should tell De Pill the truth. At least until the end of science period, as the rest of the class headed out to recess, and Mr. DeMille said, "Please stay behind, Mr. McCoy."

Nick watched his classmates file out with a sense of doom. He quickly tried to evaluate the pros and cons of being honest with

DeMille. Besides all the other issues, like the possibility of being banned from soccer for the rest of the season, he would feel like he was telling on a grown-up. He didn't want to get Officer Drybzyck in trouble.

"Nicholas, I want to talk with you about yesterday. I did reach Principal Snowe, and she agreed with me that it was entirely inappropriate for Officer Drybzyck to take you into custody. Unfortunately, the officer drove away before I could do anything, and when I went down to the station I was told that you had been taken elsewhere. Try as I might, I could not get any further information. Are you all right?"

"I'm fine, Mr. DeMille," Nick said, surprised by his teacher's tack.

"Good. And you sure you were not mistreated in any manner? He had no right to threaten you."

"He didn't."

"Well, that's a relief. I'll put that in my report to Principal Snowe."

"Uhhh, Mr. DeMille . . . ."

"Yes, Nicholas? Understand, you can tell me anything. I oppose tyranny in all its forms."

"The truth is . . . he took me to the soccer game. I didn't know he was going to do it, I swear. It was a complete surprise. But that's what happened."

Mr. DeMille looked confused and then was silent a long moment. "Well, well, well. I see. I was played the fool."

"I thought maybe I could serve my detention today," said Nick. "If that's okay, I mean. I guess I should take my punishment."

Mr. DeMille nodded his head several times, as if mulling something over, but he did not pursue the thought out loud. "Abuse of power is an ugly thing, is it not? On the other hand, I do believe you are blameless in this matter, Nicholas. And I am sorry you have been caught up in it. I think serving your detention this afternoon would be acceptable. Or we could skip it altogether if you felt . . . ."

Mr. DeMille trailed off, with uncustomary uncertainty in his voice.

"No, sir. It's okay."

"That's settled then."

"Thanks, Mr. DeMille," Nick said. "Can I go to recess now?"

"Certainly, Nicholas. Go along."

THAT AFTERNOON NICK mopped floors and emptied waste-baskets with the cleaning staff while the rest of the team played soccer. When he was done, he raced down to Caton's Field on his bicycle, hoping to catch the tail end of practice. But as he rode up, the team was already taking off their cleats.

"What's up?" Nick cried as he ran over. "There's fifteen minutes left."

"Come," J.T. said. "Tomorrow you play your third game in six days. So we have a light practice. I want to discuss what you must expect from the Green Thunder."

"Have you been scouting them?" Erik asked.

"I saw them play last week. They over-rely on their central mid-fielder. He's fast and big, with good control."

"I marked him out of the game last time," Nick said.

"You?" said Kenny. "I marked him the whole second half."

"Yeah, and we lost 6–1," Erik said. "So both of you just shut up and listen."

J.T. nodded at Erik. "Thank you. This boy is a strong player, but they have many good players, and the team is the best you have played by a good measure. But the Marauders will win. You will be the better team tomorrow."

Erik looked around at the team as J.T. talked. Thirteen seventh graders and one eighth grader. The cadaverous Parker, the tall and clumsy Jackson, the diffident Mario, the inexperienced Terry, the overconfident Gabe, the inconsistent Dylan. Erik tried to see what J.T. saw.

"In attack, Green Thunder play mostly one-on-one. Stay back and let them come to you. Force them to the outside. When help comes, switch and push them to the inside help." Dancing in his tweed jacket and green Wellington boots, J.T. crouched down to demonstrate how he wanted the defenders to move, and for the first time the team glimpsed the fierce and relentless footballer he must have been.

"If they hit a cross or through ball, Abbey will see to those. Correct?" Abbey nodded.

"Midfielders, don't get caught up. They will win their share of loose balls and you must be ready to cover. Keep the ball in front of you, and they don't score. Then you just have to break down their defense. Stay fluid in possession and your movement will confuse them. They concentrate their defense where the ball is. Keep changing sides, and the goals will come." J.T. looked around. The players were silent, hanging on his words. "Now, go get your homework done."

The players watched as J.T. left the field.

"You think he really believes it?" Jamie asked.

"Sure. Don't you?" Erik responded.

"It sounds good when he says it."

"He's right. We can beat 'em," Kenny said, unexpectedly, pausing as he stuffed his cleats and shin guards into his bag.

"What?" said Dylan. "Suddenly you're on our side?"

"Give it a rest, Dyl," Erik said.

"Hey, man, I'm just joshing around. Kenny knows that, right? I'm never serious."

"The sad thing is, you're never funny either," Kenny said, snorting at his own joke and then heading to the parking lot feeling like he had had the last word.

The team watched Kenny leave in silence. When he had slammed the door of his mother's Mercedes, Abbey said, "Hey, what about what we talked about before practice?"

"You mean about Nick?" Erik said.

Suddenly the whole team turned to look at Nick. "What?" he asked, feeling surrounded.

"How much of your Egypt paper have you done?" Erik asked.

"What does that have to do with anything?"

"A lot. We want to win the rest of the games, and we don't want you jeopardizing that because Mr. DeMille suspends you for not getting your work done."

"Come on," said Nick.

"How much have you written?" Erik insisted.

"I have some of it done."

"Beyond the bibliography?" asked Leon.

"No, but have any of you started writing?" Nick looked around. Everyone was nodding.

"We're assigning you a study partner every day to make sure you do your work," Erik said.

"Oh, for crying out loud!" Nick said.

Will laughed. "I'm on tonight. Angie and Dad have an event at Angie's school, so I'm free."

"Will?" Nick said, looking around at the others. "Come on! He's just as much of a slacker as I am."

"It's for your own good, Nicky," Abbey said. "And the team's."

"Where do you want to study?" Will asked. "Your house or mine? I'm easy as long as we have plenty of food on hand."

Nick looked resigned. "My house, I guess."

WILL AND NICK managed to get some work done, between video games and a lot of chatter, and Nick was relieved to have his project started. He went to school the next day feeling quite virtuous.

Erik greeted him at the playground. "Nick, I'm on for tonight."

"On for what?"

"Studying. We can have supper at my house and work after."

"Yeah, Erik, nice to see you too. How come with the biggest game of the year, maybe the decade, coming this afternoon, all you can talk about is my homework?"

Erik shrugged. "Just trying to keep you on the team. We have other big games after this one."

"Yeah, but if we lose this, we won't make the playoffs anyway."

"I'm just planning for the win."

"Way to get me psyched up!" Nick said sourly.

BUT NICK DIDN'T need Erik to get psyched up. Everyone in the school was talking about the game against Thunder Green, even the teachers and the younger kids. Several first graders from his sisters' class came up to wish Nick good luck on the game. So did Mrs. Tate, the reading specialist, Mr. Graber, the librarian, and Ms. DeMarneffe, the French teacher.

Principal Snowe even interrupted Mr. DeMille's math class to tell the seventh graders that she would be rooting for them.

"That's great, Ms. Snowe," Dylan said. "We'll score an extra goal for you."

"I hope so, Dylan. The Milford principal and I have a little wager on the game."

"What are you betting?" Tabitha asked.

"Just T-shirts. A Lancaster shirt from the Village Store if they win. A Hereford shirt if they lose. So don't let me down."

Mr. DeMille was the only person who seemed uninterested in the game. When Principal Snowe exited, he shot a nasty look at the door and said, "Before we were interrupted, we were considering multiplication in Base 2." He paused. "Do please pay attention; we have a lot to get through. Sports are termed *extra*-curricular activities because they are intended to take time outside of our main curriculum. And I assure you, the ability to perform arithmetic operations in different bases will be significantly more important to you future careers than any recreational athletic events."

The class tittered nervously. It was not always clear when Mr. DeMille was making a joke.

BY THE TIME the final bell rang, the school was at a fever pitch. As the Marauders gathered by the main entrance, waiting for their rides down to the field, it felt as if everyone in town had come by to wish them luck.

Although the game didn't start until four o'clock, Caton's Field was already buzzing with life by the time the team arrived at three-thirty. The field was ready for soccer. Will's father had come by on his lunch hour to mow the grass and set up the corner flags. The grass was no longer a lush green, and there were muddy patches in front of both goals, but the field had survived the season remarkably well.

On their way from the parking lot, Erik and Dylan ran into Dan Caton, carrying his ancient folding chair out to the field.

"Hey, Mr. Caton," Erik said. "A good crowd."

Mr. Caton smiled, showing several missing teeth. "It's nice to have life back here."

"Can I carry your chair out for you, Mr. Caton?" Dylan asked.

The old man looked at him scornfully. "I'm not so ancient yet that I can't take care of myself. You save your energy for the game."

J.T. was on the bench already, eating his customary sandwich. For a change, however, he was not alone. Next to him was Rory Patenaude, and they were talking quietly.

J.T. nodded to acknowledge Erik and Dylan's arrival, "Don't exhaust yourselves warming up. We have half an hour before the game begins." Then he returned to his whispered conversation with Mr. Patenaude.

Erik sat on the ground changing into his cleats. He had not had a chance to relax and listen to music before the game, and now he had butterflies. He was thinking how much depended on this one game. Suddenly the Blue Marauders meant something in Lancaster, and the crowd was already bigger than the one they'd had at the Dover game. But they weren't playing Dover, they were playing the Thunder Green. What if they got blown out? Erik closed his eyes and felt sick to his stomach.

Eyes still closed, Erik heard a voice yelling. "Hey, Coach, what the hell is going on?"

Then he heard another voice, pleading and on the verge of tears: "Dad, please don't. Please!"

"Stop whining, Kenny!" Mr. Garrity said in a commanding tone. "What's going on, Coach?"

"Mr. Garrity," J.T. said evenly. "Is there a problem?"

Erik opened his eyes as J.T. stood up.

"I thought we had a deal! But I get back from LA yesterday, and I sit him down to hear how the soccer is going. Imagine my surprise when Kenny tells me he's playing right wing. My kid is a center-half, not a goddamn winger."

"He has done a fine job on the wing."

"Don't give me that. Kenny's an all-star. He's the only thoroughbred in your Mickey Mouse organization, and you stick him out in right field."

"Not right field, Mr. Garrity. Right wing. Soccer is not baseball."

"You know damn well what I mean! You're wasting his talent and hurting his career."

As Mr. Garrity spoke, he moved in closer to J.T., his tall, well-built frame looming over J.T.'s squat body, his finger inches from J.T.'s face. Mr. Garrity lowered his voice, but Erik still heard his fierce whisper. "I have a lot to offer you, Tielemans. But if you don't play ball, you're liable to make a dangerous enemy."

As Mr. Garrity's speech concluded, J.T. reached up and grabbed his wrist. It happened so quickly, Erik hardly noticed the movement. One moment, Mr. Garrity was standing over J.T. with a finger in his face, the next his wrist was in J.T.'s grasp. From afar it would have looked just like they were shaking hands. But up close, Erik could see Randy Garrity struggling to pull away while J.T. held him close. The only sign that J.T. was straining were the white knuckles on the hand that held Mr. Garrity.

"Put your finger in my face again, and I'll tear it off and stick it down your throat," J.T. said in a quietly terrifying voice.

Mr. Garrity shook his arm and again tried to pull back, but J.T. held him tight. "Let me tell you something about soccer. Your son is a nice player, and he has some potential. He has played well the last two games. You may have heard that we won them both."

"Let go! I'll have you on assault!"

J.T. did not let go. He seemed hardly to notice Mr. Garrity's efforts to free himself. "Your son is not the best player on *this* team by a long shot. That's no fault of his own. It's a talented team. Kenny has a chance to be a nice contributor and maybe learn a thing or two." J.T. exerted a slight extra pressure on Mr. Garrity's wrist so that his knees buckled, and his face was level with J.T.'s. "You should keep your mouth shut, and try not to screw it up for him." Then J.T. let go.

Mr. Garrity rubbed his wrist and stood up straight. "You have just made a very bad mistake." He turned around and called to Kenny, who was sitting over in the bleachers, putting on his cleats. "Follow me," he commanded. "Let's see how this team fares against the Thunder without you."

"But Dad," Kenny began.

"Not now Kenny! We're leaving."

Randy Garrity went over to take hold of his son, but Kenny ducked and dashed a little ways away. "I want to play."

Mr. Garrity took a deep breath. "You can play when you're on the Thunder."

"No, Dad. I want to play today," Kenny replied, backing further away as his father advanced on him.

"Don't be stupid. We'll discuss this at home."

"But we're good. You'll see," said Kenny, dashing further away as his father approached him again, and then moving to the middle of the field where the other Marauders were warming up.

Mr. Garrity paused to review his options. He would look foolish chasing his own son in front of the whole crowd. He took another deep breath and snarled at J.T., "I blame you for this!" Then he called to Kenny. "You'll make you own way home, son! And we'll have further words about this when you get there!"

J.T. didn't blink, but Erik saw that Kenny looked pale.

MEANWHILE, THE THUNDER Green team had arrived in a small bus. The players wore forest green warm-ups over their uniforms. Their jackets read "Thunder Green" in red letters across the front, and "Thirty Years of Championship Soccer" across the back. Underneath, their uniform shirts were green with a subtle red stripe, and there was red trim on the socks and shorts.

While the Thunder Green players got ready, their three coaches huddled together on the bench, reviewing notes and flipping through charts on their clipboards. When the head coach, tall, heavy, and completely bald, blew his whistle, his players rushed out and were quickly organized into a series of shooting and crossing drills overseen by the assistant coaches.

As they began to warm up, the head coach walked over to the Marauder bench. "So you're the new guy. I'm Charles Courtland." He stuck out his hand.

"Jan Tielemans," J.T. said, taking the hand.

"I'm hoping we can have a good clean game today. No rough stuff."

"Pardon?"

"Coach Scruggs is on the Sportsmanship Committee. He tells me there have been some complaints."

"There have been no fouling issues that I am aware of."

"I don't have the specifics. We just want everyone to dial down a notch. I've talked to the refs, and they're going to call a tight game. So tell your squad, and let's everyone keep it clean. Good luck, coach!"

Coach Courtland gave a thumb's up and moved back to his bench. J.T. stared after him, nodding his head in thought.

"What was that all about?" asked Rory, still standing next to him.

"A cheap trick," J.T. replied. "He wants me to tell the team that the game will be called close. So they pull back on tackles and are less active. Stupid gamesmanship."

"I had no idea youth soccer was so cutthroat," Rory said. "They're just kids."

"Yes. Particularly the adults," J.T. said.

AS FAR AS the Marauders had come, they still felt intimidated by the Thunder Green. Even as they warmed up, they couldn't help admiring the twenty green-clad opponents moving in precise, complex patterns to their coaches' whistles.

J.T. clapped his hands loudly to call them in.

He spoke first to Kenny. "Are you okay to play, boy?" Kenny nodded. On either side of him, Dylan and Terry clapped him on the shoulder.

"Let me tell you a story," J.T. continued. "I grew up in a little town in Holland called Arlese. We had a good soccer team. We played on the village green and beat teams from the surrounding villages. One day our coach arranged for us to play in a tournament in Rotterdam. That day we lost every game. Do you know why?

"We were not worse than our competitors. But when we stepped out into the big city stadium, we knew the other teams would beat us. We lost each game before the kick-off.

"You can decide right now to lose to this team. This Green Thunder. But you don't have to. Based on my knowledge of the game, I think you can beat them. Not *can* as in a million to one. I mean you should beat them. If you want to be, you are better than they are. It is for you to decide. Is this something you want?"

The kids did not respond at once. Finally, Gabe yelled, "Hell, yeah!" and the others confirmed with a series of whoops and claps.

"I am not saying it is easy. You cannot beat this team like you beat Dover, just by showing up. You need to play smart.

"Everyone must listen to Abbey on defense. Play compact, and let the ball go to the wings. They don't cross well.

"I am asking Will to mark their central midfielder. The boy dribbles too straight ahead. Hold your ground, and he won't beat you.

"In possession, we want the ball to go through the middle and then out to the wings. Leon, you will distribute the ball out to Kenny and Matty. Nick and Erik will be in support wherever the ball goes. Use them if you get into trouble.

"Now, are there any questions?"

There were none, and for once, the Blue Marauders took the field before their opponents. Then the referee blew his whistle, and the Thunder Green huddle broke up with a roar as their eleven starters sprinted out.

Leon took the kickoff. He tipped the ball to Will, who passed back to Gabe. The Thunder Green seemed to explode at the Marauders, and when Gabe bobbled the trap, he only just had time to smash the ball down the field and out of bounds before being overwhelmed. Erik gestured to Gabe to stay calm, but Gabe yelled back, "They're freakin' fast!"

The speed and aggressiveness of the Thunder Green team kept the Marauders off balance, and it was all they could do to force the Thunder attacks to the outside. The only Marauder counter came off a long clearance from Abbey. Kenny gathered the ball and made for the goal. But before he could get a shot off, he found himself surrounded by Thunder Green defenders, with nowhere to pass. Kenny lost the ball and gestured angrily at his teammates. "Hey, I'm all alone out here."

Ten minutes into the game, on a Marauder goal kick, J.T. substituted Parker and Mario for Jackson and Leon. As they went in, J.T. stood up and whistled to get the team's attention. "Movement!" he yelled furiously.

His tone of voice shocked the Marauders out of their torpor. They began to move. Instead of knocking the goal kick to half field, Abbey slid it to Dylan on the left side of the defense. Dylan looked upfield, then hit a simple square ball across to Parker, who quickly passed it back to Abbey. And the Marauders kept moving. Nick drifted back to take the pass from Abbey and Parker moved up the wing. Kenny came back into the midfield. Erik rotated into Parker's position, and Gabe pushed forward to fill the gap Erik left. It looked like a lot of effort just to carry the ball out of the goal area, and the Thunder Green watched complacently as the Marauders approached midfield.

When at last the Thunder Green ran to challenge Nick, he was able to push it over to Kenny, who'd been left open on the right side. Dylan surged forward, taking a defender with him, and now Kenny dumped the ball into the middle of the field, where Mario had time to collect it thanks to the space created by Dylan's run. Mario took one dribble before hitting it square to Erik, who had sprinted up from his defensive position. Then Erik found Nick streaking behind the two central defenders. Instead of shooting, Nick flicked the ball back, past the charging goalie and right into Dylan's path. Dylan, the left defender, now the vanguard of the attack, met the ball solidly with the side of his foot. The ball rippled the back of the net for the first goal.

The Thunder Green were much too confident of their own ability to fold after a single goal. Instead, they redoubled their efforts. Coach Courtland sent in a raft of substitutions, a whole new set of quality players roaming around Jimmy, and they pushed the ball harder. Will, especially, was stalwart, time and again throwing his body in the way as Jimmy charged. The two boys banged up against each other and tumbled to the ground numerous times. Frustrated, Jimmy and Coach Courtland began to appeal to the referee after each collision.

But the game was no longer one-sided. For every shot the Thunder took, the Marauders returned fire. Every time Jimmy pressed the attack, Nick and Erik led a counter. Nick and Kenny, in particular, caused trouble for the Thunder Green. If Nick was covered in midfield, Kenny would come back for the ball, and Nick would take off, trusting Kenny to release him with passes behind the defense.

At halftime, it was still 1-0 and J.T. was succinct. "Pass and move. Stay crisp." The team stayed in its huddle around him, expecting more. "That's it," he said. "You're doing fine. Go!"

The team dispersed to sip from water bottles and pass in little groups. Erik and Nick listened to the Thunder huddle as they knocked a ball back and forth. They couldn't make out the words, but the voices sounded angry.

"What do you think they're planning?" Erik asked.

Nick shrugged, but Kenny came up behind to answer. "They'll come out firing. The Thunder coaches don't like to lose."

"Hey, Kenny, thanks for staying" Erik said. "I hope it's okay, with your dad, I mean."

"Forget it, Steiner. Not your business," Kenny said angrily, and moved away.

Erik looked at Nick, "I didn't mean anything."

"Touchy subject, I guess."

At last the referee blew his whistle, and the teams were ready to go again. The Thunder kicked off and their new strategy soon became clear. Jimmy and their sweeper, a tall redhead called Lane, had pushed up to play forward. Lane was good in the air and very calm on the ground. Jimmy, of course, was extremely powerful both in the air and on the ground and could control almost any ball he could reach. With these two up front, the Thunder would send long balls into the Marauder penalty area. Jimmy and Lane would win possession and score.

Martin, the Thunder Green's talented winger, had moved to Jimmy's spot in center midfield. Although he was not as dangerous as Jimmy, he was quicker, and would be able to find more space away from Will's marking. Finally, the Thunder substitute sweeper, a tall, painfully thin boy named Aaron, moved in for Lane. Although Aaron was less experienced than Lane, he had improved over the season, and the Thunder coaching staff expected he would start for the team next year.

J.T. took in all of the changes at a glance, but his team took a while to adjust. As the number of Thunder chances mounted to dangerous levels, and those of the Marauders' dwindled, J.T. moved to the edge of the field and called Nick and Erik over. "They are pushing up too far. Look for Abbey to release you."

The Thunder Green continued to press, but the Marauders' attack began to reassert itself. Whenever Erik or Nick saw the ball come loose, poked away from Lane or from Jimmy, they would turn upfield to lead a counter. And the second time Abbey hit Nick running free through midfield, they very nearly scored. Nick beat a man and then found Parker heading into the penalty area. The goal should have fallen then, but Parker's first touch was a little strong, giving the sliding Thunder goalie just enough time to knock the ball out of bounds for a corner kick.

Setting up the corner, Erik paused to wipe some mud off his cleats. When he noticed Lane and Jimmy hanging out alone at the center spot, hoping for a breakaway, he knew his target. Nick guessed it too, so just as Erik started in for the kick, Nick took off, kamikaze style, to the near post. The Thunder goalie pointed and screamed, "Mark him!" and three Thunder defenders surged to the near post. But Erik's perfect kick sailed over their heads into the large space left at the far post, where Abbey, circling in from the wing, was running to meet it unguarded. Jimmy and Lane, thinking attack, had not bothered to follow her. She jumped and hit the ball squarely on her forehead, sending it rocketing into the upper corner of the net.

But before the Marauders could celebrate, the referee ran in, blowing his whistle and waving off the goal. The Marauders were mystified but the referee indicated that Abbey had pushed off a defender. Abbey, with mud from the ball speckled over her red face, was indignant, arguing there hadn't even been a defender in the area for her to push. Nick joined her and the two of them were furious, forcing the referee to retreat under their angry pleading. When Abbey accidentally knocked up against the referee, he gave her a yellow card.

J.T. was off the bench at once, ordering his team back to their positions. That did not mean, however, that J.T. was ready to let the referee off the hook.

"It was a goal," J.T. said. "Clear as day."

Not wanting to let J.T. have an exclusive audience, Coach Courtland ran out to the field. He was red faced and sweating. "She pushed him. I saw it."

"Rubbish!" J.T. said.

"Off the field, both of you, or you'll forfeit!" the referee roared.

J.T. looked hard at him and then turned on his heels, muttering. As he walked back to the sideline, he called to his team. "Play and pass. Score another goal!"

For the next ten minutes, the Marauders played their most

beautiful soccer of the season. There were eleven passes leading to a rocket off of Nick's left foot that smashed off the crossbar. There were another seven building to a shot by Kenny that curled just outside the left post. The Marauders' third opportunity came when Erik dribbled through three defenders before hitting a cross right to Matty's head. It was just bad luck that his header hit the goal-keeper in the chest.

But the score remained only 1–0, and with time winding down, the Thunder goalie boomed a punt down the field in a desperate attempt to score the equalizer. Jimmy jumped high and headed it forward to Lane, who trapped it with his back to the goal just inside the penalty box. As soon as Lane turned, Abbey came up from behind him to poke the ball away to Nick, who cleared it back to the Thunder side of the field. There was less than a minute left, and the situation for the Thunder seemed hopeless.

But sometime between Abbey poking the ball to Nick, and Nick clearing it up the field, Lane had collapsed in a heap. The whistle blew again, and the referee ran to the penalty spot. Abbey stood stunned, her mouth open and her arms out. She hadn't touched him.

Jamie saw it all and ran to the referee screaming that it was a dive. He got a yellow card for his efforts, and once again J.T. was running onto the field. This time Coach Courtland got there first.

"Good call, ref! She clipped him!"

J.T. was silent for a few seconds.

"Do you have something to say?" The referee's voice trembled. "Or can we finish the game?"

"You know there was no foul, don't you?" J.T. said.

"I saw what I saw."

"The question is, did you call what you saw?"

"Sir!" the referee shouted. "If you do not leave the field this instant, you'll be banned from the league!"

J.T. looked around darkly, then stalked back to the sideline, and the game went on. The referee waved the players back from the penalty area and placed the ball on the penalty spot. The Thunder Green selected Jimmy to take the penalty kick, which he smashed into the upper right corner to tie the score.

The Marauders rushed to take the kickoff, but no sooner had they put the ball into play than the final whistle blew. The Marauders stood with shocked expressions on their faces, and their fans were silent. But the Thunder fans chanted, "THUNDER! THUNDER! THUNDER!"

WITH THE HELP of Rory and Georgi, J.T. gathered his team. He spoke in a hoarse voice. "I told you: Winning and losing does not matter. Today, you played soccer! Go shake hands. I'll see you at practice tomorrow."

As the players returned from shaking hands to collect their gear, Mario asked, "Does this mean we're out of the playoffs?"

Everyone looked at Erik. "Yeah, basically." The team waited for him to explain the probabilities in more detail, but for once he did not.

Nick put a hand on Erik's shoulder. "Come on, we still have to work on our reports tonight. Remember I'm going home with you so you can make sure I don't goof off?"

"Forget it," Erik said. "We can study tomorrow."

"Hey, if we don't study, we'll just have more time to think about the game and get mad. We might as well get some work done."

Erik shrugged and followed Nick over to where Mr. Steiner was waiting to take them back to Erik's house.

CHAPTER 17

Winchester

After dinner at the Steiners', Nick and Erik went up to Erik's room to work on their reports, but Erik found it difficult to study. He kept thinking about the game. "Do you think we can lodge a protest with the league?"

Nick shrugged, and kept working.

"The thing is, if we had won, we could clinch a playoff spot by beating Winchester and Thunder Red."

Nick put down his book. "Mac Scruggs is the league Mr. Big Shot. Maybe he doesn't want us in the playoffs."

"Right, because if we get in, the Thunder Red doesn't."

Nick returned to his book, and Erik was quiet for a while.

"If we beat the Thunder Red, they may still not make the playoffs," Erik said a little later. "It depends on how Bedford does. If they win their game next week, they'd be 7–5–2, the same record as Thunder Red. Then it comes down to second-half records and goal difference."

Nick said, "Look Steiner, you're supposed to help me study. I've only gotten two pages read since we sat down. Shut up and read!"

After that, Erik kept his thoughts to himself, and Nick got quite a lot of work done—until Erik said, "Nick, are you just reading?

How will you remember anything?"

"You're just reading, too."

"No, I'm taking notes. You're going to forget what you want to say by the time you get to writing."

Nick glared at Erik. "You study your way; I'll study mine."

J.T. WAS WAITING for the boys and Abbey when they arrived at Caton's Field the next day for practice. He didn't mention the previous day's game or the fact that Kenny was not at practice.

"We need to play quicker," he said. "Quicker recognition, quicker passing, better technique. Today we will play one-touch 4 v. 4 on a narrow field. No room on the sides, so you will have to be sharp. One touch, back and forth, left and right. Now, 4 v. 1 to warm up. Go!"

J.T. led the team through several different versions of the one-touch 4 v. 4 drill. He imposed a rule that the ball had to stay on the ground. "Your next opponent is Winchester. Big boys. They play Swedish style, through the air. We will play Dutch style, on the ground."

AFTER PRACTICE, NICK and Leon went to the high school library to study. Nick experimented with taking notes as he read, while Leon typed at his computer. Three of their classmates, Dylan, Laurie, and Melanie, were also at the library working on Egypt reports, and they all sat together at one of the big tables on the mezzanine.

"You finished with your research?" Nick asked Leon after a few minutes of watching him type.

"No," Leon said, "I like to get down what I'm going to say first. Then it's much easier to pick out relevant stuff while you're reading."

"That sort of seems backward," Nick commented.

"Don't listen to him," said Dylan. "Normal kids take notes first and then write them up."

"Then how do you know what to take notes on?" Leon asked, genuinely interested. "I have to know what my argument will be first."

"The point is," Dylan said, "that you don't know what your argument is until you've done the research."

"That's not true. I know what Nick's argument is, and I haven't read any of his books."

Nick was now curious himself. "What's my argument?"

"Your argument is that rich people in ancient Egypt got mummies, and poor people didn't. But that the promise of eternal life that the mummies represented was so attractive that the poor respected the rich people's mummies, because they hoped that one day their descendants would get a similar reward."

"Hey, that does sound familiar," Nick said, marveling at how easily Leon had summarized it.

Dylan said, "Yeah, but what if you start reading, and it turns out that poor people got mummies too? Or what if they defaced the mummies? What do you do then?"

"Not a problem," said Leon. "Then you just change things around a little and say that, *despite* the efforts to bribe folks with the promise of eternal life, the poor expressed their anger by attacking the rich people's mummies. And you're covered."

Dylan laughed. "Nick, pay no attention to him. That's not normal."

Nick said, "Anyway, my problem is that none of the books really talk about my topic at all."

"That is a problem," Leon agreed. "But that's why you have to do it my way. You must have a couple of books that deal with social life in ancient Egypt?"

"Yeah, because you told me to get them out when I was doing the bibliography."

"Well, they may not say a lot about mummies, but there's going to be a couple of paragraphs about the difference between rich and poor. But you have to know what you're looking for. Otherwise you'll miss it, or not know how to use it."

"A couple of paragraphs?" Nick said skeptically. "Hardly lots to go on."

"That's why most of it can be written without reading. It's mostly logic. You just have to find a sentence about how mummies were cared for to prove that the poor did most of the work."

Nick looked at Leon in admiration. "That's really how you write one of these reports?"

Dylan rolled his eyes. "Nick, I'm telling you, don't try it. It's much easier to read the books, pick out a bunch of quotes, and write 'em down. Then you shuffle them around to tell a story and write with a sentence or two to introduce each quote. Guaranteed A every time."

"Where's the fun in that?" Leon asked.

"It's not fun," said Dylan, "It's homework."

Nick was amazed at how much thought his friends put into their schoolwork. At least he'd already started working on his paper, rather than rushing everything the night before. It opened up possibilities he had not considered before. And after a while, when Nick saw that everyone had stopped paying attention to him, Nick opened his notebook and tried to write down the main points of the argument Leon had summarized. Nick was willing to take advice on studying from his friends, but he didn't want them to know that he was doing it.

ON FRIDAY, THERE was no soccer practice, but there was soccer news. Erik had realized that the Blue Marauders could still make the playoffs. He had mistakenly figured that, even if they won their last two games, the Marauders would end up with less wins than Bedford or Thunder Red. But he'd forgotten that the Marauders had a game in hand: the Braeburn game that had been cancelled. If the game was rescheduled, and the Marauders won it, they could finish tied with Thunder Red and Bedford.

"The first tie breaker is second-half records," Erik told his teammates as they shot baskets before school, "And we beat anyone on that."

"So we could really make the playoffs?" Will asked. "It seems so unlikely."

"Yeah, just three more wins."

"So how do we schedule another game against Braeburn?" Dylan said.

"My dad called and left a message with the coach this morning," Erik replied. "We should hear back tonight."

THE OTHER THING that happened on Friday was that Nick flatly refused to spend the evening studying. It was Jamie's turn to be his study partner, but Nick had other plans.

"Dad's taking me and Grandpa out for Chinese food and bowling. I'm not working tonight."

"But the paper's due on Tuesday," Erik said. "And we need you for Wednesday's game against Thunder Red. You know DeMille will bench you if you don't get it in."

"Hey, I've worked on it for three days straight. I bet I'm further along than anyone in the class, and there's still the whole weekend left."

"I've finished mine," said Tabitha.

"I have the first draft done," Abbey said.

"Me too, just about," Dylan said.

Nick looked at them like they were aliens. "Okay, I'm not furthest along, but like I said, there's still the weekend."

"We have a game on Saturday."

"So I'll study all afternoon. Who's up for Saturday?"

Abbey raised her hand. "That's me."

"Can you get a first draft done on Saturday?" Erik asked Nick.

"Sure," said Nick. "Now give me a break. Tonight is a McCoy boys' night out, and I've earned it."

WHILE NICK BOWLED that evening, Erik finished his paper and sat on pins and needles waiting for the Braeburn coach to call his dad back.

"Call him again, Dad," Erik said. "Maybe the first message got lost."

"Patience, son," Mr. Steiner replied.

IN MILFORD, KENNY sat alone in his room. His father had laid down the law: Kenny wouldn't play for the Blue Marauders, and unless Kenny shaped up, he wouldn't accompany the family to Paris over Christmas either.

Kenny was in awe of his dad. But why couldn't his father ever cut him a break? Why did Kenny have to be perfect all the time? And what was so awful about playing two more games with the stupid Blue Marauders? Kenny was enjoying it, even if they were a bunch of losers. And he wasn't sure they were losers anyway. They'd beaten the Thunder Green fair and square, even if the score said it was a tie. The fear on Coach Courtland's face had been priceless. And Jimmy had come up to him at school and said it was the toughest game they'd played all year.

Kenny knew that contacting kids on the Marauders was off limits, but he had to at least let them know he wasn't going to be there against Winchester the next day. And his dad hadn't taken his cell phone away yet.

ABBEY AND JAMIE were in Abbey's living room, playing "World of Warfare."

"Shouldn't you two be working on your reports?" Abbey's

mother asked.

"Mom, I've almost finished a draft, and I have to work tomorrow afternoon with Nick. I have to have something left to do."

"What about you, Jamie? How is your report coming along?"

"Pretty good, Mrs. Stephens. I just have to get the appendices together."

"Well, okay. But I don't want you two playing too late tonight. You have to get up early tomorrow morning for the game."

DYLAN WAS MAKING supper with his mother and feeling that all was right with the world. They were making a risotto from a recipe that Dylan's mother had found in the newspaper last Sunday. As they cooked, Dylan patiently explained to his mother the records of all the teams in the league, and what exactly had to happen for the Marauders to make the playoffs.

WILL HAD TO sit with Angie for the evening because Friday was his father's night to work late. After playing five games of "Trouble" with Angie, cheating to make sure she would win every time, he made them both macaroni and cheese from a box. Will cleaned up after supper, and then they watched one of Angie's favorite movies, an ancient collection of Pink Panther cartoons, for about the 100th time.

GABE WAS NOT working on his report. He and Terry had met in Warrick and were doing a course on gun safety to get ready for hunting season. After the course, they had a chance to shoot at Warrick's indoor firing range.

LEON'S MOTHER HAD sent him upstairs to practice violin. But Leon did not feel in the mood. Instead he sat around and reread his old comic books.

JACKSON WAS OUT with his oldest brother, making a delivery of cement.

MATTY ATE AT a pizza restaurant in Forsberg with several of his school friends. After supper, a few of them went back to Matty's house to watch horror movies.

PARKER WAS AT a concert with some ninth graders in Guilford. His mother expected him back at midnight, but she never checked, and he did not get home until three in the morning. The ninth graders had hooked up with some high school juniors, one of whom had a car and a license. After the concert, he had given everyone a ride back to his house. The junior's parents were away for the weekend, but had left the fridge and liquor cabinet fully stocked. After offering everyone some cookies and brownies, the junior got glasses out and offered shots of bourbon.

Parker took a shot glass and tried a few sips. It tasted revolting, and he did not take any more. Instead he sat quietly with the cup in his lap, a cigarette in his mouth, and his hair over his eyes, listening to the others talk about high school, girls, and bands. He realized he knew a lot more about bands than most of them, and a lot less about everything else.

By the time the junior offered rides home, Parker had gone through a couple of packs of cigarettes and was feeling pretty sick. Though it crossed his mind that he should not get in the car with the boy, who was clearly wasted, Parker was eager to get home. When he arrived safely at home and had made his goodbyes, he vaguely hoped that the rest of his friends also made it safely.

MARIO WAS AT the hospital emergency room. Although this was where his father worked as a nurse, he was not there to visit his father. He had complained of a stomachache and had a fever of a hundred and three degrees even after taking medicine. His father suggested they wait to see how he felt in the morning. His mother got upset and then very loud, insisting that they take him right away.

It turned out to be a good thing. The emergency room physician said Mario needed his appendix out and scheduled surgery for him right away. Mario's father called Leon's dad at 7:00 the next morning to let him know that Mario would miss the game, and the rest of the season.

PARKER WAS MISSING when the Marauders gathered at the Lancaster Elementary School parking lot for the drive to Winchester on Saturday morning. They called his home and his cell, but no one answered.

"Good riddance," said Gabe. "So we'll have two subs instead of three."

"Not even that," Leon said, and reported that Mario had had his appendix out and was out for the season.

"We can play with one sub," Gabe said.

Erik added to the bad news. "Kenny's not coming either. His dad won't let him play anymore."

Abbey was relieved that Erik spoke up. She'd gotten a text from Kenny too, but even though everything was supposed to be cool now, she preferred that Erik deliver the news.

"But Terry's meeting us there, right?" Dylan asked Gabe. "Otherwise, we'll be one down."

"Yeah, he's playing. His dad's driving direct from Warrick. It wouldn't make sense to come here first."

The team tried to call Parker again, and again received no answer.

"Okay," Mr. Steiner broke in. "It looks like we've got everyone we're going to get. Let's go."

WINCHESTER WAS AN hour and a half away. The field was on the south side of the city, in a park just outside the ring road. The park, surrounded by wire fencing, consisted of a bare, grassy patch encircled by a concrete track, a set of swings, and a couple of basketball courts. On the city side of the ring road, there were a series of housing developments from the 1970s. Outside was a commercial district crowded with auto dealerships.

As the Marauders reached the park, a cold drizzle began. Although the parents were dismayed, the team seemed barely to notice the weather as they gathered their stuff and headed out to the field.

The Winchester players were, if anything, bigger than the Marauders remembered.

"They're like a high school team," Jamie whispered to Abbey.

Abbey nodded without speaking as she watched three Winchester players collide in midair fighting for a cross during warm-ups.

J.T. was waiting at the visitors' bench. When he saw his team, he stepped forward and whistled loudly to call them over. He had been there a while, and small drops of rain were collecting on the brim of his hat, dripping once and a while onto his face. Dylan noticed that, for once, J.T. did not have a sandwich with him and asked him about it.

"Sandwiches don't do well in the rain," he said. "Where are the others?"

"Mario's in the hospital," Erik replied. "Kenny's dad won't let him play, and no one knows about Parker."

"And Terry?" J.T. asked.

"He's coming," said Gabe. "We were shooting last night. He'll be here."

J.T. grunted. "The rain makes it harder to play on the ground. So does the field. It's bumpy. You need start to passing. Get a sense of the conditions. Hurry."

The Marauders changed, ran out, and started their 4 v. 1 drills. The field was slick, the rain was freezing and icy, and the passes and traps were poor. But J.T. walked among them, calming them with brisk comments and making sure they focused on their own work, and not on the Winchester team.

The referee and linesmen arrived as the rain grew harder. They went to talk to the Winchester coach before coming to see J.T. "Hey, coach," the referee said. "No thunder in the forecast, so we're going to play. Okay with you?"

"Yes, certainly," J.T. said.

"Then it'll be five minutes," the referee said, and then added, "I see you only have ten kids here. You gonna have a full team?"

"I believe so. We are expecting one more boy."

"Well, the league says you can start the game with nine players on the field. So I guess it's your funeral."

At this point, the Winchester coach approached. He was six feet tall, but almost as wide as he was tall. "Hey, coach," he said in a hoarse voice, sticking out his hand to J.T. "Barry Gannetti. You only have ten kids. And one's a girl. You sure you want to play?"

J.T., whose hand had been engulfed by Coach Gannetti's, said, "Why not?"

"The game doesn't count for much. We're in the playoffs, and I guess you're pretty much out of them. We could split the teams and play a friendly."

"No, we will play."

"That's fine, then. But I warn you, my boys can dish out the hurt. And if we're playing live, it's no holds barred. I can't tell my boys to hold back, it ain't fair to them."

J.T. smiled coolly. "Then we are in agreement. I will not hold my team back either."

"Okay," Coach Gannetti said, turning to the referee with a shrug. "We're ready when you are."

The referee signaled for the players to clear the field, and J.T. called his team back to the bench. "Is Terry here yet?"

Gabe beckoned to his dad, and Officer Drybzyck jogged over to the huddle. "I just got word from Terry's dad. They had a late start and took a wrong turn. Should be here in twenty minutes."

"It does not change anything," J.T. said. "Remember, we play on the ground. The ball may be wet, but the fundamentals still apply. Take your time on your traps. Cushion the ball and look it into your feet. Make your passes quick and precise. We will run them around a little."

"What about defense?" Jamie asked.

"Nothing special is needed. If you don't win the ball in the air, win it on the ground. Jamie, you will stop their headers on the goal. But don't play their game. Work the ball out with short passes. If they are hitting long balls into the attack, there is a lot of room behind their forwards.

"We'll play with two forwards, Matty and Leon. Erik, Will, and Nick in midfield. Gabe, Abbey, Jackson, and Dylan are the defenders. Jamie in goal. Is everybody ready?"

J.T. looked around the wet, uncertain faces and laughed brightly. "Of course you're ready. This is what it is about. Freezing rain. Bad pitch. Undermanned. This is where you show what you are made of. Go."

J.T.'s voice was more urgent and filled with excitement than ever before, and the Marauders roared onto the field, feeling warmth and energy flow back into their muscles.

Winchester's strategy was anything but subtle. The kickoff was passed back to the central midfielder, who held the ball for just a couple of seconds while his attackers ran forward. Then he smashed it high and far into the Marauder penalty box. In this case, the Winchester players were a little late, and Gabe, standing his ground, put his head to the ball and sent it out of harm's way.

Will collected the ball, and following J.T.'s advice, he kept his pass to Nick on the ground. Nick also followed J.T.'s advice, trapping the wet, skidding ball carefully. Unfortunately, the extra care took extra time, and before Nick had a chance to look up the field, one of the oversized Winchester midfielders slid in from behind and took Nick's legs out from under him.

Nick collapsed onto the sodden field as the Winchester player rolled over him. There was a tense moment before Nick popped up, mud covering his shirt and much of his face. Nick was furious about the tackle, but there were positive aspects to it. First, Nick was not hurt. Second, the whistle had blown, so the Marauders received a free kick. And third, Winchester's defensive strategy was fully revealed: intimidate, intimidate, intimidate.

Nick scraped the mud off his cheek as Will and Erik came over for the free kick.

"You okay, man?" Will asked.

"Never better," Nick said, staring at the Winchester players, who had backed off a few yards. "Look, we have to hold the ball and control the midfield, right?"

"Yeah," Erik agreed.

"Then let's not mess around. If we play smart, they can't take the ball away from us."

And so it proved. The Blue Marauders dominated possession for the next fifteen minutes, until Nick got his revenge, slicing through the box to challenge one of Winchester's central defenders for a volley off a low cross from Matty. The two players arrived at the same spot simultaneously, crashing shoulders as they converged on the ball. The force of the collision sent Nick spinning backward and the Winchester defender sprawling down into the mud. The defender thought he had met the ball first and cleared it safely away, and Nick thought he had scored. But both were wrong. Nick's foot had snaked around the defender, reaching the ball first, volleying it hard toward the net. Instead of going in, however, the ball hit the goalie square in the stomach. The goalie went down instantly, crumpling into the back of the net like he'd been shot, and the ball dropped softly to the ground, rolling just a few inches from the goal line.

The rest of the Winchester defense could only look on helplessly when Leon, the closest player, stepped up and tapped the ball into the net for the first goal of the game.

Before Nick could congratulate Leon, however, he was surrounded by an angry mob of Winchester players pointing fingers in his face. They said Nick was dirty, that he'd fouled their teammate, and that he'd purposefully hurt the goalie. The second time he was pushed in the chest, Nick balled his fist, ready to attack back, but his arms were suddenly pinned to his sides.

Nick kicked out and yelled, "LEGGO!"

Holding him tight, Will dragged him from the Winchester players. "Not on your life, Nicky. I'm not letting go until you can control yourself."

"Get off me!" Nick struggled uselessly against Will's iron grip.

"You're not going to get kicked out of the game when we're already a man down," Will replied calmly.

With Nick under Will's control, and Leon having skipped away from his accusers, the angry Winchester players were now besieging the referee, pleading their case, while the Winchester coaches were sitting with the injured goalie.

Nick took a deep breath and said, "Okay, you can let go now." Will did, and Nick rubbed his arms.

"It wasn't a foul."

"I know. So does the ref. But if you had gotten in a fight, you'd have been sent out."

"I hope the goalie's all right. He took that ball pretty hard."

Will shrugged, and the rest of the Marauders now gathered with them to watch the scene. It took a couple of minutes for the referee to convince the Winchester players that the goal would not be overturned, and several more to attend to the goalie. J.T. joined the Winchester coaches as they sat around the boy, who at last stood up shakily and was helped back to the bench.

The crowd applauded as Winchester's replacement goalie ran on the field. J.T. walked over to reassure Nick. "He just had the wind knocked out of him. Don't worry."

When it resumed, the game fell into a pattern. Winchester sent players deep into the Marauder half to challenge for long balls, hoping for a lucky bounce or defensive error that would result in an open shot. The Marauders countered by holding the ball as long as possible in the open midfield areas between Winchester's forwards and defenders until they could snake a pass through to their forwards slashing behind the defense.

The Marauders had the large advantage in time of possession, but the better chances belonged to Winchester. Abbey, in particular, was the victim in Winchester's war of attrition. Often marking Winchester's tall, athletic center forward, she was pushed, jostled, and elbowed into the mud more times than she could count. After the earlier melee, the referee tried to keep control of the game, and called plenty of fouls, but the fight for the ball around the Marauder box had become a full-contact battle, and it was hard for anyone to tell who was fouling and who was getting fouled. Inevitably, much was left uncalled, and only several good reaction saves by Jamie kept Winchester from scoring.

When the halftime whistle blew, the Marauders still led 1–0, but they were tired, cold, and black and blue. And they were still a man down with another half to play. As they gathered together around J.T., they received a bit of good news. Terry arrived, running onto the field in a dry, clean uniform, looking fresh and full of energy. "I'm really sorry, guys. We got a late start and then got lost and . . . ."

"It doesn't matter," J.T. said. "You will play next to Abbey. We will play five in the back. Remember, no fouls. We do not want to give up a penalty. Also, Erik and Matty switch positions. Erik will stay up as far up as possible and the midfield will look to release him."

J.T. looked at his bedraggled team, rain dripping from their noses. "Don't stand around getting cold. Get a drink, then I want games of 4 v. 1 until the end of halftime. Keep the blood flowing."

Until now, J.T. had spoken in his usual disinterested monotone, but suddenly, just before waving the players away, his voice changed into a fierce whisper that seemed almost to escape him against his will. "Don't any of you dare *think* about being tired. You are too good not to win this game!"

The shock of J.T.'s words restored the team's energy. They rushed back on the field as ready for the second half as they were for the first. No one complained about the wet or the cold. J.T.'s praise had made them impervious to the elements.

Unfortunately, the second half began with a disaster. Abbey and Terry weren't used to playing side by side, and the first time Winchester lofted a ball into the penalty box, each waited for the other to clear it. Instead, the ball landed between them, at the feet of the Winchester center forward. He settled it with a quick touch of his right foot and slammed it into the goal. 1–1.

Abbey and Terry looked at each other accusingly. Gabe made matters worse, yelling at both of them to get their heads in the game. J.T. saw the interaction and actually ran onto the field while Winchester was still celebrating the equalizer. He went into the back of the net and collected the ball where it still lay, and then walked up to the edge of the penalty box where Abbey and Terry were standing.

"The confusion was my fault, for changing plans and not explaining properly. Talk to each other, but Terry, you take anything you can reach. Abbey, if he's there, back off and keep on your toes. You clean up anything that Terry does not get a head on. Got it?"

The players nodded. "Okay, now get playing." J.T. turned to Gabe. "You too, boy. Go help your teammates."

The game resumed and settled back into its rhythm, with Winchester lofting the ball into the Marauder penalty box and hoping for the best, and the Marauder midfielders working the ball back into the Winchester half on the ground. But with Terry added to the defense, Winchester's attack was less dangerous. And with Erik taking Matty's place up front, the Blue Marauders became more deadly.

It wasn't that Matty had been ineffective. He was a solid player. But Erik was something else again. His cuts were faster and less predictable. His traps were perfect. The ball stayed glued to his feet when he dribbled. And he could shoot with power with either foot. With the Marauders continuing to dominate midfield, it wasn't long before Nick was able to set him free behind the Winchester defense, and Erik was able to smash the Marauders' second goal into the back of the net.

Now the Marauders just had to hold onto the lead. But their legs were on the verge of giving out, and the Winchester team refused to give up. Beating the exhausted Marauders to almost every loose ball, Winchester reasserted control of the midfield and gradually ratcheted up the pressure on the Marauder goal. In the last five minutes, it was only two great saves by Jamie, and several last-minute tackles and blocks by Abbey and Terry, that prevented Winchester from scoring the equalizer. When the final whistle blew, the Marauders seemed as stunned by their victory as the Winchester players were.

Then Jamie raised his hands in the air and yelled. The team felt his exultation and ran to mob him, forming a pig pile in the goalie's crease. The mud and rain did not feel cold at all.

The Winchester players watched the celebration on their home field grimly. They were chilled by the rain and anxious to go home. When the Marauders finally disentangled from each other, the teams shook hands quickly. The parents, colder and wetter than the players, shooed their children along, urging them to hurry back to their cars.

But halfway to the parking lot, Erik realized that he had forgotten his water bottle. When he went back to look for it, there were only two figures left standing in the rain. One of them, Erik knew, was J.T., but he did not recognize the other. The man was built like J.T., short and powerful, but he was better attired for the weather, with dark blue rain pants and rain jacket, and a hood pulled over his face.

Neither man seemed to notice Erik as he searched for his water bottle, but the man in the blue rain jacket was talking to be heard over the roar of the rain, and Erik could hear what he said.

"I have plenty of contacts in Holland, and I've worked with some of your people. Van Lingen, Hoek, and the others. Not stupid by a long shot, you Dutch, but too idealistic of course. It's why Holland's never won anything. No one's willing to make the hard choices, to do the dirty work."

J.T. did not say anything and the man continued. "So I asked some of my friends about Jan Tielemans and got an earful. Everyone remembers 'the Teapot.' A solid career but overshadowed by Neeskins, so you never got your due. Then as a player-coach, you won the hardware you never could quite get ahold of as a player. A pretty fairy tale, except for the ending. Anger management issues, right? At least that's what the papers said."

If J.T. responded, Erik could not hear him, and the other man continued.

"Sounds like you've done your share of brawling. Broke your goalkeeper's nose. Numerous bar fights, all well documented. I assume you've told your team about that, and their parents."

Suddenly Erik realized who the man was. It was Mac Scruggs, the coach of the Thunder Red. Erik had his water bottle, but he stayed to hear the end of the conversation.

"But the way I heard it, there was more to the story. The fighting was a convenient cover. The league didn't want the real reason for your departure coming out. And it never did. Partly because shortly after the scandal, 'the Teapot' left coaching, left Holland, and disappeared."

J.T. must have said something then because Mac Scruggs laughed harshly in response.

"Well, maybe I was misinformed. Still, the Tri-State League may want to look into it. We have our own reputation to consider, after all." Scruggs began to walk away, then stopped and turned back. "I'd advise you to keep a low profile if you want to keep coaching in this league, Jan. That's all I'm saying."

As Mac Scruggs left the field, he noticed Erik and laughed again. J.T. saw Erik as well.

"Go home," he said over the raindrops.

Erik paused for just a moment and then ran back to the parking lot.

CHAPTER 18

Keeping a Team Together

On the way home from Winchester, the Marauders stopped for lunch at Wendy's. Erik didn't mention the conversation he'd heard between Mac Scruggs and J.T. Instead, the team discussed the likelihood of making the playoffs, and Erik explained again to his friends how that could still happen. If they beat the Thunder Red and won the rescheduled game against Braeburn, they would have the third-best record in the league and be in.

"We started 1–5," said Matty. "How we can possibly have the third-best record?"

Erik explained again. "If we beat Thunder Red and Braeburn, we'll have seven wins, five losses, and two ties. Bedford has five losses too, two to Thunder Green, two to Winchester, and one to us. They also tied Thunder Red and Braeburn. Thunder Red lost to Thunder Green once, Bedford once, Winchester twice, and, if we beat 'em, us. They also have two ties. We'll all have the same record. But our second-half record is killer, and that's what decides it."

"It won't be easy to beat Thunder Red," Leon said.

Nick laughed. "Can you imagine what Mac Scruggs would do if we knock him out of the playoffs? He'd have a cow!"

Erik kept his thoughts to himself. But suddenly he realized what

Mac Scruggs had been up to. He must want to win the game on Wednesday very badly.

BACK IN LANCASTER, Abbey's parents dropped Nick at his house. Abbey said she'd return to study in a couple of hours, so Nick had better be ready.

"Do we have to?"

"The reports are due Monday, Nick. Look, I'll see if Jamie can come over too. We'll hang out and work. It won't be so bad."

"Okay, but I've almost written the thing already. I mean, I have like three pages of notes. You guys could come over, and we could just watch a movie."

Abbey cocked her head. "I need to get *my* report done, so if you don't want to work on it, let me know, so I don't waste my time."

"Fine, fine. We'll do it. See you around five."

MOST OF THE rest of the evening was not, from Nick's point of view, particularly memorable. Jamie didn't join them, so Nick and Abbey were alone. They sat in the den, Nick working on his dad's bulky desktop while Abbey sat on the sofa typing on her Apple notebook. Nick's sisters kept creeping in to ask them questions, and Nick's mom kept shooing them away.

For Nick, it felt like a lot of work. He had expected to just transcribe his notes and be done. It turned out to be harder than that, and it took him almost two hours just to finish the first page. But it was a really good first page, he thought. He had put in some great quotes about the role that the belief in immortality played in Egyptian society. They were so killer, he barely understood them. And at least he knew what he wanted to write for the rest of the paper.

"Man, this is going to take all Sunday," he said.

"And don't forget about the footnotes."

"Is anyone assigned to me tomorrow?" Nick asked. "I mean, it's not like I need it. I know the deadline is Monday. I'm not likely to forget."

"Yeah, but you might not start work until after supper."

"Oh, come on," Nick said, and then paused to think about it. "Actually, I'd probably start in the morning, because I'd want to watch football. And I'd finish up after the Sunday night game."

"Which ends at?"

"Oh, about eleven."

"Yeah, that's why Erik assigned someone to make sure you get it done before you watch football."

"So whose turn is it?"

"Yvonne's."

"She's not even on the team," said Nick.

"She wanted to help out."

"Cool."

There was a short silence while both Abbey and Nick looked at what they had been writing. Then Abbey said, in a casual voice, "So are you and Yvonne going out?"

Nick froze, keeping his gaze on his computer screen, and thinking furiously. "Uhhh, well, I'm not sure. I mean, it's not like we have actually really gone out anywhere, at least not for a while. What do you mean by going out?"

"Come on, Nick. It's a simple question."

Nick thought. "We hang out sometimes."

"But are you going out?"

"I don't know. I've never gone out with anyone before."

"Do you hold hands? Do you kiss? Have you kissed her?"

Nick wished it wasn't Abbey asking him the question. He always sort of considered Abbey his girlfriend, at least, his girlfriend in waiting, if he was ever going to have a girlfriend. He didn't want his hanging out with Yvonne to change that. But if he and Yvonne were officially *going out*, that would muck everything up. Abbey couldn't be his girlfriend if Yvonne was, could she? But, then again, he couldn't go out with Yvonne if Abbey was his girlfriend. And he and Yvonne had kissed, twice at least. And held hands more than that.

"Yeah," Nick said at last. "I guess we're going out."

"Do you like her?"

"Yeah, I do. I like her. She's cool."

This seemed to satisfy Abbey, who turned back to her paper. But now Nick had questions. "What about you? Are you going out with Kenny? Have you kissed him?"

"Kenny and I are not going out."

"I thought you went to the movies with him. And I know you went to his parents' house for dinner."

"But that was just . . . getting to know him."

"What do you mean?"

"Like figuring out if you want to go out."

"So you didn't kiss him?"

"Maybe I did. A couple of times. Five times, actually. But only to see if I wanted to."

"You've kissed Kenny more than I've kissed Yvonne."

"Yeah, but that's different. You like Yvonne."

"I don't get it."

"You kissed Yvonne knowing you liked her. I kissed Kenny while I was finding out if I liked him."

"And you don't?"

Abbey hesitated. "It's not that I don't like him. It's just, well, I don't feel like I know him yet."

"Does that mean you can go out and kiss him some more, and it still won't count?"

Abbey grinned at Nick. "Maybe."

Nick laughed. "Look, I hope you don't mind my saying this, but Kenny's a crumb. Maybe a sad crumb, and we should all feel bad for him, but basically a crumb."

"I don't mind," Abbey said, looking down. "In fact, I'm glad you're willing to tell me what you think. And I probably agree with you, but like I said, I'm still finding out. Anyway, we haven't talked since he left the team. He's probably decided I'm not fancy enough for him. Or his dad did."

"Anyone who thinks that is crazy," said Nick hotly.

"You're sweet," Abbey said. "We should call it a night, though. You've got a lot of work tomorrow. You think your dad can give me a ride home?"

WHEN YVONNE CAME over the next morning, she did not bring her computer. Instead she had a book about zombie gymnasts.

"Aren't you going to write your paper?" asked Nick.

"I'm finished."

"So you're just going to watch me work?"

"No, I'm going to read."

"You don't have to stay," Nick said. "I'll be fine on my own."

"No, I want to stay," Yvonne said. "I promised Erik."

Nick grumbled, but sat down at his dad's desk and tried to think about work. Yvonne lay on the sofa and giggled over her book.

"What's so funny?" Nick asked.

"The zombies take over the U.S. Olympic team. But whenever they do their routines, their body parts keep flying off. So they bathe in super glue to keep it from happening."

Nick grimaced. Yvonne's book made his Egypt report sound interesting in comparison, and in the end, Nick finished more quickly that he'd expected. By one o'clock he had finished a full draft. He wanted to save going over it and doing the footnotes for later, but Yvonne wouldn't let him.

"Come on, Yvonne. I can catch the first game and finish at half-time."

"Hey, I'm not sitting around here watching football," Yvonne said. "And Erik told me I couldn't leave until you had *finished* finished."

"Man, why does everyone listen to Erik?"

"Because he knows how to get things done."

"No, he's a busybody who doesn't think anyone can do stuff for themselves," Nick said, feeling irritated. "I started the Blue Marauders without him!"

"And who got the sponsors, the uniforms, the practice schedule, and the coach?"

"He helped," Nick said. But he returned to his work, determined to finish it, if only to get out from under Erik's watchful spies. Two hours later, he presented the final copy to Yvonne.

"Satisfied?" he asked, handing her the paper.

She flipped through it and then gave it back to him. "It looks really good."

There was a moment of tension as she was standing now very close to him.

"You want to watch football now?" Nick asked.

"No," she said. "Let's go for a walk."

"It's raining out."

"So?"

Nick paused. "Okay, you can borrow a rain jacket from my mom if you want."

"I have a jacket," Yvonne said. "I'll be okay."

As they were getting ready to leave Nick said, "This is probably the furthest ahead I've ever finished a big assignment. It feels weird."

"Your paper was pretty good. You can be pretty smart, if you put your mind to it."

"Thanks," Nick said, "but I don't think you brains have anything to worry about."

"Silly," Yvonne said, and as they walked out of the door she slipped her hand in his.

"That reminds me," Nick said, "are we going out?"

Yvonne looked around at the trees in the yard, the grass and the sky. "We're out," she said.

"You know what I mean. Are we, like, *going out*?"

"Why are you asking?"

"I don't know. Abbey asked me."

"Abbey?" Yvonne frowned.

"No, not like that. She was just curious."

"What did you say?"

"Well, we had never talked about it."

"So, what did you say?"

"I said we'd kissed a couple of times so . . . ."

"Yes?"

"I said I thought we were."

"You did?" Yvonne's face lit up in a bright smile.

"Well, I wasn't sure," Nick said. "I mean, Abbey and Kenny have kissed more than us, and Abbey says they're not going out. But I sort of thought we were."

Yvonne moved close to Nick and as he finished speaking, she pressed her body up against his and kissed him on the lips.

"I think so, too," she said. Yvonne stepped back and took Nick's hand once more. They walked through the rain and talked about many things. Despite the rain, neither of them felt cold at all.

AT SCHOOL ON Monday, Mr. DeMille made a great show of reviewing his homework box to make sure that all the reports were there. He checked off names and provided commentary as he went.

"Abbey, Erik, Leon, Dylan, Michael. Good. Yvonne, you've given me eight pages. I hope you really have that much to say."

Mr. DeMille held up a report he did not like the look of. "Ryan, I see you have handed something in. But what a bedraggled thing."

The report was handwritten and ratty, with smudges all over it.

"My brother spilled milk on it," Ryan said.

"Well, don't hesitate to rewrite it next time," replied Mr. DeMille.

DeMille continued through the reports. He praised Jamie's appendix, which showed blueprints he had collected of various Egyptian monuments. He noted that Lauren was missing her bibliography. The next report he picked up was Nick's.

"Oh, my, here's a surprise. A report from Nicholas McCoy. And looking rather well formed, too." Mr. DeMille held it up. "Will wonders never cease?"

He finished going through the reports, then looked down once more at his class list. "Now, who are we missing? Aah, Parker. Where is Parker?"

No one answered. "No report and no boy? Hmm, well, there's always one. To the rest of you: congratulations. You have just completed a high school-level assignment. I should have it back to you within the week, and we'll see how you did."

Just then, Parker walked in, looking more than usually pale. He mumbled an apology to Mr. DeMille, then whispered to Erik, "Sorry, I missed the game, I was sorta sick Saturday morning."

"Mr. Bottelli," Mr. DeMille said, raising his voice, "As tragic as it may be that you missed a recreational event, it is much more tragic that you are late for school. Please sit down. I trust that you have your Egypt report to hand in."

Parker was silent, but Mr. DeMille waited him out. Nick squirmed with the knowledge that it could have easily been him on the hot seat, and felt a sudden pang of guilt. With all the help his teammates had given him, no one had thought to see if Parker needed help.

"I'm almost done," Parker said quietly.

"Close only counts in horseshoes and hand grenades, Mr. Bottelli. You are aware that it was due today?"

"Yes."

"Then you'll stay in at recess, and we can discuss the unsavory details further." Mr. DeMille turned to his math lesson, and Parker sank down in his chair.

IT WAS LUNCHTIME before Nick caught up with Parker again. Parker usually hit the bathroom before lunch, and Nick waited for him so that they would be in line together.

"Did he suspend you?"

"What do you mean?"

"From playing soccer. Because your report was late."

"No. He wants me to see a guidance counselor. He says I need *help*."

"Why?"

"You know, the whole music thing freaks teachers out. He probably thinks I'm a druggie."

"Ha!" Nick said. Then he added, "You aren't, are you?"

"No, I'm just sick of all this middle school garbage."

"Like what?"

"Homework, sports, video games. Whatever it is you and Erik sit around talking about."

"Is that why you missed Saturday's game?"

"Nah, that's different. I'm sorry about that. I meant to be there." Parker looked around and lowered his voice. "You know what the problem was Saturday? I was partying with a bunch of high school kids Friday night, and we got wasted. I didn't get to bed until four and I was totally sick the next day."

"That's why you missed the game?"

"Yeah, basically."

"That's crazy. We were counting on you."

"Right, you were counting on me. Get real! No one cares whether Parker shows up. Not like the great Nicky McCoy!"

"Hey, why are you attacking me, man? We need the whole team. I can't win the games alone."

"Nick, you're a good guy, but don't be so naive. You don't need me. And this whole *team* thing is just propaganda. Keeps everyone in line."

"I don't get it. You said you'd play for the season."

Parker rolled his eyes. "It's just kid stuff. It doesn't really matter."

"Like you know what matters?"

"You guys are such babies." Parker stood up and picked up his tray. "Grow up a little, and you'll find out I'm right."

As Parker walked away, Nick sat back, stunned by what had happened. Since when had Parker been so angry at everyone? Nick was just trying to be friends.

BECAUSE THE WEEKEND rain had passed and the sun was out, Nick and Erik elected to walk down the hill to Caton's Field. Dylan and Leon joined them while Abbey, Jamie, and Gabe caught a ride with Will and his dad.

Nick recounted his conversation with Parker to Erik. Erik didn't seem to think it was a big deal. "He's been like that for a while, Nick."

"Parker?"

"Yeah. Wearing black and not talking to anyone. I'm surprised he's played as many games as he has."

"How come I never noticed?"

"You and Leon were the only ones he acted normal around. I guess because you grew up together. Forget it. Anyway, I have something important to tell you about what happened after the game on Saturday. I haven't told anyone else." Erik sketched out what he had overheard Scruggs say.

"Wow!" Nick said.

"Do you think he's trying to get J.T. to throw the game?"

"No way J.T.'d do that. Besides, he couldn't. We're the ones playing."

"That's what I thought."

"What do you think got J.T. fired in Holland, if it wasn't the fighting?"

"I don't know."

"You think it was criminal?"

"I don't know. Scruggs said it was never made public."

THE FIELD LOOKED beautiful in the late October sun. The remaining leaves on the oak, birch, and maple trees glowed orange and red under the sunshine. Water droplets on the grass and on the pine trees glistened like silver.

The kids were in a goofy mood. The Egypt report was off their backs, and it was a short week, with no school on Thursday and Friday while the teachers did their in-service training. Of course, Mr. DeMille had tried to ruin their anticipation of the October break by scheduling a big math test on Wednesday morning, but even that could not dampen their mood. The mid-term vacation was close enough to taste.

On top of which, Erik's dad had rescheduled the game against Braeburn for the Wednesday after they got back from vacation, and they were sure they were going to make the playoffs.

As Dylan asked, "Who can stop us? We're the best team out there!"

"It'd be nice to have a sub," Leon said. "Mario's out, but what's up with Parker and Kenny?"

"Come on," said Gabe. "What has Parker ever done? We're better off without him."

Dylan jumped up and began imitating Parker's gangly run, limbs flying everywhere. He tried to kick a ball but missed it on the forward swing of his foot and knocked it backward as his foot swung back into position. Then, in a classic stoner voice, Dylan said, "Hey, man, what happened to my ball?"

The imitation was so accurate that everyone, with the exception of Nick, laughed. Nick felt terrible. Parker had been right. No one else on the team thought he mattered much.

"Hey, Park can be a solid defender when he wants to be," Nick said.

"Yeah," said Dylan, "when he wants to be."

"What about Kenny?" Jackson asked. "A horse's ass, but sort of useful at times."

"His dad won't let him play again," Erik said.

"Not for us, anyway," Gabe said. "I wouldn't put it past him to figure out a way to play for the Thunder Red, though."

"He was great the other day," Will said.

"All I'm saying," Gabe said, "is he never wanted to play for us, so good riddance."

The boys were still lolling on the grass when they suddenly became aware that J.T. was standing behind them.

"Are you here to talk, or are you going to play football today?"

Dylan had a funny remark on his lips but then fell silent when he saw J.T.'s face.

"I never agreed to babysit a group of spoiled children. Either you work and learn to play proper football, or you might as well quit right now."

The boys and Abbey exchanged questioning looks as they quickly finished getting ready. Out on the field, they waited hesitantly for J.T.'s instructions.

"You don't have to wait for me!" he barked. "You know what to do. 4 v. 1. Play!"

The team quickly organized itself and started warming up.

"Faster, faster!" J.T. shouted, and when Leon hit a pass astray, J.T. pounced. "The side of your foot, boy! Can't you understand that? We've worked on this for weeks!"

Shocked, the team wore itself out trying to satisfy J.T., while he urged them to run harder and berated them for their mistakes.

When Erik dribbled around his defender instead of passing the ball off, J.T. whistled play to a halt. "Make the pass, boy. The man on your left was open. Why can't you pass him the bloody ball, instead of showing off like a bloody prima donna? Any real defender would take your legs out from under you before you had a chance to blink." Erik looked down and blushed.

When Abbey backed off a challenge from Jackson, J.T. stopped play again and demanded to know exactly what Abbey thought she was doing on the field if she was going to play like a piece of puff pastry. "You have skills, but I have yet to see any evidence of courage." Abbey's eyes welled and she couldn't reply.

Nick stepped up to defend her. "It was a tough play, coach. I think Jackson had the angle."

J.T. turned on him. "You talk to your coach, but you never talk to your teammates. Let's see some leadership on the field, and maybe we'll see a team. Instead you squabble and joke around like a baby. Come, start again. Let's see some effort."

Whipped on by J.T.'s sarcasm and anger, the team played the entire practice at full speed and with full contact. The play grew sloppier and more aggressive as practice wore on, but any attempt to hold back drew J.T.'s vehement scorn. The scrimmage at the end of practice, a blur of sprinting runs, hard-fought challenges, and ill-tempered tackles, seemed to go on forever. Finally, after a particularly ugly collision between Dylan and Matty, J.T. whistled the melee to an end. Matty rolled on the ground clutching his knee, and the other players clutched at their shorts, glassy eyed and panting.

J.T. roared, "Practice isn't over yet. We end with sprints. Five sets. Erik, lead them."

The team groaned, but lined up at the goal line, even Matty, who was still limping, and began to run again. They might die, but at least practice would be over that way.

It was during the second set of sprints that Rory Patenaude and Georgi approached J.T. "Working them awfully hard, aren't you?" Rory asked.

J.T. didn't reply.

"What grade are these boys in, Rory?" Georgi asked.

"Seventh grade, Georgi."

"Nicholas," said Georgi. "A good Greek name. He reminds me of a young Pampedreou. When I was growing up in Athens, he was the only bright spot in Greek football."

"Rubbish! He doesn't play at all like Pampedreou," J.T. said.

"Now Erik, he's more of a Nordic player, like your Bergkamp," Georgi continued. "They're good, aren't they, for ones so young? It would be a shame to dampen their love of the game."

"Winning doesn't dampen your love of the game."

"That's funny," Rory said. "I could have sworn I heard someone tell the boys that winning wasn't important."

"The focus must be on beautiful football," said Georgi. "I've heard that too, Rory."

"Discipline is not inconsistent with beauty," J.T. said.

"But it is hard to find beauty without joy."

J.T. looked angrily at Rory and Georgi. "I understand what you're doing." He threw his whistle at Rory. "You can end practice if you think you can do better."

J.T. stomped away, and a moment later Rory blew the whistle to spare the kids their last set of sprints.

THE NEXT DAY the team approached practice with more trepidation. The players had joked with each other after practice, of course, and spent some time wondering what had happened to turn J.T. psycho. But behind their joking was a sense of guilt. J.T. had been a great coach since he took over, winning the players' trust. If he was angry, they figured, it was probably something they did.

Erik and Nick considered how J.T.'s sudden transformation was related to the information about him Erik had overheard, but they did not share their thoughts with the rest of the team. Knowing that he had a history of violence made his demeanor at practice that much scarier. Erik was worried that someone would decide that he should not be coaching the team.

"Well, if he's going to haul off and punch the lights out of someone," Nick pointed out, "maybe he shouldn't be."

"He won't punch anyone," Erik said.

"How do you know?"

"Come on, be serious."

"I am," Nick said. "And we still don't know what the other thing he did was."

"Was supposed to have done. We only have Scruggs's say so."

"Maybe he killed someone," Nick grinned.

Erik rolled his eyes. "The thing is, I think he was mad at Scruggs, not us. Scruggs threatened him, and he snapped."

"Well, why doesn't he kill Scruggs? Why does he take it out on us?"

"That's what he's doing, idiot. He's pushing us, so we crush Thunder Red."

"Yeah, if we even survive. I am not looking forward to practice today."

AS IT TURNED out, the boys had nothing to fear because J.T. wasn't there. Rory and Georgi were sitting on the bench when the team arrived at practice, and they explained that J.T. would be a little late.

"Did he quit?" Erik asked

"We said he'd be late, not that he wasn't coming. My goodness, have a little faith," Rory said.

While they waited, Rory and Georgi had the kids circle up and do some gentle stretching exercises. Abbey and the boys laughed to see the two heavy men trying to touch their toes. Each time they moved, their bellies fell out of their shirts, but the men didn't seem to mind.

After stretching, Georgi organized a penalty shot competition, with himself in goal. He turned out to be a surprisingly good goalie, although he wouldn't dive for the ball. When Will complimented his skills, Georgi looked offended. "Of course, what do you think? I played semi-professional in Greece."

Half an hour later, J.T.'s truck drove into the parking lot. He sat on the bench next to Rory, watching the boys play with Georgi for a few minutes before calling the team in.

"Sit, sit," he said. "I have just come from visiting Matty. He strained his knee yesterday in his collision with Dylan. He cannot play with us tomorrow."

The team realized at once what that meant. With Kenny, Mario, and possibly Parker out too, they might only have ten players against Thunder Red.

"It is my fault, of course, and I want to apologize. I am not a perfect person. No one is, of course, but I am particularly imperfect. I have always been very competitive, and this has often gotten me in trouble. I received a lot of yellow cards, and no few red cards. I've had a share of stupid fights. All of this, I thought, would not come up working with . . . ," J.T. held out his hand and gestured around, "American seventh graders. I never thought that I would care if you won or lost. I thought I would show you how to play properly, but I never dreamed . . . you would actually start to do it."

J.T. scratched his eye and paused. "Are you a hundred percent, Dylan?"

"Sure, coach," Dylan said.

"Well, as it turns out, you have. Started to play properly, that is. When I saw what you were capable of, I began to care about the results. I wanted to beat the other teams. I wanted you to win every game. Particularly, for my own reasons, which I will not go into, I wanted you to win tomorrow.

"But, as Georgi and Rory have helpfully pointed out, I pushed too hard. I'm to blame for Matty's getting hurt. Now we need to get some of our players back, or we have to face the Thunder without a full squad. As usual, I talk too much. If you accept my apology, let's go out and scrimmage." J.T. paused but no one said anything. "Georgi, you play goal with Nick, Erik, Terry, Jackson, and Leon. Jamie, you play goal with me, Will, Abbey, Dylan, and Gabe. Rory, you too, play with us."

"I don't play soccer."

"You'll learn."

The scrimmage, informal and at times silly, lasted the rest of the practice. Rory looked ridiculous whenever the ball came near him; Georgi turned out to be even better in a game than he was at penalty shots; but Erik kept his eyes on J.T. Despite the fact he was in Wellington boots, he won every challenge and no one could take the ball away from him. The only exceptions were one time that Nick flat out beat him to a loose ball, and one move Erik made that seemed to catch him wrong footed, although, in the latter case, J.T. had grabbed Erik's collar before Erik could run free. J.T.'s team also won the game.

At the end of practice, J.T. called the team together again. "We play tomorrow at four o'clock. Mario and Matty are out for the game. We will see about Parker and Kenny. We'll play with whoever's available. And, maybe, we will have fun."

ON THE WAY home, Nick asked his father if they could swing by Parker's house. "I want to see if I can convince him to play tomorrow."

"Sure," Charlie McCoy said.

Five minutes later, they pulled into Parker's driveway. His mother's ancient Chevy Malibu was in the driveway, so someone was home. Nick's dad picked up the copy of the paper that sat between the driver and passenger seats. "Okay, kid. I'll be here when you come out."

Nick nodded and jumped out. Parker's mother answered the door. Nick liked her. She was still young, in her thirties, and had always been up for a game of something when he and Parker were kids. But she was always fat, and in the last couple of years, she had become obese. She and Parker made an odd pair these days. Parker, skinny as a rail, dressed in black and mostly silent. His mother, fat, in bright colors and make-up, and hyper-friendly.

"Nick!" she exclaimed. "What a wonderful surprise. I was just getting dinner on. Parker will be so glad to see you. You can stay and eat if you like. Parker likes to eat in his room, but I can bring a tray in for both of you."

"No thanks, Mrs. Bottelli," Nick said. "My dad's waiting in the truck."

"Oh, you silly! Since when was I Mrs. Bottelli? You've called me 'Suzie' since kindergarten. And your dad is welcome too. We'd love to see Charlie."

"I think Mom's expecting us back. I just need to talk to Parker for a minute. Is he through here?" Nick asked, pointing in the direction of Parker's room.

Mrs. Bottelli waved him on, and Nick went back and knocked on Parker's door. "Go away!" a voice from inside said.

"Parker, it's Nick. Can I come in?" Nick tried the door but it was locked. "Open up!"

There was a sound of scrabbling and then the door opened. "I thought you were my mom," said Parker. "What do you want?"

"Matty got hurt yesterday."

"Matty?"

"Hello? Matty Hall from Forsberg. Ponytail and glasses. You played soccer with him all season."

"Oh, yeah. So what?"

"Well, Mario is sick, and Kenny's out. So without you, we'll only have ten players against the Thunder Red tomorrow."

Parker sighed deeply and rolled his eyes.

"Don't be like that," Nick said. "You told me at lunch that we didn't need you, and I'm here to say we do. No one else can help us. Come on and play!"

"Look, Nicky, I didn't mean all those things I said at lunch. I just get so angry sometimes."

"Forget it. I don't care. Anyway, you're right. The other kids do think you're weird, but it's not like you give them much to work with. You think everything they care about is stupid. None of it matters. Just come and play soccer."

"It's not like I add much."

"You're just as good as some of the players out there. I'm serious. Anyway, you're a whole lot better than no one. Besides, it'll feel good to beat the Thunder. Even for you."

Parker bit his lip.

"My dad's waiting," Nick said. "I've gotta go. Sleep on it, but you should play."

Parker watched Nick leave. After Nick had shut the door, he said quietly, "Okay, Nicky. Just this one time."

THAT EVENING, ERIK received an e-mail from Kenny: *Dad's out of town tomorrow. I'll play if I can get a ride to Lancaster.*

Erik e-mailed back at once: *Great! I'll work on a ride.*

Erik hurried to ask his dad if he could pick up Kenny in Milford the next afternoon.

Larry Steiner sat back in his seat smiling. "As it happens, I have a noon meeting in Milford with some of Randy Garrity's technical contacts. It'd be easy to pick Kenny up afterward and bring him to the game."

"Is that wise?" Mrs. Steiner asked. "I mean, taking the boy without his parents' consent. Isn't that kidnapping?"

"Oh, I don't think there's any question of lack of consent. Erik, read Kenny's e-mail again." Erik did.

"He says he can play and needs a ride," Mr. Steiner said to his wife. "Kenny's still a member of the Blue Marauders. I haven't received any paperwork saying he's withdrawn from the team. So it's just a matter of a coach picking up his player for a game. Nothing to worry about."

Mrs. Steiner shook her head. "Well, don't have an accident. That's all I'm saying."

CHAPTER 19

The Last Game

At school on Wednesday, the only thing that intruded on Nick's anticipation of the game, other than Mr. DeMille's math test, which, honestly, did not intrude very much because Nick felt the whole thing was hopeless, was Parker. That morning Parker had approached Nick at the line-up before school to let him know he was going to play. The problem was that Nick had just learned from Erik that Kenny was going to play too, which meant that the team didn't need Parker quite as much as Nick had suggested to him yesterday. One substitute was better than none, Nick thought, so he still wanted Parker to play, but he worried Parker might think he'd been lied to and quit again. He waited until lunch before he finally told Parker that Kenny was back on the team, so they'd have eleven players after all.

"Duh," Parker said. "You think I'm deaf? It's all anyone is talking about."

"Well, I just wanted to tell you because, yesterday, I said we'd only have ten men."

"So now you don't need me anymore?"

"No, we still need you. I just didn't know about Kenny when we talked before."

"Yeah, I figured that already."

"So you'll play?"

"I guess," Parker replied indifferently, and Nick went away, as confused as ever about what motivated Parker.

Meanwhile, for everyone else at school, the day raced by and excitement mounted. Kids in the younger grades offered the Marauder players and the other seventh graders (most of them had only a fuzzy idea of who was actually on the team) high fives as they passed in the hall. The teachers inquired about the kickoff time and league standings. Then, wonder of wonders, Mr. DeMille himself interrupted his usual end-of-day procedures, usually consisting of a monologue on the importance of some virtue he felt the students lacked, to ask:

"Am I correctly given to understand that there is a sporting event of some significance this afternoon?"

The students took a moment to work through the grammar of his question, and another to absorb the shock that he was acknowledging the existence of the soccer team.

"Come, now, has the cat got your tongues?"

It was Tabitha who recovered first. "Yes, sir, Mr. DeMille. The Blue Marauders are playing after school. Winner makes the playoffs."

"Not necessarily, ..." Erik started to correct her before everyone hissed him to silence. He had fought a losing battle all day against this simplified version of the story. He kept trying to explain that the Marauders still had to beat Braeburn to get in, and he couldn't understand Dylan's simple point, "No one cares!"

Mr. DeMille looked at his watch. "I suppose from a certain point of view that might be considered thrilling. I don't wish in any way to shortchange your education but, under the circumstances, I will be forgiven for releasing you ten minutes early today. If only to ensure all of the necessary padding and equipment are properly donned and adjusted before you take the field of battle."

The kids again paused to work through the syntax.

"Well, go on! Class dismissed!"

THE SEVENTH GRADERS raced out of class in a wild horde. The soccer players went over to the bathrooms by the gym to "don and adjust" the necessary equipment, while their comrades hung out and basked in the reflected glory.

Too eager to wait for their rides, the team and their classmates walked the fifteen minutes down to Caton's Field en masse. The road running down the hill from the elementary school to the Lancaster town center was fairly narrow, so the gang of seventh graders, laughing, joking, and walking three or four across, caused some traffic slow downs. Fortunately, most of the cars passing seemed to know what was happening and did not seem put out by the delay. As they passed, the cars honked or rolled down their windows to offer good luck wishes. Sometimes they offered rides, but these were refused.

Thanks to Will's dad, the field was in pristine condition. When Pat Cooper had arrived to work that morning, Tim Thomas had sent him to Caton's right away. "You have just one job today," he had said. "I want that place to sparkle for the game." And, in the late October sunshine, it did.

Mr. Cooper had mown the field in an elegant crosshatch pattern and painted the lines with fresh white paint. He had put up the corner flags, carefully centered the goals, and retacked the nets. He had collected two extra bleachers from the high school and placed them neatly on the sidelines. He had even set up a scorer's table and a portable scoreboard between the team benches.

When the Blue Marauders arrived, Pat Cooper and Dan Caton were making a final walk around the field. The team looked around in astonishment.

The adults went over to the kids, and Will's father asked them how they liked it.

"It's beautiful," Eric replied.

"Better than it ever was," said Dan Caton.

Will beamed at his father as the other members of the team added their thanks and praise. "The field looks amazing." "How'd you make that pattern?" "It's just like Wembley." "It's so awesome."

Dan Caton grinned, and Pat Cooper blushed. "Well, it's time I went and got Angie. You boys have fun today. We want to see a good game."

AS THE BOYS rushed through their final preparations, Mario showed up in street clothes, looking pale, followed by Matty wearing a knee brace. Erik and Leon helped them over to the scorer's table that Pat Cooper had set up.

"You guys okay?" Erik asked.

"The knee'll be okay. I'm just bummed to miss the game," Matty said.

Mario said that he was meant to still be in bed. "But papa knew he couldn't keep me away."

HALF AN HOUR earlier, Mr. Steiner had been parked outside the library in Milford when he saw Kenny walking toward him. Mr. Steiner honked and Kenny ran over and climbed in the car.

"Thanks for picking me up, Mr. Steiner."

"No problem, Kenny. We're all pleased you can play."

"I can't believe you guys beat Winchester without me." Kenny paused a second. "I didn't mean that like it sounded. I just meant, winning short-handed and all. Like, with anyone missing."

"I know," Mr. Steiner said. "I got it. Say, Kenny, will you need a ride home?"

"No, thanks. My friend Tommy is on the Thunder Red. His mom'll be late for the game, but she can get me back to the library before six. That's when my mom's picking me up."

"Fine. I hope Tommy still lets you ride back with him if the Marauders knock the Thunder Red out of the playoffs." Mr. Steiner smiled to show he was joking, but Kenny took him seriously.

"We can't do that," he said. "The kids at school were talking about it. Even if we win, they'd be tied with Bedford. Both teams have the same second-half records, so it would come down to goal difference, and Thunder Red has a big advantage. We'd have to beat 'em by six goals to knock them out of the playoffs. And that *won't* happen."

"Well, as I understand it from Erik, if we beat both Thunder Red and Braeburn, we'll have a better record than both of them."

"Braeburn?"

"Yes, we rescheduled the game that was cancelled."

"I didn't think about that," Kenny said. "I don't think any of the Thunder kids did either. Wow, that'd be amazing."

They rode in silence for a while and then Kenny said, in a shy voice, "Mr. Steiner?"

"Yes, Kenny?"

"Are you still talking to my dad about your business?"

"More or less," Mr. Steiner said.

Kenny hesitated, his face flushed. "I don't think he'll give you any money."

"Why do you say that, Kenny?"

"Uhh, I've heard him say some pretty mean things about you. Like you don't know what you're doing."

"That may be, Kenny. Your father has a lot more experience than me," said Mr. Steiner evenly.

"I guess I just wanted you to know. I've heard my dad sometimes likes to string people along so he can find out their ideas and use them himself."

"Listen, Kenny. I appreciate your trying to help me out. But remember, your dad is a very successful business man, and he's helped a lot of people grow their companies over the years."

Kenny didn't say anything, so Mr. Steiner continued.

"He's helped me too, whether he intended to or not. He's made me think more clearly about what I need, and he's introduced me to some fairly prominent folk. I know you're trying to do the right thing, Kenny, and I won't pretend your father is my favorite person, but he's done a lot you can be proud of."

WHEN MR. STEINER and Kenny arrived at Caton's Field, the parking lot was already filling up, so they parked in Georgi's lot despite the unfriendly sign: "PARKING FOR CUSTOMERS ONLY. TRESPASSERS WILL BE TOWED NO QUESTIONS ASKED."

Kenny hurried out of the car and ran to the field to join his teammates. The Marauders were warming up with small games of 4 v. 1, looking relaxed and confident. When Kenny took the field, his teammates greeted him with a cheer. Gabe hit a ball over to him, and he knocked it on to Leon. The ball rolled true.

A few minutes later the three vans holding the Thunder Red team arrived, maneuvering through the crowded parking lot. A thrill ran through the crowd as the twenty-one boys in shiny red uniforms, with matching red-and-white-striped socks, jogged toward the field. The boys quickly formed a circle around two assistant coaches and began their well-choreographed calisthenics routine.

In the crowd, Lancaster townspeople with some experience of the local soccer world turned to their friends and warned them not to get their hopes up. The Marauders had done well this year, but the Thunder had first pick of the best players from the entire region. Their coach, Mac Scruggs, was a legend in boys' soccer. He had won five regional championships and a national championship with his Thunder teams. The Marauder fans should just hope for a good game.

Scruggs himself was aware of his standing, and he jogged out to greet the referees with a good deal of complacency and theatre. After a brief conversation, feeling the eyes of the crowd on him, he headed over to the Marauder bench to shake hands with the opposing coach. To the spectators in the bleachers, it looked like a fine gesture. The old coach welcoming the upstart.

Of course, the crowd could not hear what was said. Neither could most of the team, because when J.T. had seen Mac Scruggs approach, he got up and walked away from the Marauder bench. He doubted it would help his team to overhear the conversation. The coaches met at midfield, where Mario and Matty were sitting at the scorer's table. J.T. nodded at them, but then ignored their presence.

"Heard you almost broke a boy's leg at practice on Monday," said Scruggs. "I'm surprised you're here. I pegged you for someone who ran away from his mistakes."

J.T. made no response, except to hold his hand up to stop Matty from interrupting to protest Scruggs's version of events.

"Don't think you can knock us out of the playoffs," Scruggs continued. "Your game against Braeburn won't count. Coach Flynn could have told you that, he knows what he's doing. Used to be one of my assistants. He knows the Tri-State rules require all league games to be completed before the October break, beginning tomorrow by the way. Any exceptions have to be approved by the Competition Committee."

"Of course, you are on the Competition Committee," J.T. said.

"I recused myself from the final vote."

"But you convinced them that permitting the game would upset important league traditions."

"That is how the committee saw it. They should be alerting your Coach Steiner of the decision." Mac Scruggs paused and looked at his watch, smiling unpleasantly. "Any time now."

"I expected something of this sort," J.T. said. "I saw you for what you were right away."

"Yeah, what's that?" Having won the day, Mac Scruggs was more than happy to entertain the frustrated insults of his opponent.

"A bully and a coward. In fact, I'm the one who is surprised that *you* are here. If you forfeited, I understand that the league would record a 3–0 loss, and you would be guaranteed to make the playoffs."

"It's already guaranteed. I'm resting my starters."

"Perhaps. But I believe Bedford can still edge you out if you lose to the Marauders by more than five goals."

Mac Scruggs clapped J.T. on the back and barked with laughter. "Now that is a joke. I always heard the Dutch had no sense of humor."

"We don't," J.T. said.

THE BLUE MARAUDERS were gathered in their pregame huddle when Larry Steiner came up to J.T. "Jan, can I talk to you for a second? I've just talked to the league and there's something you should know."

"Not now, Larry," J.T. said, turning to his team. "Terry and Kenny at wing, Leon at center forward. Erik, Will, and Nick in the midfield. Jackson, Gabe, and Dylan on defense. Abbey at sweeper. Jamie in goal. Parker, you start off but remember, equal playing time for all. Let me know if you need a rest."

The referee's whistle blew, but the Marauders waited for more from their coach.

J.T. looked annoyed. "I have no big speech. Play your game and you'll be fine. Focus on converting your chances, and don't muck around." He lowered his voice. "Let's see how much we can win by."

Now the Blue Marauders sprinted onto the field as the crowd roared to life. When the Thunder Red followed them out, three things happened. First, J.T. noticed that Mac Scruggs had sent his starters in after all. Second, Erik realized that, for the first time all season, he did not feel like an underdog. In fact, it was the Thunder Red that looked a little unsure of themselves. And third, scanning the fans to see who had shown up, Nick saw the one person he never expected. Dressed in a grey trench coat, and hidden further behind wrap-around dark glasses, Mr. DeMille stood at the far end of the bleachers. Nick almost pointed him out to Erik and Will, but then decided that it might make De Pill more uncomfortable than he already looked. In the end he just smiled and said to himself, "Okay, DeMille, now you'll see what Nicky McCoy is really good at."

And if Mr. DeMille was paying attention, it would not have taken long for Nick's talent to be revealed to him. Nominally at right midfield, Nick was everywhere, always ready and open to receive a pass. As a result of Nick's omnipresence, the Marauders could keep possession as long as they wanted. A player under pressure could always pass to Nick who, that day, at least, would not lose the ball as he made space and found the next open man.

In the previous game, the Thunder Red had closed on the Marauders so quickly that there never seemed to be time to breathe. But with J.T.'s coaching, and Nick always available as an outlet, the Marauder play was faster and smoother than it had been before. Even Leon was snapping passes with barely a thought. As a result, the Blue Marauders were able to move the ball around until they found the most dangerous point of attack, usually one with Erik in the vanguard. The Marauders had a chance to score on almost every possession.

The game might have been less one-sided if the Thunder Red had found their own avenues of attack. But as Tommy, the on-field general for the Thunder Red, moved the ball back and forth across the field, trying to find space and time, there were no open teammates. Over the last couple of weeks, Abbey had relived every moment of the earlier defeat, and she remembered all of the

Thunder Red formations and tendencies. She knew where every ball was headed long before the play developed, and she barked commands to Jackson, Gabe, and Dylan so they easily disrupted each Thunder Red probe.

The first goal fell after ten minutes. Nick took the ball from Jackson, burst up the left wing, and hit Will in the middle. Will found Erik, cutting across Leon's center forward space. Erik took the ball with his momentum heading to the right, but with a beautiful touch trap changed his direction straight to the goal, leaving one defender behind and only one more and the goalie to beat. Slowing down as the defender rushed out, Erik hit a simple pass into space on the right side of the penalty box, where Kenny smashed his shot past the goalie from ten yards out.

The second goal fell after Parker came on for Leon. Nick found Kenny breaking up the wing and Kenny hit a low cross that ricocheted off Parker's shin into the top left corner of the net. Nick was the first up to congratulate him, ruffling his hair. "Way to go, Park!"

"It was lucky. It bounced off my shin," Parker said.

The third goal came just before halftime, with Will heading in a cross by Erik. Mac Scruggs cursed his team loudly from the sidelines, and when the whistle blew, J.T. walked coolly over to the Thunder Red bench.

"There's still time to withdraw, Scruggs." He looked up at the clear blue sky. "You can say you feared your boys might get struck by lightning."

"Two of those goals were luck," Mac Scruggs spit back. "You only have one sub. You can't keep it up. The second half is going to be thirty minutes of hell for your boys."

Meanwhile, the Marauders were standing in a circle, drinking water and sucking on oranges provided by Polly's Café. Little was being said. The game was magical, and none of the players wanted to break the spell by talking about it. They held their breath when J.T. came over to them, wondering if he would say something to jinx them. But he just said, "You're doing fine. Keep it up. Erik starts out next half. Kenny, you're in midfield. Terry, you are up at wing."

For the Marauders, halftime never felt so long. They wanted to get out there and continue the game. Instead, they sat silently and listened as snatches of Mac Scruggs's halftime oratory reached their ears. "Never so disappointed . . . supposed to be the cream of the crop . . . can't play with second stringers . . . 120% . . . thirty minutes of hell."

Finally, the whistle blew, and the Marauders went out, conscious that they were without their most deadly weapon, Erik. But even that turned out not to matter much. The Thunder Red did indeed charge at them. They came in waves, sprinting hard, tackling hard, attacking on attack and attacking on defense, but the Marauders were beyond being intimidated. They were matadors with the ball, waiting patiently for the charges, and passing it skillfully away out of danger.

The fourth goal fell while Erik was on the bench, this time as Dylan made a run overlapping Kenny, got the ball free behind the defense, and took it to the goal, for once without toeing it beyond his own reach. The goalie was forced to come out to narrow Dylan's shot options. A month ago, Dylan might have panicked and slammed a shot at the goalie's chest, but today he just slipped the ball to one side and sped past the goalie to tap it into an open net.

That's when Mac Scruggs made his last tactical change. There were fifteen minutes left to play, and Mac Scruggs substituted a fresh cadre of players. The boys took up their positions deep in the Thunder Red half. Six defenders and three midfielders crowded into their own end to prevent a fifth goal, leaving only one attacker standing near midfield.

Play resumed, and the Marauders discovered that they could take the ball almost unmolested to within twenty-five yards of the Thunder goal, but beyond that there were ten Thunder Red defenders waiting for them, making it impossible to get closer. J.T. sent Erik back in, but even he found it impossible to weave through the confusing jumble of legs and bodies around the box. Every attempt ended in another long clearance from the Thunder Red defense, and the Marauders had to begin the build-up again.

With the middle clogged, the Marauders instead passed the ball out to the wings, to Terry and to Parker, for crosses into the middle. But as the minutes passed without the Marauders scoring, the Thunder Red felt like they might have stopped the bleeding. Indeed, with the Marauders pushing ever further up to try to get their heads on the crosses, the Thunder Red began to use their speed to counterattack. The attacks became more pointed when Thomas came back in the game as the midfield connector to the lone center forward. Several times, Abbey, Dylan, and Jackson had to win close sprints to stop a dangerous opportunity. Once Jamie made a diving save. Although the ball was around the Thunder goalmouth for most of the time, the better chances belonged to the Thunder Red. Mac Scruggs finally sat down on his bench.

Nick and Will and Erik paused before a throw-in to talk tactics. "Will, you can't lose track of Thomas now," Nick said. "Hang back and take care of the counterattack. Erik, take the ball to the wing. We'll do better with you hitting the crosses than Terry. I'll crash the goal, so look for me coming near post."

"Who'll cover back for you, Nick?" Will said. "The counters are killing us."

"I'll get back," Nick said grimly. "You wait and see."

And he did. Somehow Nick was both fighting for every cross, and, by the time the goalie had taken a couple of steps to throw or kick the ball, was back in the midfield fighting for the ball. So the

Thunder Red countermeasures became less effective, and the Marauder attack became more dangerous. With Erik hitting the crosses, they actually went where they were intended. The goal came when Erik faked the cross, moved past his defenders, and found room to dribble toward the goal close to the endline. The goalie moved to protect the near post, and two Thunder Red defenders ran over to stop his progress. But they left Nick open, and when Erik slotted the pass back to him, he hit an easy shot into the back of the net at the far post. It was 5–0 with almost seven minutes to play.

On the sideline, Mac Scruggs sat rigid on the Thunder bench. He let one of his assistants handle the substitution. But with a five-goal lead, the Marauders saw no urgency to score. Instead of pushing forward, they simply knocked the ball around the midfield, retaining control, and earning roars of appreciation from the crowd for each pass. As the seconds ticked away, J.T. seemed content. He made no attempt to encourage his team to renew their attack.

Mario and Matty, on the other hand, were shouting their heads off. They had overheard J.T.'s conversation with Scruggs about the Competition Committee's decision to disallow the rematch with Braeburn, and they knew both that the Marauders were out of the playoffs, and that a sixth goal would eliminate the Thunder Red as well. Finally, Matty could stand it no longer. When the ball rolled out of bounds near the scorer's table for a Marauder throw-in, he hobbled over in his knee brace and picked it up. And he refused to give it up until Erik came to take the throw.

"The Braeburn game's been cancelled," he said, as Erik came over to take the ball out of his hands.

Erik froze.

"It's true. Scruggs arranged it with Competition Committee last night."

Erik understood at once what Matty was saying. If Braeburn was cancelled, the Marauders couldn't make the playoffs. And if the Marauders were out, it was between the Thunder Red and Bedford, and it would come down to goal difference. The Thunder Red was up five goals, so to knock Mac Scruggs out of the playoffs, the Marauders had to win by six. They needed another goal, and they had just two minutes to score it.

Erik beckoned to Nick, and Nick ran toward him. Erik threw him the ball, and Nick neatly volleyed it back to Erik's feet. Erik surveyed the field. The Thunder Red remained in their defensive crouch, not bothering to exert pressure on the Marauders beyond shooting range. At any rate, they assumed that the Marauders would be content to play keep-away at midfield until time expired, so Erik met little resistance as he began to carry the ball upfield.

There was something in his body language, however, perhaps a glint in the eyes, that alerted Mac Scruggs to danger. As Erik moved toward the Thunder Red goal, Scruggs sprang from his bench.

"Stop him! He's wants to score!"

But the Thunder Red did not react. There was no reason to fuss. The game was lost and nothing was on the line. Scruggs himself had assured them they were in the playoffs no matter what happened today. Anyway, they were confused about who should go out and challenge Erik.

Erik was just about twenty-five yards from the goal, and the defenders were still dropping back, when he realized that, tightly packed as they were, they had left him a lane to shoot. It was a tough shot, leaving a small window in the upper right corner of the goal. It would help if Erik could curve the ball a little from right to left. On the other hand, the goalie's view was blocked, and he'd never see the ball coming. Erik's body had made the decision before his head. He nudged the ball forward to his right, looking left so the defenders would not guess what he had seen, and then cracked a shot that exploded off his boot. The ball was hit perfectly, curling just around the heads of several Thunder Red defenders into the top right-hand corner of the net before the goalie even moved.

The score was 6–0. While the Marauders celebrated again, the Thunder Red walked the ball up slowly to the center spot, ignoring Coach Scruggs's screams to hurry. The referee looked at his watch and, just as the ball came back into play, blew his whistle to signal the end of the game.

IMMEDIATELY, MAC SCRUGGS rushed out to the referee to ask for clarification about the final score. "No, no, you miscounted," he said, when informed of the 6–0 result. "There were only five goals." But J.T. was right behind him to say that the Marauders had been shortchanged and the real score was 7–0. Confused, the referee reviewed the goals and came up with six again, which number anyway seemed like a safe compromise between the two coaches.

When the matter was settled, to Mac Scruggs's intense dissatisfaction, he turned to J.T.

"You'll pay for this. Mark my words. I'll have you out of this league."

"We'll see," was all J.T. said. "We'll see."

THE TWO COACHES separated as their players were coming together to shake hands. Most of them were confused about the meaning of the game. The Marauders, other than Erik, thought the win would send them to the playoffs, assuming they could knock off Braeburn. The Thunder Red players thought they would be headed to the playoffs despite the loss. But when the Thunder goalie congratulated Erik and said, "I'm sure glad we won't see you in the playoffs," all Erik said was, "You won't."

After the handshake, it seemed like the entire town of Lancaster descended on the Marauders, and it was some time before J.T. was able to pull his players away from their friends and families and gather them around for a final word. Even then, before he could say anything, Georgi interrupted.

"No, no. Not here. Come over for pizza. On the house. Any talking, we do there!"

J.T. held up his hands in surrender. "Okay, we talk at Georgi's."

The players cheered and went to gather their sweats, water bottles, and backpacks. As they were doing so, Kenny approached Erik and Abbey to say good-bye.

"Can't you come for pizza?" asked Abbey.

"No, I'm getting a ride from Thomas. You know how it is. Mom doesn't know I'm here. Dad'll kill me if he finds out. I've got to get back. But do we have another game next week or not?"

"It was cancelled by the league," said Erik. "So we can't make the playoffs, but at least we knocked the Thunder Red out. Bedford beats 'em on goal difference now."

"I see. That makes sense." Kenny hesitated. "Well, then, good-bye. Thanks for the season, I guess. It was great."

"Thanks for playing," Erik said.

"Yeah. I'll see you around then. You too, Abbey," said Kenny.

"Sure," Abbey replied. And she and Erik watched Kenny walk away to find Thomas.

"What?" asked Erik, noticing the iciness of Abbey's posture.

"*You too, Abbey*," she said. "Ha! All he cared about was the stupid season."

Erik thought for a while and then said, "Well, it was a good season."

Abbey punched him hard in the arm.

GEORGI'S PLACE WAS packed. In addition to the team and their families, Georgi had invited all the other people who had helped the Marauders over the season. Heidi, the recreation department coordinator, was there. Dan Caton and Rory Patenaude, of course.

Tim Thomas was at a table with Pat Cooper and Charlie McCoy, talking about drainage. Even Mr. DeMille was there. He had been cornered by Parker's mother, Suzie Bottelli, and Officer Drybzyck, and looked as if he was trying to disappear into his raincoat.

In addition, most of the rest of the Lancaster sixth and seventh grades had joined the celebration. Georgi did not discriminate. He provided free pizza and soda to everyone, including some people who were completely unaware of the game. The only price they paid was having the action described to them in great detail while waiting to pick up their food.

Larry Steiner was the first to make a short speech. He thanked everyone for their help over the year and explained the playoff situation and the league's decision about the game with Braeburn. There was brief outrage and a discussion about appealing the decision, but while Mr. Steiner promised to look into the matter, most people realized that nothing was likely to come of it. And it did little to dampen the mood. Knocking the Thunder Red out of the playoffs seemed consolation enough.

Then J.T. stood up and called for quiet.

"Let us not worry about results," he said. "What matters is that this group of boys and girls have worked hard and played beautiful football. They may not play another game this year, but I know one thing. Everyone in the league is scared of playing them."

There were a few scattered cheers and he called for silence again. "Next year," he said, "they will have to wrap up their spot in the playoffs earlier."

Dylan shouted out the obvious question. "Will you coach again?"

J.T. looked at his wife, and she nodded to him before he replied. "My trophy case still has room for the Tri-State League championship."

"And next year, you need real uniforms, socks and shorts, not just cotton T-shirts." The team looked around and was shocked to see that it was Georgi speaking.

"Whole uniforms run into real money," Rory Patenaude said. "We'll have to see what we can afford."

"Money, money, money," said Georgi. "It's just money. Our team has to look good."

Erik and Nick looked at each other and started to laugh.

AS THEY LEFT the pizzeria, Nick felt his father's hand on his shoulder. "So, Nicky, was it worth it?"

"What?"

"The team, the whole Blue Marauders thing. You put a lot of work in to get it off the ground."

"Yeah, it was." Nicky shrugged his father's hand off his shoulder because it always made him feel like a kid. But as he did so, he turned and looked at his father in the face with the ironic expression that the two of them always used when communicating something important. "Thanks, Dad."

AND THAT NIGHT, as he got ready for bed, Larry Steiner told his wife about his conversation with Kenny in the car.

"Oh, the poor boy," Mrs. Steiner said. "Imagine being so ashamed of your father you have to warn people off doing business with him."

"That's what I thought," Mr. Steiner said. "That's why I defended him."

Mrs. Steiner thought for a second and then said, "But do you think Mr. Garrity might try to steal your software?"

"Not a doubt in the world. But, darling, it never occurred to me otherwise. It took him a month to send back the confidentiality agreement, and then he set me up to meet with people who weren't bound by it."

"Oh, dear," said Mrs. Steiner, "you and your partners have worked so hard on it. What'll we do if they steal it? We don't have the resources to fight a lawsuit against someone like that."

Mr. Steiner smiled and climbed into bed next to his wife. "Darling, I may be an incompetent soccer coach, but I'm not a total idiot. The only thing I told Garrity about was a project we worked on two years ago that never went anywhere. If he thinks it's worth stealing, he's welcome to it. I'll wait for him to introduce me to someone I trust before I show the good stuff."

THE END

Acknowledgments

I have had a lot of help in getting this book ready. I would like to thank my many friends and readers who provided comments, encouragement and/or expert advice. These include, at the very least: Karen Marks, Emily Rhinelander, Jason Overdorf, Dean Conway, Dino Koff, Bill Miles, Rick Greenwald, Clay Block, Ron Rainey, Corisande Albert, Justin Albert, Nick Silitch, Diana Burnham, Ben Milligan, Sam Atkinson, Josh Kim, Jeff Vaughn, Dirk Koppers, Jim McCracken, Charlie Boyd, Isabel Taylor, Kevin Brooker, Mike Pepe, Ann Bumpus, Mark Schiffman, Moira Burnham, David Herrington and Kevin Mills. If there are some people I've forgotten, I am sorry.

I also want to thank my brother, Lincoln, who did a thoroughgoing edit/re-write of the whole book, and who is not responsible for the length.

High-quality, professional copy-editing and advice was provided by Alan Berolzheimer at just the right time, and beautiful text and cover designs, as well as the all-important author photo, were provided by the talented Linnea Spelman. Of course, even they could not stop me from continually fiddling with the wording and punctuation, and I am responsible for any of the errors that remain in the book.

I also want to thank all the people I have played soccer with over the years. The kids in Hyde, Holland and Central Parks, as well as all the rest of the pick-up soccer joints across the U.S. and the world. The evening games in Dublin were magical. The Praterkickern in Vienna were life-savers. As were Watt, Jared and the

Huntley Meadow pick-up group. Thanks to all the Norwich and Thetford futsal players for providing winter ball. And Kris and the gang from Norwich United for age-appropriate competition.

Thanks to Dean, Dino, Bill, Rob, Doug, Ron, Chan, Charles, Dylan, Mike, Matt, Brian, Jen, Kevin, Bill, Patty, Jeff, Ray and all the other quality coaches, particularly in the Upper Valley Lightning program, who have shared their expertise, or even just let me watch them work, over the years.

Most of all, thanks to my mother and father, my first readers, and longest supporters. And to my kids, Alex, Lily and Casey, fabulous soccer players and even better company. And Katy, who doesn't even play soccer.

Ted has worked a lawyer, teacher, consultant, paralegal, recep-
tionist and soccer coach in Boston, New York, Ann Arbor,
London, Philadelphia, Hamburg and Berlin. Now he lives with
his wife and three teen-age children in Thetford, Vermont. He
writes whenever he is not cooking for his family, driving his
kids to sporting events, or playing pick-up soccer.

CPSIA information can be obtained at www.ICGtesting.com
Printed in the USA
BVOW03s2151170816

459375BV00001B/8/P